2nd Edition

EXPLORING
JUVENILE
JUSTICE

Cliff Roberson LL.M., Ph.D.
Washburn University

 **WADSWORTH** CENGAGE Learning™

Australia • Brazil • Japan • Korea • Mexico • Singapore • Spain • United Kingdom • United States

**Exploring Juvenile Justice,
Second Edition**
Cliff Roberson

For product information and
technology assistance, contact us at **Cengage Learning
Customer & Sales Support, 1-800-354-9706**

For permission to use material from this text or product,
submit all requests online at **www.cengage.com/permissions**
Further permissions questions can be emailed to
permissionrequest@cengage.com

Library of Congress Control Number: 95-83952

ISBN-13: 978-1-928916-09-3

ISBN-10: 1-928916-09-0

Wadsworth
20 Davis Drive
Belmont, CA 94002
USA

Cengage Learning is a leading provider of customized learning solutions with office locations around the globe, including Singapore, the United Kingdom, Australia, Mexico, Brazil, and Japan. Locate your local office at **www.cengage.com/global**

Cengage Learning products are represented in Canada by Nelson Education, Ltd.

To learn more about Wadsworth, visit
www.cengage.com/wadsworth

Purchase any of our products at your local college store or at our preferred online store **www.cengagebrain.com**

Printed in the United States of America
8 9 10 11 12   23 22 21 20 19

To Lynne B.

Acknowledgments

I would like to thank the following criminal justice professionals who have contributed to this project: Glenda Hunt, Pama Zacek Hencerling, Rob Hawkins, Ruth Masters, Harvey Wallace, Tom Dull, and Robin Button. In addition, a word of thanks to the many manuscript reviewers.

A special thanks to Professor Gary Bayens, Washburn University, for his assistance on this second edition.

Preface

The purpose of this text is to provide the reader with an introduction to, and a balance between, juvenile justice theory and practice. Not only will we examine how the system began, but also its current state and the direction it appears to be heading.

In our exploration of juvenile justice, we will examine the history of juvenile justice, philosophy of the system, police involvement, detention, diversion, and the processes involved. Included are chapters on causation, drugs, and gangs. An attempt has been made to present the material in a context that is content balanced and value free. In a few places, however, it has been necessary to interject value elements.

To paraphrase and misquote the late U.S. Supreme Court Justice Oliver Wendal Homes' definition of *due process* —

The development of the juvenile justice system is based more on life experiences than on logic.

Acronyms and Abbreviations

(COMMONLY USED IN THE JUVENILE JUSTICE SYSTEM)

ABA	American Bar Association
ACA	American Correctional Association
APA	American Psychological Association
BJS	Bureau of Justice Statistics
CHINS	Children in need of supervision
CHIPS	Children in need of protection or services
CIC	Children in custody
DARE	Drug Abuse Resistance Education
DSO	Deinstitutionalization of status offenders
DUF	Drug Use Forecasting Program
EBD	Emotionally and behaviorally disturbed
FAS	Fetal alcohol syndrome
FINS	Families in need of supervision
IACP	International Association of Chiefs of Police
MINS	Minors in need of supervision
NAC	National Advisory Committee
NCCD	National Council on Crime and Delinquency
NCJRS	National Criminal Justice Reference Service
NCPCA	National Committee for Prevention of Child Abuse
NCS	National Crime Survey
NCVS	National Crime Victims' Survey
NIBRS	National Incident-Based Reporting System
NIC	National Institute of Corrections
NIJ	National Institute of Justice
NJDA	National Juvenile Detention Association
OJJDP	Office of Juvenile Justice and Delinquency Prevention
PINS	Persons in need of supervision
POST	Peace Officer Standards and Training
PSI	Pre-sentence investigation
RICO	Racketeer Influenced and Corrupt Organizations Act
UCR	Uniform Crime Reports

Juvenile Justice on the Web

Listed below are some of the most popular web sites for students interested in searching for information on juvenile justice on the World Wide Web.

Coalition for Juvenile Justice

Access: AOL, keyword *cjj* or *legal*, then select *Juvenile Justice*

e-mail address: *JuvJustice@aol.com*

Juvenile Justice and Delinquency Prevention Act

Access: *http://www.ncjrs.org/docfiles/ojjjjact.wpd*

National Criminal Justice Reference Service

Access: *http://virlib.ncjrs.org/JuvenileJustice.asp*

Juvenile Justice Newsletter by e-mail

To subscribe: *listsproc@aspensys.com*

Office of Juvenile Justice and Delinquency Prevention

Access: *http://ojjdp.ncjrs.org*

National Criminal Justice Association

Access: *http://www.sso.org/ncja*

e-mail: *ncja@sso.org*

Gang Crime Prevention Center

Access: *http://www.gcpc.state.il.us*

Table of Contents

PART 1
OVERVIEW

Chapter 1

An Introduction to Juvenile Justice 3

PART II
DELINQUENCY AND ABUSE

PART III
THE JUSTICE SYSTEM

Chapter 6
Police and Juveniles 131

PART IV
JUVENILE DISPOSITION
AND CORRECTIONS

PART 1

OVERVIEW

Chapter 1

An Introduction to Juvenile Justice

The juvenile justice system has evolved as the result of attempts to deal constructively with the problems of delinquent, neglected, and dependent youths. During the last 30 years, the research on juvenile justice has undoubtedly exceeded the total of all research accomplished on any topic prior to the 1960s. Yet, despite all the research, our juvenile justice problems appear to be worsening.

One of the goals of this text is to introduce the reader to as many key issues as possible and to assist the reader in gaining a greater and broader understanding of youths, their needs, the community's needs, and the juvenile justice system in general. In this area, there are no easy, quick, or cheap solutions. For edification, included at the end of this chapter is a summary of the recent *National Report on Juvenile Offenders and Victims: A Focus on Violence* (Summer, 1995) published by the National Center for Juvenile Justice.

In studying the juvenile justice system, keep in mind that there are no provisions in the United States Constitution that guarantee a separate court or system of justice for juvenile offenders. The juvenile court systems in all fifty states and the District of Columbia were created by statutes. Accordingly, they may be eliminated by state legislatures.

Few social problems arouse as much concern as the problems associated with our youths and, to a great extent, we expect the juvenile justice system to deal with them efficiently. The concerns range from protection from child abuse to appropriate punishment of young violent criminals. Often, we are critical of the present system and the dedicated persons working in it without realizing that the system is extremely complex and is taxed with responsibilities that other elements of society, such as the family, have failed to accomplish. In many respects, we are requiring too much of our juvenile justice system.

The juvenile justice system is responsible for controlling and correcting the delinquent behavior of youths. The problem is that the system does not operate in a vacuum. There are many conflicting and complex forces that intrude on any attempt by the system to control and correct delinquents. These forces are partially responsible for the failure of the system to develop effective philosophies and strategies for solving the juvenile crime problem. The conflicting and complex forces include: youth gangs, the drug problem, declining family influences, social and economic problems facing America and the "get tough" vs. the "go soft" approach.

As we will discuss in Chapter 2, there are currently many "get tough" strategies being used with juvenile offenders. These are a few of those strategies:

> The movement of the juvenile justice philosophy away from saving the youth and toward protection of the public.

> Making the dispositions of juvenile court more punitive.

> Automatically removing serious offenders from the juvenile justice system and transferring them to adult criminal court.

> Advocating the use of the death penalty for the most serious juvenile offenders.

Children are not small adults. They are infants, lacking the maturity to make important judgments...

Judge Lindsay G. Arthur

DEFINING JUVENILE JUSTICE

The phrase "juvenile justice" appears to be self-explanatory. Juvenile refers to a person who is not yet considered an adult, and justice refers to fair treatment. That definition, however, does not fully describe the vast responsibilities of our current juvenile justice system. In many states, the juvenile justice system is also responsible for handling those adults, including the elderly, who are incapable of taking care of themselves. In all states, the juvenile justice system is responsible not only for those individuals involved in delinquent behavior, but also for those children needing protective services.

For purposes of this text, the juvenile justice system consists of the agencies and institutions whose primary responsibility is dealing with juvenile offenders and those juveniles in need of supervision. Our present juvenile justice system focuses on the 2.5 million youths per year who are either taken into custody, diverted to other programs, processed through the court system and placed on probation, referred to community-based programs, placed in group homes, or placed under the care of a public or private agency.

The juvenile population in the U.S. will increase gradually into the next century

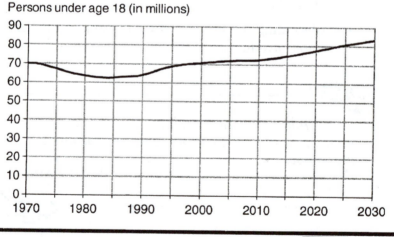

Persons under age 18 (in millions)

Juvenile Offenders and Victims: 1999 National Report   **NCJJ/OJDP**

In any text regarding juvenile justice, the concept of juvenile delinquency must be addressed. Juvenile delinquency is a broad and generic term that includes all of the diverse forms of antisocial behavior in which youths are involved. The United States Children's Bureau defines juvenile delinquency cases as noted below:

> Those cases referred to courts for acts defined in the statutes of the State as the violation of a state law or municipal ordinance by children or youths of juvenile court age, or for the conduct so seriously antisocial as to interfere with the rights of others or to menace the welfare of the delinquent himself or of the community.

There are two primary types of juvenile delinquency cases. The first type involves conduct that is considered criminal regardless of whether it is committed by an adult or a child. Such conduct includes murder, rape, robbery, theft, etc. The second type involves conduct that is considered wrong only because of the age of the offender. Such conduct includes truancy, curfew violations, running away from home, etc. These types are commonly known as status offenses. About one-half of the states include both types of cases in their definition of juvenile delinquency. The remaining states distinguish between the handling of the two types. In these states, status offenders are viewed as individuals "in need of supervision." They are commonly referred to as PINS (persons in need of supervision), CHINS and CINS (child or children in need of supervision), MINS (minors in need of supervision) and JINS (juveniles in need of supervision).

All states have statutes that define an upper age limit for juvenile court jurisdiction. The upper age limits vary from 19 to 16 years with 18 being the most common. Many states do not designate a lower age limit and use the common law approach that a child below the age of seven is not criminally responsible for his or her behavior. However, there is generally a *presumption* that children between the ages of seven and 14 years of age are not criminally responsible for their acts. To hold a juvenile in that age range responsible for a criminal offense, the state needs to establish that the child understood the nature of his or her conduct.

In general, juvenile court has primary jurisdiction over youths under 18 years of age who have committed serious crimes. In most states, the juvenile court must waive jurisdiction before the juvenile may be tried in an adult criminal court. The jurisdiction of juvenile court is discussed in greater detail in Chapter 8. The methods by which juvenile courts waive jurisdiction are by legislative or judicial waiver. Legislative waiver is accomplished by a state law or penal code provision that provides that youths being tried for certain offenses may be tried originally in adult criminal court. For example, in Washington, D.C., by statute, children over the age of 14 who are charged with murder are tried in adult criminal court. The judicial waiver requires that the juvenile court hold a hearing to determine if the juvenile court should waive jurisdiction and allow the juvenile to be tried in adult criminal court (waiver hearing).

FAMILY AUTHORITY

The juvenile justice system is based on the concept that the state has a right and duty to assure the health, safety, and welfare of children. The Latin term *parens patriae* is roughly translated as the right of the government to take care of minors and others who cannot legally take care of themselves.

When the juvenile justice system first started, society was built around the family. The family was the primary social control of children. Wayward children or delinquents were generally returned by the police to the family. The family was then expected to correct the children. Starting in the early nineteenth century, the authority of the family began to decline and the state began to take more authority away from the family. There is a debate about which was first, the decline of family authority or increasing state influence. In either case, the shift of authority has continued to the point where now primary social control of children is thrust upon the state which in turn has established the juvenile justice system to act as the social control agent. (Clemens Bartollas and Jerry Stockdale, *Social Problems*, New York: Harper/Collins, 1994).

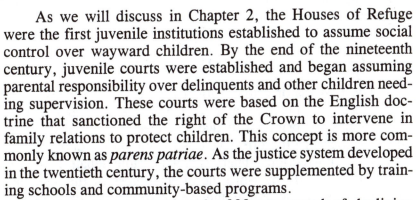

One of the major problems in the history of juvenile justice is that the system has attempted to be both the "super parent" and the criminal court for juveniles.

Source Unknown

As we will discuss in Chapter 2, the Houses of Refuge were the first juvenile institutions established to assume social control over wayward children. By the end of the nineteenth century, juvenile courts were established and began assuming parental responsibility over delinquents and other children needing supervision. These courts were based on the English doctrine that sanctioned the right of the Crown to intervene in family relations to protect children. This concept is more commonly known as *parens patriae*. As the justice system developed in the twentieth century, the courts were supplemented by training schools and community-based programs.

It does not appear that the 300-year trend of declining authority of the family will change in the future. All indicators seem to point to even greater state involvement and control. With the declining authority, the American family is beset with increasing divorce rates, one-parent families, increasing number of children being born out of wedlock, rising rates of child abuse and neglect, and the drug problem. In addition, for many youths, the influences of street gangs are prevalent.

MEASURING DELINQUENCY

The measurement of crime committed by persons under the age of 18 years is difficult. Various measurement methods yield different absolute levels of delinquency, thus researchers are vexed in their attempts to discover the extent and nature of juvenile delinquency in the United States. In addition to differing measurement methods, accurate data may be difficult to obtain. For example, in a case where the offender is unknown, it is impossible to determine if the crime was committed by a juvenile or an adult. Also, many victims are reluctant to report offenses which were known to be committed by juveniles. Data on juvenile crime tends to deal with crime in local areas only.

Juvenile crime sources are either from official or unofficial statistics. Data regarding juvenile crime is varied depending on the data source, the time frame, and its scope. It appears that at best, the statistics reflect trends in the various categories involved and at worst, they confuse to the point of uselessness. While the data is not perfect, it gives us a glimpse of the extent of juvenile crime.

SOURCES OF JUVENILE CRIME DATA

The first major crime statistics were used to measure the society's moral health. Later they were used to measure the effectiveness of criminal justice agencies. They are still used today to measure the effectiveness of our police departments, courts, and corrections. There is considerable debate as to their ability to correctly measure the effectiveness of the agencies. While the public holds the agencies responsible for the crime problem, seldom do those same agencies receive any credit when crime rates drop.

The United States Department of Justice uses the Uniform Crime Reports (UCR) and the National Crime Victimization Survey (NCVS) to measure the magnitude, nature, and impact of crime in the United States. The two measures are different in the methodology used to collect the data and their coverage of crime. Accordingly, there are inconsistencies between their results. Looking at both together, however, enhances our understanding of the crime problem. While these reports contribute to our knowledge of crime, crime victims, and offenders, none portrays completely and accurately the kinds and amounts of crime that go unreported and unrecorded. The phrase "dark figure of crime" is commonly used to refer to crimes that are committed but not discovered, reported, or recorded by law enforcement agencies.

The Uniform Crime Reports were criticized because they failed to provide critical data on crime. Starting in 1988, the FBI announced its new approach to collecting crime data. The new approach was the National Incident-Based Reporting System (NIBRS). The NIBRS views crime, along with all of its components, as an incident and that those components should be collected and organized for the purpose of analysis. Under NIBRS, the elements of the crime include the following:

➤ Any alcohol or drug influence

➤ Specified location of the crime

➤ Type of criminal activity involved

➤ Type of weapon used

➤ Type of victim

➤ Relationship, if any, of victim to offender

➤ Residency of victim and offender

➤ Description of property and its value

The NIBRS collects data on 22 crime categories; whereas, the Uniform Crime Reports focus only on the eight Part One crimes. At the time of the announcement, the FBI hoped that the new system would be fully implemented in five to ten years. Now, over a decade later, the system is still being implemented.

Drug Use Forecasting Program

Since 1987, the Drug Use Forecasting Program (DUF) has collected data on drug use from booking facilities throughout the United States. The purpose of DUF is to provide cities with the necessary information for the early detection of drug epidemics, planning and allocation of law enforcement resources, and for determining local drug abuse treatment and prevention needs. The data is collected for approximately 14 consecutive evenings each quarter through voluntary and anonymous interviews and urine specimens from selected arrestees. According to the reports received in this program, cocaine is the most frequently used drug.

More high school seniors use marijuana on a daily basis than drink alcohol daily

	Proportion of seniors who used			
	in lifetime	in last year	in last month	daily*
Alcohol	81.4%	74.3%	52.0%	3.9%
Been drunk	62.4	52.0	32.9	–
Cigarettes	65.3	–	35.1	22.4
Marijuana/hashish	49.1	37.5	22.8	5.6
Stimulants	16.4	10.1	4.6	0.3
Inhalants	15.2	6.2	2.3	0.2
LSD	12.6	7.6	3.2	0.1
Cocaine, not crack	9.3	5.7	2.4	0.2
Tranquilizers	8.5	5.5	2.4	0.1
MDMA (ecstasy)	5.8	3.6	1.5	0.2
Crack cocaine	4.4	2.5	1.0	0.1
PCP	3.9	2.1	1.0	0.3
Steroids	2.7	1.7	1.1	0.3
Heroin	2.0	1.0	0.5	0.1

■ More than 1 in 5 high school seniors smoked cigarettes on a regular basis, with more than 1 in 10 smoking half a pack or more per day.

*Used on 20 or more occasions in the last 30 days.

–Not included in survey.

Source: Authors' adaptation of Johnston, O'Malley, and Bachman's *Drug use by American young people begins to turn downward.*

Juvenile Offenders and Victims: 1999 National Report

During the first few years under the DUF, the data indicates that between 54 and 82 percent of men arrested for serious offenses in 14 major cities tested positive for illicit drugs.

VOLUME AND RATES OF JUVENILE CRIMINAL ACTIVITY

An Overview of Juvenile Crime

The most frequent juvenile arrests occur for curfew and loitering, runaways, vandalism, arson, and burglary. Approximately 18 percent of all index crimes that were "cleared" were committed by offenders under the age of 18 years. Only about nine percent of the violent crimes were committed by juveniles, whereas approximately 40 percent of the arson crimes and 22 percent of the burglaries were committed by juveniles. It is estimated that approximately one out of every six males and one out of every nine children will be referred to a juvenile court before their eighteenth birthday. Approximately 47 percent of all arrests are of persons under 25 years of age.

A review of the UCR trends for the past two decades indicates that although female juvenile crime involvement is still less than those of the male juvenile, there has been an increase in arrests of female juveniles (approximately 20 percent) and a decrease in the number of male juvenile arrests (about 10 percent). It is also interesting to note that the median age of juvenile males arrested is approximately 15 years and almost 16 years of age for female juveniles.

Individual Crimes and Misconduct

Curfew: Curfew violations are commonly used by the police to disperse juveniles who are gathered in areas such as fast food stores and convenience-type grocery stores. Many United States cities are imposing curfews on youths as a method to reduce teenage violence. For example, New Orleans has a dusk-to-dawn curfew for youths under 16 years of age. In the first week, over 200 youths were cited for curfew violations. Curfews are denounced by civil libertarians as a violation of civil rights, but tend to be applauded by parents and judges.

Runaways and Truants: Runaways have a distinct age pattern when compared to other crimes or juvenile misconduct. It appears that both female and male juveniles start runaway activity at about 12 years of age and reach a peak at 16. After age 16, the numbers of males that run away sharply declines, whereas the numbers of females continue to increase. Also, the older the juveniles are, the longer they tend to stay away from home. Closely related to runaways are truancies. Truancy is the failure to attend school as required by state law. Many state laws now hold the parents responsible for the failure of their children to attend school. For example, in Houston, Texas, both parents may be fined up to $100 per day for a child's truancy.

Vandalism: Vandalism is defined as the mischievous destruction to get attention, for revenge, or to vent hostility. Vandalism can also send a message that the juvenile has personal problems.

Murder: Murders occur less often than any other index crime. Murder is defined as the unlawful killing of a human being. Deaths caused by negligence, suicides, accidental deaths, and justifiable homicide are excluded. Traffic fatalities are also excluded. The typical pattern is that more murders occur during August than any other month of the year, with the fewest occurring in February.

More than three out of four murder victims are male. The overall murder rate is approximately 10 per 100,000 per year. On a regional basis, the South's murder rate was 12, the West's was 10, and the Midwest's and

Homicides of juveniles peaked in 1993 and by 1997 had fallen to their lowest level in the decade

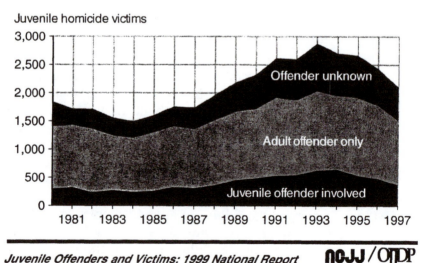

Juvenile homicide victims

Juvenile Offenders and Victims: 1999 National Report   **ncJJ/OJDP**

Homicides of juveniles ages 15 to 17 were more likely to involve a firearm than were homicides of adults

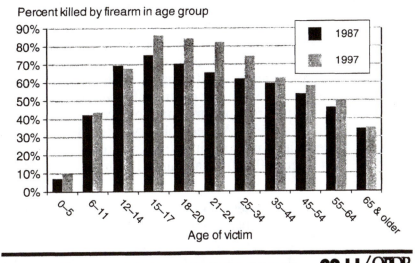

Percent killed by firearm in age group

Juvenile Offenders and Victims: 1999 National Report **NCJJ/OJJDP**

Northeast's were each eight. Approximately 58 percent of the known murderers were relatives or acquaintances of the victims. About 20 percent occurred as the result of some felonious activity, such as robbery.

Criminal homicide has the highest clearance rate of all the index crimes. The police generally clear about 67 percent of the cases. It appears that juveniles are responsible for approximately 6.5 percent of all murders.

Forcible Rape: Forcible rape, the carnal knowledge of a female forcibly and against her will, mostly involves a lone victim and a lone offender. It is the least reported of all violent crimes. Statutory rape differs from forcible rape in that it involves sexual intercourse with a female who is under the legal age of consent, regardless of whether or not she is a willing partner.

It appears that approximately 80 percent of the rapes are acquaintance rapes (rapes in which the victim knows the offender). The police clear about 50 percent of reported rapes. Of the persons arrested for rape, 55 percent are white and about 43 percent are black. Approximately 9 percent of the rapists are under the age of 18 years of age.

Robbery: Robbery is the violent crime that most often involves more than one offender. It is defined as the taking or attempted taking of anything of value from the care, custody, or control of a person or persons by force or threat of force or violence or by putting the victim in fear. Armed robbery refers to the use of a weapon. In metropolitan areas, the robbery rate is about 341 per 100,000 inhabitants. In rural areas it is about 70 per 100,000.

Sixty-one percent of those arrested for robbery are black and about 38 percent white. Males account for over 90 percent of those arrested for robbery. Most (62 percent) are under 25 years of age. Over 10 percent are under the age of 18 years of age.

Assault: Assault is the unlawful attack by one person upon another for the purpose of inflicting severe or aggravated bodily injury. There are two types of assaults— aggravated and simple. Aggravated assaults usually involve the use of a weapon or means likely to result in death or great bodily harm.

Simple assaults occur more frequently than aggravated assaults. Simple assault may be described as "second degree" assault which may involve fistfights and scuffles. Most assaults involve one victim and one offender.

Males constitute about 86 percent of those arrested for aggravated assault. Approximately 60 percent of those arrested are white and about 38 percent are black. Approximately 9 percent are under 18 years of age.

Burglary: Burglary is the unlawful entry of a structure to commit a felony or a theft. Attempted forcible entry is included under the burglary definition. Burglary may include violence or personal encounters; however, it is most often a property crime. Of the individuals arrested for burglary, 19 percent are under the age of 18. Approximately 91 percent of those arrested are male. Whites accounted for 69 percent of those arrested and blacks accounted for 29 percent.

Motor Vehicle Theft: Motor vehicle theft is relatively well reported to the police, probably because of insurance requirements. It is defined as the unlawful taking or attempted taking of a self-propelled road vehicle owned by another, with the intent of depriving him or her of that vehicle permanently or temporarily. Ninety percent of the people arrested for this crime are male and 21 percent are under 18 years of age.

Arson: Arson was the latest crime added to the index. Arson involves the unlawful, willful, or malicious burning or attempted burning of property with or without intent to defraud. Single family residences are the most frequent targets of arson. About 16 percent of the structures where arson occurred were vacant. Only about 18 percent of the arson cases are cleared by the

The proportion of violent crimes committed by juveniles that victims reported to law enforcement has changed little since 1980

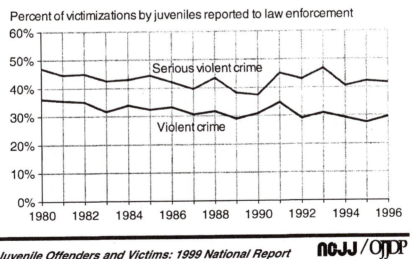

Percent of victimizations by juveniles reported to law enforcement

police. About 40 percent of the arson crimes that were cleared involved offenders under 18 years of age, a higher percentage of juvenile involvement than for any other index crime. Seventy-seven percent of the people arrested for arson are white.

Victimization by Race, Gender, and Age

Race: Generally, blacks have the highest victimization rate for crimes of violence. Hispanics have the next highest rate for victimization, and whites have the lowest. In rural areas, however, whites tend to have higher rates of victimization for crimes of violence than nonwhites. For crimes of theft, whites have a greater victimization rate than blacks.

Gender: Women are generally less likely than men to be crime victims. Their rate of victimization is about 60 percent of that of men. In two classes of victimization, however, female victims predominate. The two classes are rape and violence between intimates. Violence between intimates refers to crimes committed by one spouse against the other, by ex-spouses, and by live-in partners. Women are three times more likely than men to be victims in crimes involving intimates. Among crime victims, 25 percent of the women and only 4 percent of the men were victimized by persons whom they knew intimately. About 85 percent of the crimes against a female by an intimate involved assaults and/or batteries, and 11 percent involved robberies.

Age: In general, the higher the age category, the lower the probability of both violent and theft victimization. Individuals between 12 and 24 years of age have the highest rate of victimization while those 65 and older have the lowest rate. Females under the age of 35 have a higher rate of victimization than men or women above the age of 35. Men between the ages of 12 and 34 have the highest victimization rates.

Seventeen is the most common age to be arrested for a violent offense. Eighteen is the most common age to be arrested for property offenses. Nineteen is the most common age to first be imprisoned as an adult.

COHORT STUDIES OF JUVENILES

As noted earlier, cohort studies examine a selected group of youths, born at the same time and living within the same area over a period of time. Since Word War II, there have been major studies in three cities in the United States. Each of these studies is discussed in this section.

The Philadelphia Cohorts

In the 1960s, Marvin Wolfgang studied some 10,000 males born in Philadelphia in 1945. He concluded that by the time of their eighteenth birthday, some 627 youths had been arrested five or more times. He also concluded that less than 7 percent of the youth were responsible for nearly 70 percent of the crimes attributed to the 10,000. He repeated his study later for youths born in 1958 with similar findings. They were published in his book *Delinquency in a Birth Cohort*. Similar studies were conducted for other cities in the United States.

Delinquents who committed five or more crimes made up only about 6.3 percent of 1945 cohort (birth year of individuals in this group). This small group, however, accounted for over 51 percent of the delinquent acts. The factors of race and education figured heavily in delinquency. Nonwhites showed up almost twice as often in police contacts, were more likely to be recidivists, and were more likely to become chronic offenders (five or more offenses) than whites. Nonwhites also had less education than their white counterparts.

While the two cohorts' characteristics and involvement were similar, the 1958 cohort group was more likely to have committed more violent crimes and to have more repeat offenses.

The general findings of these studies are as follows:

> Juvenile violent offenders were a very small fraction of the total number of youths.

> As a rule, juveniles did not typically progress from less serious to more serious crimes.

> It was difficult to predict which juveniles would progress to more serious crimes.

> A relatively small number of juveniles were responsible for most of the arrests involving juveniles.

> Violent juveniles did not generally specialize in the types of crimes they committed.

> Most violent juvenile crimes did not involve the use of weapons.[7]

The Columbus Cohort

In Columbus, Ohio, the records of all juveniles born between 1956 and 1960 who had been arrested for a violent offense were examined. The researchers also continued to look at the group after they had reached adulthood. The backgrounds of the 1,138 arrestees were compared. Researchers found that males outnumbered females by about six to one and that only a small percentage of the total youth population was involved in serious crimes (2.3 percent). About 12 percent of the youths who had committed one or more serious crimes had brothers or sisters who had also committed a serious crime. Of the arrestees, 42.1 percent had been arrested for property crimes and 12.6 percent had been arrested for violent crimes. The researchers concluded that:

> The frequency of arrests declines with age.

> Most adult crimes committed by juvenile offenders are not violent crimes.

> Four out of ten adult offenders were arrested at least once as a juvenile for an index crime.

> Almost half of the arrested cohort members were imprisoned as an adult. (Donna Martin Hamparian, et al. *The Violent Few: A Study of Dangerous Juvenile Offenders*, Lexington, MA: Lexington Books, 1980).

The Racine Study

This study looked at juveniles born in Racine, Wisconsin in the years 1942, 1949, and 1955. Its findings published in Lyle Shannon's, *Assessing the Relationship of Adult Criminal Careers to Juvenile Careers* were similar to those of the other two cohort studies. The main conclusions of this study were that most violent juvenile crime was committed by a relatively small percentage of youths and that those individuals generally continued their criminal activity as adults. While the cohort studies are valuable and add insight to the data, their weakness is their inability to project the findings beyond the members of the cohort.

Twentieth Century Fund Task Force

The Twentieth Century Fund Task Force, a group of experts who studied the juvenile justice problem, concluded in 1978 that:

> Most young people violate the law at some point during adolescence, but relatively few young people are repetitive, serious criminals.

> Most youth crime is not violent crime.

> Most young persons who commit crime as juveniles outgrow the propensity to commit crimes in the transition to adulthood. A small number, however, will persist in criminal careers.

While the study is about 20 years old, the above conclusions regarding juvenile crime appear to be valid. Two other researchers concluded that:

> ➢ Today's youth are no more seriously delinquent than youths of 10 years ago.

> ➢ Juvenile offenders primarily victimize other juveniles, and they victimize males about twice as often as females.

> ➢ While the at-risk juvenile population is shrinking and the arrest rate is declining, juvenile detention and training school populations are growing. (Robert Trojanowicz and Merry Morash, *Juvenile Delinquency: Concepts and Control* 4th ed. Englewood Cliffs, NJ: Prentice-Hall, 1987).

JUVENILE OFFENDERS AND VICTIMS: A FOCUS ON VIOLENCE

Included below is a partial reprint of a statistics summary of the *National Report- Juvenile Offenders and Victims: A Focus on Violence*. The report was published in June, 1995, and deals with violent juvenile crime.

Until their teenage years, boys and girls are equally likely to be murdered

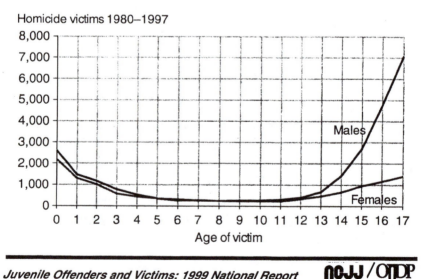

Homicide victims 1980–1997

Juvenile Offenders and Victims: 1999 National Report   **NCJJ/OJJDP**

A Focus on Violence

The information contained in the *National Report* can be juxtaposed and reordered to provide a detailed summary of a particular topic. This OJJDP Statistics Summary has sections from the full report that focus on violence by and against juveniles. (Howard N. Snyder and Melissa Sickmund, *Juvenile Offenders and Victims: A Focus on Violence,* Office of Juvenile Justice and Delinquency Prevention, May, 1995).

As this *Summary* and the *National Report* show, the proportion of violent crimes committed by juveniles is disproportionately high compared with their share of the U.S. population and the number of these crimes is growing. Between 1988 and 1992 juvenile arrests for violent crime increased nearly 50 percent.

Even with these large increases, however, juveniles are not responsible for most of the increase in recent years. If juvenile violence had not increased between 1988 and 1992, the U.S. violent crime rate would have increased 16 percent instead of 23 percent.

Additionally, as the accompanying figure from the *National Report* shows, a very small percentage of juveniles are arrested for violent crime. However, these violent juveniles and the system's response to them are driving very broad changes in juvenile justice policy and legislation in states and at the federal level.

While juveniles may not be responsible for most violent crime, the growing level of violence by juveniles does not bode well for the future. If violent juvenile crime increases in the future as it has for the past 10 years, the authors of the *National Report* estimate that by the year 2010 the number of juvenile arrests for a violent crime will more than double and the number of juvenile arrests for murder will increase nearly 150 percent.

DISCUSSION QUESTIONS

Answer the following questions and provide justification for your answers.

1. Compare and contrast the Uniform Crime Reports with the victim surveys.

2. What are the problems with our present crime reporting databases in attempting to determine the rate and level of juvenile crime?

3. Explain the various classifications of crime.

4. What steps should be taken to improve our knowledge regarding the amount of juvenile crime that exists in our society?

5. Why are juvenile crime data considered to be "soft" by most researchers?

6. What have we learned from the cohort studies?

7. You have been asked by your state legislature to research the following issues:

    a. What is the correct definition of delinquency?

    b. How much delinquency is there in this state?

    c. What characterizes the typical juvenile offender?

    d. What delinquency measures would you use to answer the above questions?

Chapter 2

History of Juvenile Justice

A society that doesn't know its past cannot understand its future.
                    Studs Terkel, Historian

ny understanding of the present juvenile justice system needs to begin with an analysis of the past. The history of juvenile justice is a relatively short one with the first juvenile courts established only about 100 years ago. Throughout most of history, children have not enjoyed the special legal status that they presently hold. Youths were generally under the same statutes and guidelines which were used with adult offenders.

EARLY HISTORY

Even primitive tribes exercised some form of social control over the behavior of their members. Generally, children were subject to the same control as the adult members. Banishment was one of the primary forms of punishment. When a person was banished from the tribe, that person was considered outside of the law (an outlaw). The banished person received no protection, survival or help from the tribe and was left unprotected against wild animals.

Little has been recorded about youth crime in our early history. Children, like adults, were subject to banishment for failure to obey tribal rules and customs. Later, ancient societies confined to dungeons and cages individuals, including children, who did not abide by societal rules. Such social vengeance was the forerunner of our practice of using punishments to enforce criminal laws. The general view that regarded juveniles as nothing but "little adults" extended to the realm of legal punishments.

It appears that there was a state of indifference toward youth. From a historical setting, it is easy to understand the absence of a separate status for juveniles until the late nineteenth century. The infant mortality rate exceeded 50 percent. Each child represented a burden on the family. The failure to develop a personal, caring attitude toward youth may be viewed as a defense mechanism. Often families lived from day to day on what they could hunt, make, or produce. The inability to provide economically for new children often lead to infanticide (killing of infants) or the abandonment of unwanted children. A third method of handling an unwanted child was by the use of an apprenticeship. In many cases, an apprenticeship amounted to nothing more than the selling of a child into slavery.

Code of Hammurabi

The first major code of laws is believed to be the Code of Hammurabi established in about 1752 BC by the Babylonian King Hammurabi. This code set forth rules for the kingdom. It established offenses and set punishments. The main principle of the code was that the strong shall not injure the weak. The family portion of the code was based on the patriarchal system whereby the father was the head of the family unit. Rebellion against the father by the children, even adult children, was not tolerated. For example, item 195 of the Code stated that if a son struck his father, the son's hand could be cut off. Compared with such punishment of children by their parents, today's practice of referring children to juvenile court seems rather meek.

The code also provided for the adoption of children. Children who were adopted were expected to be loyal to their adoptive parents as payment in return for their new homes. If an adoptive child was disloyal to his new parents, they could cut off the child's tongue or have his eye plucked out. While the code had many regulations regarding the care of children, it was not concerned with behavior within the family. It appears that the family unit was the primary agent in the supervision and punishment of the child. For misconduct outside the family unit, it appears that children faced the same rules and punishments as an adult. In fact, if anything, it appears children faced even harsher rules and punishments than adults.

The Concept of Childhood

The concept of childhood did not begin to emerge until the seventeenth century. During this same time, medical advancements greatly increased the life expectancy of youths. The churchmen and schoolmen of the time led the movement to view children as different from adults and in need of special protection. The leaders used the youth as a source to attack the immoral and sinful aspects of society. According to them, the youth needed to be protected from corruption and trained for their future role in society. This movement established the concept that childhood was the period of time during which the young could receive moral and educational training without the pressures of adulthood.

The English Experience

Starting in England, about the year 1300, there developed a considerable body of law regulating apprenticeships. These laws affected freeborn English children. The minimum age limit for apprenticeship was eventually established at 12 years of age. An apprentice was expected to be obedient, industrious, orderly and not wasteful of his or her master's goods. By 1600, if an apprentice was delinquent, he or she could be sued in the Mayor's Court. Later, Chamberlain's Court (Gentlemen of the King's Prince Chamber) was used to handle matters between masters and their apprentices. Many researchers consider this court the forerunner of our present juvenile court.

During the sixteenth, seventeenth, and eighteenth centuries, the churches played an important role in controlling the behavior of delinquent children. Examples of harsh punishments of children during this period are many. For example, in 1716, in England, a mother and her 11-year-old daughter were hanged for witchcraft. In Halifax in the 1690s, children less than 14 years of age were put in debtor's prison and forced to work for their creditors until their debts for food and lodging were paid.

Other changes during this era included the concept that special discipline is needed for youthful offenders and the idea that responses to misconduct should be tailored to fit the age of the offender. The English common law rule regarding the age of responsibility was also developed. Under this rule, youths under seven years of age could not be held criminally responsible for their actions. Youths between the ages of eight and 14 could be held criminally responsible only when it could be shown that they understood the consequences of their actions. Youths over the age of 14 were considered adults and therefore responsible for their criminal acts. While the concept of childhood developed during the seventeenth century, punishment sanctions against offenders remained the same regardless of the age of the offender.

In the early 1700s, the English began to express concern regarding the growing population of vagrant, destitute, and delinquent children. In 1756, the English Marine Society was founded. One of its goals was to provide apprenticeships to sea service for vagrant and delinquent boys. At that time, England was at war with France and Spain and needed to increase its naval force. A stated objective of the society was to reclaim delinquent boys and make sailors out of them. Even after youth were committed to prison, they were often released to the Society. Magistrates were encouraged to commit young delinquents to the Marine Society rather than to prison. The Society claimed to take no runaway apprentices nor any boys whose parents did not consent. The Society was probably an early forerunner of our present- day industrial schools.

By the 1700s, it was generally acknowledged that apprenticeships often failed to control the criminal youth of the country. Accordingly, the community leaders began a search for new solutions. In 1758, Sir John Fielding, a British magistrate, established a group home to rescue vagrant girls from almost certain lives as prostitutes. The group home was known as the House of Refuge for Orphan Girls. Later in the 1780s, public asylums for destitute and neglected children were founded by the Philanthropic Society in London.

Transportation

Transportation to Australia was also used to remove delinquent children from London. It appears that during the period from 1787 to 1797 at least 93 children were transported. Generally, during transportation, the delinquent children were confined. The records of one ship indicate that on one voyage there were two delinquent youths who were only nine years old. The English government recommended in 1829 transportation for life for the growing number of juvenile delinquents.

Youth Institutions In England

The first private prison for young offenders was established in England in 1788. The institution was established by Robert Young to educate and instruct the children of convicts or such other infant poor that are engaged in a vagrant and criminal course of life in some useful trade or occupation.

In 1818, the English established the Warwick County Asylum with the help of generous contributions from citizens. The asylum's goal was to provide a place where a criminal boy could escape the ways of vice and corruption. This reform effort, like many present- day efforts, suffered from the lack of funds. The public soon lost interest in the project, and it was able to survive only by showing the public that it saved them money.

It was common practice in England for the head of the house to discipline all youths living in the house. Punishment for juvenile delinquents was generally carried out within the family. It was not unusual for children brought before a magistrate to be sent home for a court-observed whipping.

PARENS PATRIAE

The concept of *parens patriae,* the state as guardian and protector of all citizens who are unable to protect themselves, can be traced back to the Chancery Court of England. Under the guidance of the king's chancellor, the Chancery Court was originally created to grant relief to needy subjects of the kingdom. Based on the right of the king, the Chancery Court exercised the right of *parens patriae* (parent of the country) to allow the court to act in place of the parents (*in loco parentis*). This concept permitted the Chancery Court to assume parental authority over neglected youths. However, the court did not deal with criminal youths.

The English Parliament passed the Statute of Artificers in 1562. This act provided that children of paupers could be taken involuntarily from their parents and apprenticed to others. Later, the Poor Law Act of 1601 also provided for the involuntary separation of children from their pauper parents and allowed such children to be placed in bondage to others. Both of these statutes were based on the concept that the king has a primary interest in the welfare of children and the right to ensure such welfare.

The Growth of *Parens Patriae*

- *1500s*—English Chancery Court, as a representative of the king (father of the country), develops the right to intervene for the welfare of children, especially in the cases of orphans and children of paupers.

- *1562*—English Parliament passes the Statute of Artificers. This act permits the government to involuntarily separate children from their pauper parents.

- *1601*—English Poor Law Act allows government to place poor children in bondage to local residents as apprentices.

- *1838*—Pennsylvania Supreme Court in *Ex Parte Crouse* holds that *parens patriae* provides sufficient basis to intervene in the lives of juveniles without parental consent.

- *1870*—Illinois Supreme Court rules that *parens patriae* is not sufficient grounds to allow the government to intervene in the lives of juveniles without parental consent. (Note: the decision was largely ignored by the courts.)

- *1905*—The Pennsylvania Supreme Court holds that courts can intervene in child custody and discipline matters if the intent of the courts is to help the youth.

- *1966-1967*—The U.S. Supreme Court seriously questions the doctrine of *parens patriae* and establishes due process requirements on juvenile courts.

AMERICAN JUVENILE INSTITUTIONS AND COURTS

The custom of permitting boys to ramble about the streets by nights, is productive of the most serious and alarming consequences to their morals.

Dunlap's American Daily Advertiser
August 5, 1791

Like the English, the American colonies attempted to use apprenticeships to control delinquent youths. When they failed to control the criminal youths, the colonists turned to incarceration. It was during the 1700s that the phrase "juvenile delinquency" ceased to mean misbehavior common to all children and started to be used to describe poor children who were involved in criminal behavior. There was a rising distrust of the abilities of poor families to raise their own children. By 1800, "juvenile delinquency" was a label applied mainly to children of the poor. When confined for criminal misbehavior, these children were imprisoned with hardened criminals.

During the early 1800s, America started a transformation from a rural to an urban society. Industrialization resulted in families moving from rural farms into urban areas. As the cities grew in size, they also became diverse. Individuals moving to the cities brought with them a variety of outlooks, customs, and ideas. At the same time, the cities were attracting immigrants from a wide range of European countries. With industrialization and diversity also came poverty.

Houses of Refuge

Dissatisfaction with the way young criminals were being handled increased in the United States during the 1800s. While many juveniles were being confined, few appeared to benefit from that confinement. For example, in 1849, the Mayor of New York City, George Matsell, publicly warned that the numbers of vicious and vagrant youth were increasing and that something must be done regarding the gangs of criminal boys roaming the streets of New York City.

By the mid-1800s, state and local governments started funding reform schools. Like the reformatories, these reform schools emphasized formal education and the teaching of middle-class values to the lower-class youths. Many of the reform schools were designed as cottages where the boys could be classified and segregated according to criminal misconduct.

The movement to establish separate institutions for juvenile criminals started in New York City in 1819. That year, the Society for the Prevention of Pauperism publicized the plight of young children who were confined with adult prisoners. The Society contended that there was a definite correlation between crime, delinquency, poverty and parental neglect. In 1823, the Society became known as the Society for the Reformation of Juvenile Delinquents. In 1825, in New York, the first juvenile prison was opened under the name of the House of Refuge. Similar institutions opened in Boston and Philadelphia by 1830. By 1854, many other cities opened similar houses of refuge for juvenile offenders.

The first houses of refuge were built by child-saving organizations primarily concerned with the poverty, vice, and neglectful families which were considered breeding grounds for crime. The houses were designed to provide a home for the delinquent youth where they could be reformed, educated and disciplined. In addition, children were also placed in the homes to protect them from immoral, unfit, and neglectful families. The houses were built as secure facilities. The basic schedules and routines required of the children were similar to those required in prisons. Silence was maintained at all times. Youth who broke rules were punished. Punishment ranged from depriving the child of any food except bread and water to whippings with a leather whip.

While the period of confinement for the youths was indeterminate, the average youth stayed in the home about two years. Few stayed as long as four years. Often, youths who showed no signs of improvement were exiled to whaling ships for extended voyages. Finding employment for the youths who appeared to be improving was difficult. The depression of 1857 resulted in the homes becoming overcrowded. Most reformers contended that the houses of refuge were nothing but prisons for the young.

Charles Loring Brace, Director of the New York Children's Aid Society, contended in his book, *The Dangerous Classes of New York and Twenty Years Work Among Them* that the rigid punishments, strict schedules, and military regimentation of the houses prevented any meaningful chance to reform the youths. Brace stated: "The longer the youth is in a refuge, the less likely he is to do well in outside life." Brace advocated the placement of youths with farm families. According to him, the dirty city with its taverns, gambling halls, and gangs was no place to reform wayward youths.

Reformatories flourished in the late 1800s. The controversial Enoch Wines was considered by many as the leader of the reformatory movement. Others have a lessor opinion of him. In 1872, he became the first president of the International Penal Congress. The underlying philosophy behind the reformatory movement was that proper training in a residential environment would offset the early experiences of poverty, poor family life, and corruption. The youths were to be protected from idleness and laziness by means of military drill, physical drill, and continual supervision. The youth would be separated from the corrupting influence of adult prisoners.

Although the goals appeared to be reasonable and workable, it was not long before the theoretical and abstract philosophies developed into an actual system that was very different from what was intended. For all practical purposes, the reformatories were no different from the prisons they had replaced.

For example, the Elmira Reformatory in New York was designed as the model reformatory. It was constructed with 500 cells. Shortly after it opened, it was jammed with over 1500 juveniles.

During the Civil War, most jails and prisons were practically empty as prisoners were paroled to fight in the war. The reform schools, however, were overcrowded. Many attributed this overcrowding to the absence of family authority as many fathers were in military service.

The new reform schools were not effective in preventing juvenile delinquency. This failure increased interest in the legality of the proceedings that allowed youths to be placed in reform schools. The procedures for placing youths in reform schools permitted the commitment decisions to be made in non-judicial proceedings.

In 1855, Illinois passed the Chicago Reform School Act which was followed in 1879 by the establishment of industrial schools. The establishment of these schools did not have the unanimous support of the courts. In 1870, the Illinois Supreme Court ruled the Chicago Reform School Act unconstitutional in that it placed a restraint on the natural liberty of children who had not been convicted of a crime. In 1872, the same court ruled that the state had a right, under the concept of *parens patriae*, to divest a child of his liberty if no other lawful protector could be found. Later in 1879, the court ruled that the Illinois Industrial School Act, which was enacted to replace the Chicago Reform School Act was also unconstitutional.

JUVENILE COURTS

During the early 1800s, state legislatures began to delegate the role of *parens patriae* to the court systems. The delegation of this responsibility to the court systems was taken from the English experience.

By 1880, several states had passed statutes providing for the separate trials of juveniles. The first juvenile court, however, did not appear until 1899. The first court was established in Cook County, Illinois, as a family court to handle juvenile concerns. For several years prior to 1899, Colorado Judge Ben

Lindsey, a leading advocate of juvenile courts, operated an unofficial juvenile court. After the establishment of the Cook County juvenile court, other states quickly followed in establishing separate juvenile courts. By 1920, only three states did not have separate juvenile courts. In 1932, there were over 600 independent juvenile courts in the United States. By 1945, all states had established separate juvenile courts. From the 1920s to the 1960s, the emphasis in dealing with juveniles was for the most part on attempting to understand the delinquent as a member of society rather than on punishment. The establishment of the juvenile courts created a whole new vocabulary. No longer was there a finding of guilt, but an adjudication. An adjudicatory hearing was substituted for a trial. However, in recent years there has been a greater tendency to use adult criminal terms when referring to juvenile justice.

The basic philosophy contained in the first juvenile court acts was the right of the state to act *in loco parentis* (in place of parents) in cases involving neglected or delinquent children. Under the doctrine of *parens patriae,* the courts were to act in the best interests of the children. The courts operated on the concept that the juvenile ceased to be a criminal and had the status of a child in need of care, protection, and discipline directed toward rehabilitation.

The original Illinois juvenile court jurisdiction allowed for juvenile court intervention only in cases involving criminal activity, dependency, and neglect. Later, the jurisdiction of the courts was extended to include such actions as curfew violations and status offenses. In 1903, the Illinois juvenile court's jurisdiction was also extended to include handling youths who needed to be removed from their families.

The period between 1899, when the first juvenile court was established, and 1967 when the U.S. Supreme Court placed certain due process requirements on the courts, has been referred to as the era of "socialized juvenile justice." During this era, the legal rights of the juvenile were ignored and emphasis was placed on determining how best to treat the juvenile and rehabilitate him. Since the juvenile courts were based on many of the same ideas originally used by the early reform schools, they were subject to the same problems.

The courts were generally designed to operate in an informal manner. The representation by attorneys was discouraged.

Selected Terms Used in Juvenile Court

JUVENILE COURT TERM	ADULT COURT TERM
Adjudication: Judicial determination that the juvenile has committed a delinquent act.	**Find of Guilt**
Adjudicatory Hearing: A hearing to determine whether the allegations of misconduct are supported by the evidence.	**Trial**
Adjustment: Settlement of matters before the court by agreement of the parties.	**Plea Bargaining**
Aftercare: Supervision given a delinquent after the individual is released from training school but is still under supervision of the court or the training school.	**Parole**
Commitment: Order by the judge that the child should be committed to a training school.	**Imprisonment**
Delinquent Act: An act that if committed by an adult would be called a crime. Does not include status offenses.	**Crime**
Delinquent: A youth who is adjudicated to have committed a delinquent act.	**Criminal**

Detention:
Temporary holding in custody
of a child.

Holding in Jail

Dispositional Hearing:
A hearing held to determine
the disposition of a delinquent
youth.

Sentencing Hearing

Hearing:
The presentation of evidence
to the court, his or her consideration of the evidence, and
the judge's decision.

Trial

Petition:
An application for an
order of the court.

**Indictment or
Accusation**

Take Into Custody:
Act of the police in
securing the physical
custody of the child.

Arrest

Source: National Advisory Commission on Criminal Justice and Goals

The rules of evidence and the requirement to take testimony under oath were eliminated. Judges were encouraged to take a paternal stance toward the juvenile and focus on assisting the youth rather than on punishing the youth for misbehavior. Originally, in most states, the juvenile courts had primary jurisdiction over youths under 18 years of age.

Problems of the original juvenile courts included the fact that many of the courts, and agencies dealing with the courts, relied on untrained volunteers to perform key functions. For example, in 1920, at least 40 percent of the courts did not have full-time probation officers. In 1918, there were only 23 full-time juvenile court judges in the United States. The new agencies created to assist the juvenile courts, such as child guidance clinics, had similar problems.

While most historians generally hold that the development of juvenile courts was a progressive, humanitarian development, others contend that the courts were developed as a means of preserving the existing class system in the United States. The latter group saw the courts as a vehicle of the upper class for controlling the dangerous lower classes in society. To support their argument, they point out that the driving force in the development of the houses of refuge and juvenile courts was the middle- and upper-classes; many of the women involved in the movement were wives and daughters of industrialists and landed gentry. They also established that these systems developed during the time that the lower-class ranks were growing with new, poor immigrants and that this growing lower-class was seen as a threat to the status quo. In addition, they point to the exploitive use of the children (generally from lower-class families) who were incarcerated or under the care of the system. The systems provided cheap labor and indoctrinated the youth in the capitalistic ideology of the upper class.

THE SECOND REVOLUTION

In 1965, President Johnson established the President's Commission on Law Enforcement and the Administration of Justice. His reasons for establishing this commission included the rising crime rates, the fear of crime, increasing social disorders and riots related to the Vietnam War protests and the Civil Rights movements, and pressure from the conservative wing of the Republican party to address the crime issue. (John A. Conley, ed., *The 1967 President's Crime Commission Report: Its Impact 25 Years Later*, Cincinnati, Anderson, 1994). The Commission was staffed primarily by social scientists rather than attorneys and focused on crime control issues. The Commission published numerous task force reports on various topics including juvenile justice and a summary volume, *The Challenge of Crime in a Free Society*. The commission report led to the passage of the Omnibus Crime Control and Safe Streets Act of 1968. This act created the Law Enforcement Assistance Administration (LEAA). During its seven-year existence, LEAA spent $7 billion. Many people feel that much of the money was spent unwisely. After it was dissolved, the National Institute of Justice and Delinquency Prevention and the Bureau of Justice Assistance were formed.

One of the Commission's task force reports was *Task Force Report: Juvenile Delinquency and Youth Crime* (1967). This report is considered by many as one of the pivotal events in the history of the American juvenile justice system. According to many researchers, this report transformed America's approach to thinking about youthful offenders and treating delinquency. Some have referred to the results as the "second revolution."

The task force report concluded that:

> The great hopes originally held for the juvenile court have not been fulfilled. It has not succeeded significantly in rehabilitating delinquent youth, in reducing or even stemming the tide of delinquency, or in bringing justice and compassion to the child offender. To say that the justice courts have failed to achieve their goals is to say no more than what is true of criminal courts in the United States. But failure is most striking when hopes are highest.

The Commission proposed a two-pronged strategy for combating youth crime. First, a series of community-oriented prevention proposals that were largely based on the strain, subcultural, and control theories of criminal behavior. These proposals were aimed at increasing opportunities and attacking the root causes of deviance. The second strategy was grounded upon the labeling theory and was aimed at reforming the juvenile justice system. The reforms included expanding diversion programs, decriminalization of certain crimes, de-institutionalization of juvenile offenders, and providing juveniles with certain due process rights.

The task force report, however, focused attention on juvenile crime. As a result of the report, practitioners, politicians, and others gained a greater appreciation of the seriousness of the youth crime problem. LaMar Empey reported that many persons felt that the system as it existed in the 1960s tended to evoke and make worse many of the problems it was designed to correct.

Prior to 1967, the U.S. Supreme Court had adopted a "hands off" policy towards juvenile courts apparently under the assumption that the juvenile court system was working. Between 1966 and 1975, the Court issued a series of cases that followed the Commission's call for due process reforms for juvenile offenders. In the first major case, *Kent v. United States*, Justice Fortas's opinion indicated that the Court no longer believed that the concept of *parens patriae* was working. Justice Fortas stated:

> There is evidence, in fact, that there may be grounds for concern that the child receives the worst of both worlds: that he gets neither the protection accorded to adults nor the solicitous care and regenerative treatment postulated for children. *383 U.S. 541 (1966).*

The Court's rulings during that period transformed the juvenile courts from informal proceedings dominated by the personality and good will of the judge to more formalized hearings with attorneys involved. The justice courts were directed to focus their primary attention on the legal aspects of the case and reduce their reliance on hearsay evidence. In theory, the courts were to balance the public's need for social defense with the child's need for rehabilitation.

States following the recommendations of the Commission revised their juvenile codes to decriminalize and create special categories of status offenders such as CHINS, MINS, etc. In addition, many states moved away from institutionalization toward more humane, effective, and cost-efficient alternatives. For example, in Massachusetts the secure institutions were closed by Jerome Miller. Finally in 1974 after five years of debate, congress passed the Juvenile Justice and Delinquency Prevention Act (JJDPA). This act was based on the theory that the present system of juvenile justice was failing miserably. The act created the Office of Juvenile Justice and Delinquency Prevention (OJJDP). The OJJDP was mandated to discourage the use of secure institutions and to promote community-based programs that provided more sensible and economical alternatives for youths in the justice system.

PUNISHMENT OR REFORM

During the years 1975 to 1979, there was a serious debate over the question of whether to punish or reform. The conservative politicians and practitioners started a counteroffensive against the liberal recommendations of the Commission. Robert Martinson, Douglas Lipton, and Judith Wilks were commissioned by the New York Governor's Special Commission on Criminal Offenders to review the literature and determine which strategies lowered recidivism. The three researchers studied several thousand evaluations of adult and juvenile treatments in an attempt to determine what works. Martinson's article regarding the study was published in the 1974 issue of *The Public Interest*. The group had concluded that with few and isolated exceptions, rehabilitative efforts that have been reported so far have had no appreciable effect on recidivism.

James Q. Wilson, using the findings of the Martinson study, blasted the liberal approach to crime control as recommended by the President's Commission. According to Wilson, the Commission's recommendations were based on unconventional wisdom and were biased, misleading, and empirically shallow. Wilson, following the classical school approach, contended that criminals were free, rational, hedonistic persons who needed and deserved punishment. Wilson dismissed the labeling theory (*Thinking About Crime*, New York: Basic Books, 1975) by stating:

> To destigmatize crime would be to lift from it the weight of moral judgment and to make crime simply a particular occupation or avocation which society has chosen to reward less than other pursuits. If there is not a stigma attached to an activity, then society has no business making it a crime.

In addition to the conservatives, several prominent researchers believed that the labeling theory was theoretically flawed. Since many of the President's Commission recommendations were based on the labeling theory, this cast doubt on the validity of the task force report. About the same time, there were several studies that demonstrated that some of the key programs established as a result of the task force report were not working.

The efforts to remove status offenders from adult jails were ignored in many jurisdictions. Despite the U.S. Supreme Court decisions, many juveniles were still not receiving the due process rights that were being given to adult criminals. Perhaps the biggest failure was in the diversion area. Cases that were selected for diversion included, to a great extent, those youths who formerly would have been screened out or released after a brief contact with the police. Community corrections, an important aspect of diversion, was being used generally only for minor offenders.

By the time the Juvenile Justice Delinquency Prevention Act was passed, the optimism of the President's Commission was on the wane and many viewed it as a bad joke. Ronald Reagan's 1980 election platform included the concept that social welfare programs were aggravating the plight of the poor and that we needed to get tough on crime. The new punishment-oriented perspective was clearly noted by Reagan's appointment of Alfred Regnery as administrator of the OJJDP. Regnery believed that juvenile delinquents, like adult criminals, were free, rational, and hedonistic actors. Regnery stated in "Getting Away With Murder: Why the Juvenile Justice System Needs an Overhaul," *Policy Review*, Vol 34. 1985, pp. 65-68:

> Thus, we must begin to tell our young people, no matter what their background and no matter why they committed an offense, that they must obey the law and that, if they violate the law, they will be held accountable for it.

Following the lead of the national government, legislatures in many states including Arizona, California, Texas, and Florida, again revised their juvenile codes. Included in the codes was the statement that one of the primary purposes of the juvenile courts was to protect public safety. As discussed earlier, the juvenile statutes had indicated that the primary purpose of the juvenile court was to rehabilitate youth. Now, judges are instructed to consider protecting the public safety from juvenile crime as an equal concern. The indeterminate sentencing concept, one of the cornerstones of the individualized treatment of juveniles, was replaced in most states with determinate sentences.

By the end of the 1980s, at least one-third of the states had some form of punishment-oriented sentencing statutes for juvenile offenders. In those states, the treatment concept has, to some extent, been replaced by the just deserts concept. The just deserts approach is based on the theory that criminal offenders should be punished because they violated the law and deserve punishment. The 1960s movement of de-institutionalization and decriminalization had been replaced by a punishment-oriented focus. As Alexander Pisciotta in "A Retrospective Look at the Task Force Report on Juvenile Delinquency and Crime" in *The 1967 President's Crime Commission Report: Its Impact 25 years Later* (Cincinnati: Anderson, 1994) observed, "After 200 years of thinking about crime and dealing with delinquency, the American juvenile justice system was where it started—in the eighteenth century."

Children Not Escaping the Tough-on-Crime Climate

The above caption was the title of the lead article in the July 25, 1995, *California Bar Journal*. The article pointed out that effective in 1995 California had enacted the below changes to its juvenile justice laws:

- The age that a child could be tried as an adult was lowered from 16 to 14.

- Some 16-year-olds could be sent to state prison, and some California Youth Authority inmates could be transferred to state prison at the age of 25 instead of being automatically released.

- Law enforcement officers could make public the names of some juvenile offenders upon request if certain conditions are met.

Other proposals being considered by the California state legislature include:

- Permitting the paddling of youths for graffiti offenses.
- Allowing the use of juvenile convictions as sentence enhancements in adult criminal cases including the habitual criminal statutes.
- Permitting prosecutors to take juvenile cases directly to adult criminal court rather than conduct transfer hearings.

One juvenile justice expert remarked that the 1994 California legislative session was "a freight train that rolled right into the juvenile justice system."

It appears that our juvenile justice system has been driven by cycles that fluctuate between harsh punishment and rehabilitation-oriented treatment. There have been three such cycles in the past 200 years. As many researchers have stated, the juvenile justice system has a long history or promising much but delivering little. As stated by Pisciotta, "If the past is a prelude of what is to come, future generations of delinquent, dependent, neglected children may be in serious trouble."

DISCUSSION QUESTIONS

1. Explain the importance to juvenile institutions of the concept of *parens patriae*.

2. What does the term *in loco parentis* mean?

3. What were some of the major issues that led reformers to develop a separate juvenile justice system?

4. Explain the role that apprenticeships played in the development of our present system.

PART II

DELINQUENCY
AND
ABUSE

Chapter 3

Causes of Delinquency

In this chapter, we will take a brief look at the causes of juvenile delinquency. While there are many theories advocated to explain why juveniles break the law, most theories can be divided into either the classical or positive school of thought.

According to the classical school, human behavior is rational and the product of free will. Thus, the juvenile chooses to commit his or her criminal acts. The other school of thought, the positive school, contends that juvenile conduct is determined by internal and external influences. Rather than a juvenile choosing between right or wrong, the juvenile's conduct is determined by biological, psychological, or social factors which may be beyond the juvenile's control. While the classical school focuses on the concept of free will, the positive school focuses on the biological, psychological, or sociological influences that affected the conduct in question.

Roots of Delinquency

In 1995, Penn & Schoen Associates Inc. of New York conducted a poll for the National Law Journal. They polled 250 judges who hear juvenile delinquency cases. The judges were asked their opinion of the most significant contributors to violence by kids. The results of the poll showed:

Single parent/family breakdown   26%

Drugs   21%

No jobs	17%
Poor housing	15%
Poor education	7%
All these factors	5%
Don't know	5%
Other reasons	4%

CLASSICAL SCHOOL

The classical school sees human behavior as a product of rational decision making. People, including juveniles, choose between alternate courses of conduct. Their actions are based on a judgmental decision as to which course of conduct will cause the greatest pleasure and produce the least pain. Cesare Beccaria and Jeremy Bentham are credited with founding the classical school. The school was the first organized school of thought on the causes of criminal behavior. Hence, it was named the classical school. The classical school of thought is embodied in our *Declaration of Independence* which is based on the concept that "all men are created equal."

According to the classical school of thought, all people are equal in their capacity to reason. People, however, are naturally hedonistic and desire to maximize pleasure and minimize pain. Therefore, law and social controls are necessary to keep people from interfering with the freedom and rights of others. Without law and social control, individuals seeking the enjoyment of their pleasures would conflict with other individuals seeking similar pleasures. To this line of thinking, the criminal is no different from the noncriminal; he just made wrong choices.

CESARE BECCARIA

Cesare Bonesana, Marchese di Beccaria 1738-1794

Cesare Beccaria was the son of a wealthy family in Italy. His mother, concerned that he lacked the drive and intensity to be a successful businessman, secured for him a professorship at a university. It is reported that he was lazy and preferred to discuss world problems at the local beer pubs rather than engage in other more boring matters.

In 1764, Beccaria published a 17 page essay, *An Essay on Crimes and Punishment*. The essay was very critical of the present criminal justice system in Italy and the judges who conducted the criminal trials. Accordingly, when this document was first published, it was published anonymously. The document, the only significant article ever published by Beccaria, is probably the most exciting article on crime published in the eighteenth century.

To Beccaria, laws are the conditions whereby free and independent men unite to form society. In the essay, Beccaria proposed that criminal laws and punishments should be directed toward humanistic goals. He advocated that the crimes be set forth in statutes that are specific to enable an individual to understand what conduct is prohibited and what conduct is not prohibited. He contended that judges should interpret the laws not make them. According to Beccaria, the real impact of crime was its danger to society. The essential end of punishment is not to torment offenders nor to undo a crime already committed, but rather to prevent offenders from doing further harm to society and to prevent others from committing crimes.

Jeremy Bentham (1748-1832) followed Beccaria as the spokesperson for the classical school. Bentham was a prolific writer and was often described as an "armchair philosopher." His writings covered a variety of topics including those of prison building and the purpose of law. He has been considered by many as the greatest legal philosopher and reformer the world ahs ever seen. Bentham's great-grandfather was a prosperous pawnbroker in London. His father and grandfather were attorneys. Betham studied law and was admitted to the "bar." Bentham, however, had great scorn for the legal profession. He once commented humorously that "only lawyers escape punishments for their ignorance of the law."

Jeremy Bentham
(1748-1832)

Unlike Beccaria, who enjoyed being with people, Bentham was ill at ease in public and preferred books to social outings. His mother died when he was young, and he did not like his stepmother. Apparently, he had his first and only relationship with a woman at the age of 57. When she refused his proposal of marriage, he had nothing further to do with her. Jeremy Bentham died in 1832. Following the terms of his will, his body was dissected. His skeleton was dressed in his usual attire and is on display at the University College in London. For over 160 years, the fully-dressed skeleton has attended the college faculty assemblies. Speakers at the assembly traditionally first voice recognition to Bentham and then to the other members of the assembly and guests.

Bentham was intensely influenced by the times in which he worked. He undertook the task of expounding a comprehensive code of ethics, but later, believing that such an undertaking alone was sterile and too non-utilitarian, he then put great emphasis on the practical problem of eliminating or, at least, decreasing crime. He was aiming at a system of social control that would be a method of controlling human behavior according to a general ethical principle of utilitarianism. This principle of utilitarianism is that an act is not to be judged by an irrational system of absolutes but by a supposedly verifiable principle of the greatest happiness for the greatest number. Bentham said that an act possesses "utility" if it tends to produce benefit, advantage, pleasure, good or happiness or prevents pain, evil, or unhappiness. According to him, the "goodness" or "badness" of an act should be judged by its utility. To Bentham, all human action is reducible to one simple formula of motivation—the pursuit of pleasure and the avoidance of pain. He contended that motive necessarily refers to action. Pleasure, pain, or other events prompt the action. There is no such thing as any sort of motive that is bad; it is only the consequence of the motive that can be bad because of its effect on others. Bentham contended that it was obvious that all persons might derive considerable pleasures from uncontrolled orgies of criminal behavior if there were no pains attached to this criminal behavior. Bentham recognized that any legal sanction must be acceptable to the majority of people before it would be effective. He advocated social engineering to establish effective punishments for criminal behavior. He dismissed any recourse to natural law. He caustically labelled "natural law" as "nonsense on stilts."

Bentham saw punishment as an evil, but a necessary evil to prevent greater evils from being inflicted on society and thus diminishing happiness. According to him, punishment should not be an act of anger, resentment, or vengeance. Punishments should not produce any more pain that necessary to accomplish its purpose. He advocated two principles regarding punishment:

1. The general concept that the less certain the punishment, the more severe that it must be to have any possibility of deterrence.

2. Overtly equivalent punishments are not really equivalent because of the variations among the offenders. Regarding the second principle, a fine to a rich man is a mild punishment compared to similar fine against a poor man.

Bentham contended that extensive capital punishment statutes produce contempt for the laws and make perjury appear meritorious by founding it on humanity.

Classical thinking dominated criminal law during the nineteenth century. To a great extent, even today it dominates our adult penal statutes. In theory, because all people were equal, the law should treat all people equally. The appropriate punishment for a criminal act, therefore, should be based on the crime committed. Putting a price tag on each crime would discourage persons from committing that crime. The more serious the crime, the more serious the punishment should be. According to the classical theorists, if people are aware of the penalty for committing a criminal act, they would be less willing to commit the act. The punishment should be greater than the pleasure received in order to discourage people from committing that particular offense.

Classical thinkers contend a punishment's only purpose should be to protect society. To make punishment effective, it should be prompt, certain, and not unduly harsh. An old Chinese proverb states that "it is better to hang the wrong fellow, than no fellow." Many classical school followers would embrace this proverb since they consider it important in crime prevention that no crime go unpunished.

POSITIVE SCHOOL

By the end of the nineteenth century, the influence of the classical school had declined. As crime continued to increase, people became dissatisfied with the classical school's concept of free will. It was also during this period that Charles Darwin and his book, *The Origin of Species*, gained popularity. Darwin advocated the concept of evolution through natural selection. Darwin had developed his theory based on observations of animals.

Emile Durkheim, considered by many to be the founder of sociology, studied the variations in suicide rates in France's provinces. Based on his observations, Durkheim developed theories on why people commit suicide. Both Darwin and Durkheim were considered to be leaders in the development of scientific knowledge by use of evidence gained through observation. Their approach gave rise to the positive school of thought. Cesare Lombroso is, however, considered the founder of the positive school for proposing one of the first empirically-based theories on the cause of criminal behavior.

Cesare Lombroso
1835-1908

Cesare Lombroso was born in Verona, the second of five children, to Jewish parents. At 15 years of age, he wrote two historical papers that received wide acclaim. He graduated from medical school at the University of Pavia in 1858. During his student days, Lombroso found himself in disagreement with the free will philosophy that dominated Italian academic circles. After graduating from medical school, he volunteered for duty with the Italian army. As an army doctor, Lombroso's assignments included treating persons confined in Italian prisons. Later, he was in charge of several hospitals for the insane. His contributions to the methods of identifying dead bodies have ranked him as one of the innovators of scientific methods in pathology and police work.

Cesare Lombroso is credited with being one of the first researchers to use scientific methods of biology and physics in an attempt to explain human behavior. In his book *The Criminal Man*, Lombroso stated that criminals were atavistic or throwbacks to their ape ancestors. According to Lombroso, certain bodily characteristics indicated a born criminal. Lombroso surmised that criminals were distinguished from noncriminals by the manifestation of multiple physical anomalies.

The positive school focuses not on choice, as does the classicist, but on the influences that cause certain behaviors. According to the positive school, human behavior is determined by internal and/or external influences. Unlike the classical school, the positivists suggest that all men are not created equal and that there are fundamental differences between criminals and non-criminals. According to the posivitists, a criminal act is not the result of a free will decision, but is a symptom of some underlying problem. Thus, the only way to prevent future crime is to correct the underlying problem.

THE SOCIAL THEORIES

Social theories tend to focus on the collective behavior of individuals rather than on individual behavior. Sociologists tend to view delinquent behavior as learned social behavior. A person learns social behavior norms, values, etc. as a result of that person's socialization process. The concept of socialization refers to the process by which a person learns and internalizes the ways of society. The mechanisms of socialization include family, friends, peers, and schools. Many social theorists contend that many types of deviancy and criminality are the result of inadequate or inappropriate socialization experiences during childhood.

Strain Theories

Strain theories assume that excessive pressures or strain on the juvenile often result in criminal conduct. According to strain theorists, people are basically good. Excessive pressures placed on us by society cause some people to commit criminal acts. The basic assumptions of the strain theories include:

- If the juvenile fails to conform to social norms and laws, it is because of excessive pressures that compel the juvenile to commit criminal behavior.

- People are basically moral and desire to conform to society's laws.

Emile Durkheim
(1858-1917)

Emile Durkheim was a French sociologist credited with teaching the first sociology course in a university. His theory of anomie was originally developed to explain suicide.

Durkheim was concerned primarily with the transformation of villages into modern societies and the attendant problems including social disorganization resulting from that transformation. He defined *anomie* [a Greek term meaning *lawlessness*] as a state or a condition that exists within people when a society evolves or changes from primitive to modern. *Anomie* is a condition in which norms of behavior have lost their meaning and become inoperative for large numbers of people. Anomie includes the feeling of social isolation, social loneliness, collective sadness, aimlessness, frustration, and hopelessness.

Between 1978 and 1997, poverty rates increased for juveniles while declining for the elderly

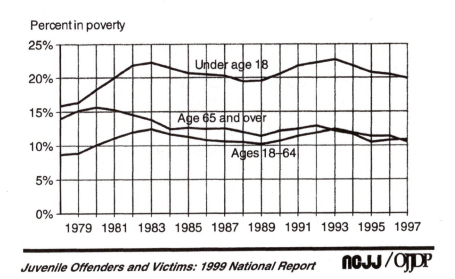

Percent in poverty

Juvenile Offenders and Victims: 1999 National Report   **ncJJ/OJJDP**

Structural Approaches

Emile Durkheim was one of the first researchers to examine the effects that particular social structures have on social deviancy. He disagreed with those who blamed the causes of crime on external characteristics such as economic conditions, population densities, climate, or ecological circumstances. For Durkheim, crime was normal. A society exempt from crime would be a society with no room for individual differences. People in such a society would suffer an even greater crime—boredom.

As Durkheim noted, crime has a functional purpose. Presently, it is one of our largest industries in the United States. More money is spent on crime prevention, courts, and corrections than on education. If the crime problem is eliminated, many people, including this author, would be unemployed.

Robert Merton, building on Durkheim's theory of anomie, contended that individuals live by two sets of criteria: goals and the means to achieve them. Thus, one set [goals] defines the socially acceptable end results and the second set [the means to achieve the goals] defines the socially acceptable methods of achieving the end results. Most individuals in society accept the two sets of criteria. Anomie is experienced when either one or both of the sets is rejected.

Merton theorized that there were five possible adaptations that could develop between cultural goals and the means to achieve them. The adaptations are also viewed as five methods used to deal with anomie. The five are listed below:

1. **Conformity:** In this mode, the individual accepts both the goals and the means to achieve those goals that are accepted by society at large. For example, financial security is a socially accepted goal. The accepted means of achieving this goal is by obtaining a good education. Conformity usually does not lead to deviance and is often considered society's middle-class response.

2. **Innovation:** In this mode, the individual accepts the goals, but not the means to achieve them. Innovation is likened to taking a shortcut. Merton believed this mode of adaption was greater among the lower-socioeconomic status groups, but felt that it could also apply to white-collar crime. For example, in the goal of achieving financial security, the individual may use innovative rather than traditionally accepted means of achieving the goal (i.e., fraudulently obtaining money or property to achieve financial security.) Another example would be where the goal is to make good grades in college, the student, rather than applying the acceptable means of attaining that goal—studying—cheats to obtain good grades.

3. **Ritualism:** In this mode, the individual rejects the accepted goal, but accepts the approved means for achieving that goal. Merton believed that this response, like conformity, does not seem to be a deviant response. For example, parents who want their children to be college educated force their children to go to college. The children go through the ritual of attending classes, but do not apply themselves because they have not accepted the goal of attaining a college education.

4. **Retreatism:** This is when the individual rejects both the accepted goals and the means to achieve the goals. Retreatism is an escape response. Addicts, alcoholics, vagrants, and people who are mentally ill could be viewed as retreating.

5. **Rebellion:** In this mode, the individual rebels against the accepted goals and defines his or her own goals and means to achieve them. Rebellion is an angry, revolutionary response. It differs from retreatism in that rebels generally have strong feelings about their goals. An example would be the outlaw motorcycle gang that has replaced accepted societal goals with their own goals.

Durkheim saw anomie as a temporary state. Merton, in contrast, saw anomie as a permanent feature of all modern societies. Accordingly to Merton, as long as society elevates goals and there are limited means to attain them, anomie will exist.

Albert Cohen, another strain theorist, applied the anomie theory to juvenile delinquency. He saw American society as being comprised primarily of the middle and working classes and felt society placed high premiums on ambition, getting ahead, achievement, and education. These values transcended one's class and were therefore coveted by all. Cohen believed that the middle and working classes were in conflict due to the difference by which they socialized their children. He contended that lower-class boys are taught a different value system and, thus, are not properly socialized to meet the requirements of middle-class society. While Cohen's theories may explain delinquency by the lower-class youths, it fails to explain delinquency by middle- and upper-class youths.

Control Theories

Social control theorists contend that individuals are by nature amoral and will commit deviant acts if they have the chance. They contend that people are born to break the law but will refrain if societal controls are present. Accordingly, if socialization is effective, people will not normally become criminal. Social controls tend to be more effective in small, homogeneous communities than in groups of larger, heterogeneous communities. Social controls that restrain persons from committing criminal behavior include controls that are both external (i.e., police, peers, family, etc.) to the person and those that are internal (i.e., attachment, commitment, involvement and belief).

David Matza and Gresham Sykes, two leading control theorists, contend that juveniles who have no commitment to either societal norms or to criminal norms will drift in and out of delinquency. Matza states that most delinquents spend the majority of their time in law-abiding activities and that the majority of delinquents are drifters who drift into and out of delinquency. In essence, most delinquents are not committed to criminal behavior but rather experimenting in it.

According to Matza and Sykes, people do not commit crimes when they are controlled by morals. When morals are neutralized, people are more apt to commit crimes. Some "techniques of neutralization" are as follows:

1. **Denial of Responsibility:** The delinquent contends that he or she is not responsible for his or her conduct. Bad acts are the result of unloving parents, bad companions, etc.

2. **Denial of Injury:** There was no injury or harm to the victim. For example, gang fighting is seen as a private quarrel and no one else's business. The delinquent feels that that particular behavior does not create any great societal harm.

3. **Denial of Victim:** The victim deserved to have something bad happen to him or her. This technique transforms the victim into the wrongdoer and the offender becomes Robin Hood. Thefts are justified because the store owner sells his products at an outrageous price. Rape is justified because the woman dressed provocatively.

4. **Condemnation of the Condemners:** The offender contends that the police are corrupt, stupid, and brutal. The who-are-they-to-accuse-me syndrome.

5. **Appeal to Higher Loyalties:** The norms of the gangs or peer group are more important than society's norms. "I did it for the benefit of the gang" syndrome.

Travis Hirschi believes that juveniles will break the law and will only refrain from breaking it if special circumstances are present. The special circumstances exist only when a person's bonds to mainstream society are strong. A person's bonds to mainstream society are based on four elements:

1. **Attachment:** Attachment refers to the person's ability to be sensitive to the thoughts, feelings, and desires of others.

2. **Commitment:** Commitment is the rational component in conformity. If a person is committed to society, that person is less likely to commit criminal behavior.

3. **Involvement:** The more a person is involved in the community and conventional things, the less likely a person is to commit a crime.

4. **Belief:** When a person's belief in the values of society or group is strong, the person will be less likely to commit criminal acts.

Cultural Deviance Theories

Cultural deviance theories assume that juveniles are not capable of committing deviant acts, and what are considered deviant acts are deviant only by mainstream standards, not by the offender's standards. According to cultural deviance theories, when a person's cultural values and norms conflict with those of mainstream society, cultural conflict occurs. Cultural deviance theorists accept that lower-class youths have separate identifiable cultural values and norms that are distinct from those of the middle-class and contend that the lower-class youths have a value system that emphasizes aggression and violence in resolving problems.

Social Disorganization Theories

Social disorganization theories hold that there is a relationship between increasing juvenile crime and the increasing complexity of our society. They also contend that social disorganization is a causal factor in juvenile crime. Social disorganization is defined as a breakdown in the bonds of society, especially those involving relationships, teamwork, and morale. In addition, they hold that in communities where the traditional clubs, groups, etc. are no longer in existence, the community is disrupted and there is a lack of consensus of values and norms. Subsequently, this lack of consensus causes higher incidences of delinquency.

Symbolic Interactionist Theories

The two leading symbolic interactionist (SI) theories of delinquency causation are differential association and labeling. The SI theories examine the process of becoming a criminal. Both SI theories hold that criminal behavior is a learned activity. Both theories also place the causes of our behavior in our interpretation of reality.

Differential association (DA) has been the most influential social-psychological theory of crime causation for the past sixty years. According to DA, a person learns to commit criminal acts the same way we learn to play basketball, baseball, and other childhood games. The learning also includes the manner and techniques of committing the crime. Criminal behavior is learned from the message we receive from the people with whom we associate. Some associations, however, have greater effect on us than others. For example, the messages we receive from our close friends or family have more impact on us than those we receive from the media.

Differential Association Propositions

1. Criminal behavior is learned, not inherited; hence, anyone can learn to be a criminal.

2. Criminal behavior is learned with other persons in the process of communication. According to Edwin Sutherland, founder of differential association theory, both criminal and noncriminal

behavior are learned through our associations with others.

3. The principal part of learning criminal behavior occurs within intimate personal groups. We identify with our reference groups and they, in turn, guide our values. The contacts that a juvenile has with his or her peers, family, and friends have the greatest influence on the juvenile's behavior.

4. When criminal behavior is learned, the learning includes: (1) techniques of committing the crime, which can be very complicated or very simple; and (2) the specific direction of motives, drives, rationalizations, and attitudes. Our associations with others influence not only whether or not we commit criminal acts, but also the methods we use to commit crimes.

5. The specific direction of motives and drives is learned from definitions of the legal codes as favorable or unfavorable to violation of the law.

6. A person becomes delinquent because of an excess of definitions favorable to violation of the law over definitions unfavorable to violation of the law.

7. Differential associations vary in frequency, duration, priority, and intensity.

8. The process of learning criminal behavior by association with criminal and noncriminal patterns involves all of the mechanisms that are commonly involved in any other learning.

9. Although criminal behavior is an expression of general needs and values, it is not explained by those general needs and values since noncriminal behavior is an expression of the same needs and values.

Labeling

The followers of the labeling theory contend that society labels certain people as deviant. The selected persons accept the label and thus become deviant. For example, if we consider a youth bad and the youth subconsciously accepts that label, he will become delinquent. As Frank Tannenbaum in his book, *Crime and the Community* states:

> The process of making the criminal...is a process of tagging, defining, identifying, segregating, describing, emphasizing, making, conscious, and self-conscious; it becomes a way of stimulating, suggesting, emphasizing, and evoking the very traits complained of. . .The person becomes the thing he is described as being.

When a person commits a crime, there is no automatic process that labels the person a criminal. Accordingly, the labeling theory focuses not on why a person commits a criminal act, but rather on how the individual becomes labeled as a criminal or juvenile delinquent.

Hypotheses of Labeling Theory

No act is intrinsically criminal. A person does not become a criminal by violation of the law, but only by being labeled a criminal by society. We all commit criminal acts; therefore, people should not be dichotomized into criminal and noncriminal labels. The act of getting caught starts the labeling process. The criminal justice system makes differential decisions regarding the handling of delinquency based on the juvenile's race and socioeconomic class.

BIOLOGICAL THEORIES

Biological theories are more popular in Europe than in the United States. The biological theories are based on the concept that the juvenile delinquent is biologically inferior to the nondelinquent youth. The biological process may be the result of our genetic makeup or brought on by the things we eat. Biological theories are concrete, simple, cause-and-effect answers to the complicated crime problem. There are four subdivisions of biological theories:

1. Inferiority theories that suggest the criminal is inferior in a biological way from the noncriminal.

2. The different and defective theories which see the criminal as different from the noncriminal.

3. The body-type theories which contend that a person's body type is a factor in whether or not that individual commits a crime.

4. Nutrition and vitamin theories which scrutinize our diet to locate causes of criminal behavior.

PSYCHOLOGICAL THEORIES

The psychological theories were developed from the fields of psychiatry and psychology in the early twentieth century. They are based primarily on the works of Sigmund Freud. Freud believed that aggression and violence have their roots in instinct. According to Freud, violence is a response to thwarting the pleasure principle. He developed the concept that each of us has a "death wish" that is a constant source of aggressive impulses and that this death wish tries to reduce the organism to an inanimate state. The death wish may be expressed directly, manifested indirectly as in hunting, or sublimated into sadomasochism.

Sigmund Freud
1856-1939

Sigmund Freud was born in Freiberg, Moravia, of Jewish parents. In his youth, he was interested in philosophy and humanities. He was a distinguished graduate of the medical college at the University of Vienna. From 1881 to 1902, Freud was in private practice with an emphasis in neurology. In 1902, he was appointed a professor of neuropathology at the University of Vienna. Freud remained there until 1923, when he was forced to retire due to cancer. In 1938, he fled Vienna to escape the Nazis and moved to London. He was one of the most controversial and influential persons of the twentieth century. Freud was a person of great industry, learning, and extraordinary eloquence. He was also witty and expansive. Until 1902, however, he primarily worked in isolation and shrank from those who opposed him. After 1902, he worked with other famous scholars including Carl Jung and Alfred Adler. However, later in his life, Freud considered them bitter enemies.

Psychoanalytic and personality theories concentrate on the causes of crime as arising within the individual. The causes are not, however, seen as inherited or biologically determined. Generally, they are seen as the result of a dysfunctional or abnormal emotional adjustment or of deviant personality traits that were formed in early socialization or childhood development (Ronald L. Akers, *Criminological Theories*, Los Angeles: Roxbury, 1994).

Sociopathy

Some theorists contend that delinquent behavior is the result of a particular personality structure known as the "sociopathic personality." The terms "sociopathy," "psychopathy," and "antisocial personality" are interchangeable and tend to refer to the same personality disorder. These terms refer to a pattern of behavior exhibited by many juvenile delinquents and non-juvenile delinquents. Some researchers contend that the sociopath is mentally ill; others do not. Many people who are identified as sociopaths do not commit criminal behavior. As James Q. Wilson and Richard J. Herrnstein (*Crime and Human Nature: The Definitive Study of the Causes of Crime.* New York: Simon and Schuster, 1985) stated: "Psychopathy only overlaps with criminality; it is not identical with it. If for no other reason than the vagaries of the criminal justice system, there would be many non-psychopathic offenders and many psychopathic non-offenders."

There are several theories regarding the causes of sociopathy. Some researchers believe that the personality disorder is biological, physical, and\or genetically based. Others contend that it is the result of the person's emotional development caused by poor relationships and faulty child-parent relationships in the person's early years. A third group sees the personality disorder as the result of the person's social environment (i.e., poverty, racism, disrupted family life, poor housing, and/or limited education).

Thinking Pattern Theories

The thinking pattern theorists study the offender's cognitive processes. These theorists contend that the delinquent juvenile has different thinking patterns from the non-delinquent juvenile. They focus on the offender's intellect, logic, mental processes, rationality, and language usage. The mind of the delinquent is affected by his or her cognitive processes, and it is, in turn, the cognitive processes that influence behavior. Accordingly, the way that delinquents think and what they tell themselves in their minds will determine the offender's behavioral choices.

The most detailed study regarding the thinking patterns of criminals was by Samuel Yochelson and Stanton E. Samenow. Their longitudinal study took place over a 15 year period and involved intensive interviews and therapy of criminals. Yochelson and Samenow concluded that criminals think differently from noncriminals.

DYSFUNCTIONAL FAMILIES

The family has long been viewed as one of the most important factors in the socialization process of juveniles. The family originally provides the child's identity, teaches social roles, moral standards, and moral obligations. The relationship between broken homes and juvenile delinquency has been the focus of many studies in the twentieth century. Most early studies concluded that there was a direct relationship between broken homes and delinquency. Therefore, most researchers believe that the family has failed to provide for the child's emotional, intellectual and social needs. Other studies, however, have concluded that the effects of a broken home on juvenile crime have been negligible. There is also evidence that broken homes have had a greater impact on African American youths than on other racial groups.

However, recent studies tend to indicate that the quality of home life is more important than whether or not the child's family is intact. The most important factors in determining the quality of home life are presence or absence of family conflict,

The teen birth rate in the United States is far higher than in many other countries

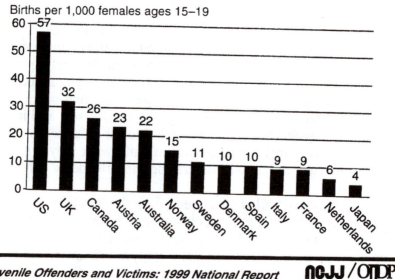

Births per 1,000 females ages 15–19

Juvenile Offenders and Victims: 1999 National Report   **ncJJ/OJDP**

poor marital adjustment, rejection in the home, and lack of or inconsistent discipline. The studies tend to indicate that when discipline in the home is punitive and/or lax, and erratic, high rates of delinquent behavior result. Shelon and Eleanor Glueck studied marital relationships and family cohesiveness. They concluded that the better the marital relationship and family cohesiveness, the less likely there was to be delinquency.

There appears to be a direct relationship between child abuse or neglect and involvement in criminal behavior. The extent of this relationship will be difficult to establish. It is now a common practice for anyone arrested for a serious or violent crime to blame child abuse or neglect as the problem. Accordingly, it will be difficult for any researcher to establish whether or not child abuse or neglect was a factor. Child abuse and neglect are further discussed in Chapter 5.

Homes in which substance abuse or mental health problems exist also have a higher incidence of delinquency. This is not surprising, since these families are more likely to also be dysfunctional.

Over half of all black children lived with only one parent in 1997

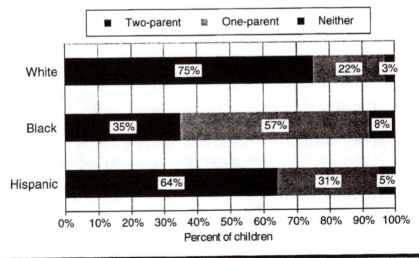

Juvenile Offenders and Victims: 1999 National Report   NCJJ/OJJDP

Children and Justice

Three out of four students said that they generally feel safe on campus.

One student in five has seen guns on campus, excluding weapons carried by the police.

Four out of ten students have family members who have been in prison.

More than 40% of students have tried drugs, while less than 15% use drugs every week.

Only one student in ten has been involved in gangs.

One student in four is sometimes too afraid to use the school restrooms.

1995 survey of 1,200 plus students at Lincoln High School in Los Angeles, California.

Out-of-wedlock births are increasing, especially for minority females in the inner cities. It appears unlikely that many children growing up in these families will have their emotional, physical, and moral needs met. Therefore, this increasing trend would indicate another group of delinquents emerging.

SCHOOLS

Children were once expected to work on the family farm or in the family business. Now, with most families living in urban neighborhoods and child labor laws preventing their working in businesses, the only major place in society for most youths is school. Accordingly, it should not be surprising that there is a direct relationship between failure in school and involvement in juvenile delinquency. Success in schools is not easy for many youths, particularly those children who lack the support of a stable home environment. Children who do poorly in school tend to be more disruptive and many drop out of school. Those who are labeled "dropouts" by society generally have low self-esteem which is conducive to involvement in criminal behavior.

Dropouts generally lack employment skills and have low employability. The likelihood of low-level jobs and welfare dependency increases the chance of involvement in criminal activities and the search for illegitimate job opportunities.

Outside the family, the school has the greatest influence in the lives of children and adolescents. School profoundly influences the hopes and dreams of youth.

Many of America's children bring one or more risk factors to school with them, and these factors may hinder the development of their academic and social potential. School prevention programs, including traditional delinquency prevention programs not related to the school's education mission, can assist the family and the community by identifying at-risk youth, monitoring their progress, and intervening with effective programs at critical times during a youth's development. [OJJDP Summary, *Comprehensive Strategy for Serious, Violent, and Chronic Juvenile Offenders*, June, 1994.]

The Relationship Between Lower Grades and Delinquency

In 1980, Josefina Figueira-McDonough conducted research to explore the usefulness of Robert Merton's Anomie Theory in explaining delinquent behavior among high school students. Using data collected from self-administered surveys of 1,735 tenth grade students, the findings suggested that all types of delinquency increased inversely with grade average: the lower the grades of the students, the more their involvement in delinquent behavior.

In sum, the results of this study support the hypothesis that failing students are under high strain. A conclusion is drawn that more attention should be paid to the strain of failing students as a motivating force for delinquency.

Source: On the Usefulness of Merton's Anomie Theory: Academic Failure and Deviance Among High School Students, (1983), Youth and Society, 14(3), 259-279.

High school completion rates among persons ages 18–24 were consistently lower for Hispanics than others between 1972 and 1996

Percent of youth ages 18–24 completing high school

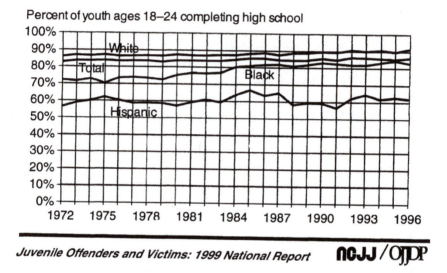

DISCUSSION QUESTIONS

1. The classical school followers believed that in order to prevent crime, punishment should be swift and certain. What can we do to make our punishment swifter and more certain?

2. Distinguish between the primary purposes of punishment as advocated by the classical school and the positive school.

3. Why are juveniles likely to be involved in delinquent activities?

4. Discuss the importance of the family and school and their relationship to delinquent behaviors.

Chapter 4

Juvenile Gangs

No discussion of the juvenile justice system is complete without an examination of the juvenile gang problem. The problem of youth gangs is both a long-standing and costly one. First, there is the direct cost to individual victims resulting from delinquent acts by youth gangs. Second, the community, as a whole, pays significantly for gang related activities (i.e., the cost of law enforcement, judicial proceedings, etc.). No one can place a dollar amount on the loss of life and the physical and emotional suffering experienced by the victims of gang crimes. In addition, there is a loss to society of the youth's potential skills and contributions due to his or her gang involvement. Juvenile gangs are the subject of many present-day research endeavors.

WHAT CONSTITUTES A GANG?

According to West Virginia University Professor R.J. Fox, everyone has their own definition of gangs. The definition depends on who you talk to. A California police detective, in summing up the state's two-page definition of what constitutes a gang, stated: "Three or more who join, act in consort, find a gang name, find a gang territory, commit criminal acts for the further enhancement of antisocial behavior. It is the criminal acts that separate many gangs from other youth groups." Juvenile gangs are defined by *The Encyclopedia of Crime and Justice* as:

> ... self-formed associations of youths distinguished from other types of youth groups by their routine participation in illegal activities. They differ from other

types of law-violating youth groups by manifesting better developed leadership, greater formalization, more clearly defined identification with localities or enterprises, and a greater degree of deliberate intent in the conduct of crime (Sanford H. Kadesh, ed., vol.4, New York: Free Press, 1983).

For purposes of our discussion, a juvenile gang is defined as a group of youths which has formed an allegiance for a common purpose and which engages in unlawful or criminal activity. In this chapter, we will examine juvenile gangs. Parts of this chapter repeat material in other chapters. This is considered necessary in order to provide a complete view of the gang problem in this chapter.

GANG CATEGORIES

As will be discussed later, there are many types of youth gangs existing in the United States today. Most of the gangs, however, may be grouped into certain predominant categories. These gang categories include:

- **White Supremacist:** This gang is typically a drug-abusing and racially motivated gang that is also frequently involved in satanic worship and practice in the occult. Some of the white gangs are called "skinheads." They are repeatedly involved in hate crimes against minorities.

- **African American:** The two prominent African-American gangs are the Crips and the Bloods. These gangs are identified by the colors they wear. They are rival gangs originally from Southern California and are connected with drugs, robberies, and street violence.

- **Hispanic:** Hispanic gangs tend to be territorial turf- and neighborhood-based street families. They tend to stress extreme loyalty and machismo. They are known to commit burglaries and crimes involving street violence. They also deal in drugs.

- **Asian:** Asian gangs are harder to identify since they do not have a particular dress code. They tend to be violent and prey on their own culture, especially new immigrants.

- **Multiracial:** In recent years, there appears to have been an increase in multiracial gangs that tend to be neighborhood-based in poor communities.

HISTORY OF JUVENILE GANGS

Juvenile gangs have been responsible for an integral part of our American history. John Hancock, the largest signature on the *Declaration of Independence*, is rumored to have made a fortune using youth gangs to smuggle goods into the colonies. New York has had problems with youth street gangs since the 1820s. One of the first gangs in New York City was the Forty Thieves. This gang murdered, robbed, and mugged. The gang members came from areas that were overcrowded with substandard housing, broken homes, and limited opportunities to gain lawful employment. The predecessors of today's youth gangs used extortion, intimidation, robbery, murder, and other acts of violence for purposes of gain.

Frederic Thrasher conducted a classic study of 1,313 juvenile gangs in Chicago in the 1920s. (*The Gang*, Chicago, University of Chicago Press, 1927). His conclusions were as follows:

➤ Gangs are merely loose federations of individual boys who are trying to work out emotional problems.

➤ There is little consensus, little identification, and rapidly changing leadership in gangs.

➤ Most gangs are really "cliques" involving quasi-permanent relationships between individuals interacting as a social unit.

➤ Gangs become the primary social group and replace the family in the psychosocial development of the person who feels the need for acceptance and finds it in the delinquent gang.

Youth gangs started on the East Coast. Soon they were present in Los Angeles and Chicago. Now, young gangs are present in every major city in the United States and in many of the smaller cities as well. Recently, it was estimated that there were over 950 different youth gangs in Los Angeles with an estimated membership of over 100,000.

Black Gangs

Black gangs have existed in the Los Angeles area for many years. They concentrated their activities mainly within their own neighborhoods. For many years, the gangs went virtually unnoticed by the general public. Most of the gangs were originally social groups that evolved into gangs. The early gangs were the Gladiators, Slausons, Pythons, Rebel Rousers, Businessmen, and Watts' Farmers. By the 1970s, most of these gangs had disappeared.

Present-day black gangs started in the early 1970s. Today, they are divided into two separate and major gangs—the Crips and the Bloods. The Bloods are also known as the Pirus. Each of these gangs is subdivided into different sets that identify themselves by local streets or landmarks. Various sects or factions of the Crips often have altercations. The Bloods do not seem to have this problem.

The most commonly accepted version of the origin of the Crips is that they were started by Raymond Washington in the West Los Angeles area and preyed on other African-Americans who were not gang members. They established a reputation as the strongest of the black gangs. Later, other gangs started renaming themselves and adopting "Crips" into the new names. For example, the Main Street gang became the Main Street Crips. While the gangs may have adopted the Crips' name, they tended to retain the same leaders and membership. They remained independent but shared a common name.

The Bloods (or Pirus) evolved later than the Crips. Their development, however, was very similar to that of the Crips. Sylvester Scott and Vincent Owens are generally given credit for developing the Bloods in the early 1970s known then as the Compton Pirus. This gang originated on West Pirus Street in the California city of Compton. The Bloods grew quickly and became extremely strong. While the Crips outnumber the Bloods, the Bloods make up in violence what they lack in numbers.

The Bloods identify with the color red and refer to each other as "Blood." They will normally carry a red rag and wear articles of clothing that are red. Generally, they write their graffiti in red. Frequently, they will use the terms "Blood," "Piru," or "C/K" (Crip killer). The Crips identify with the color blue. They will usually have a blue rag in their possession. In addition, they will normally wear articles of clothing that are blue or have blue shoelaces. They refer to one another as "Cuzz."

Hispanic Gangs

The Hispanic gangs originated in the 1930s or 1940s with the influx of Mexican nationals into California. Like the African-American gangs, they originally were not noticed outside of their own neighborhoods. The Hispanic gangs stress loyalty to the gang and will often do newsworthy acts such as drive-by shootings to demonstrate their loyalty. Gang members usually are required to earn their placa and the right to wear the gang logo.

Hispanic gangs tend to dress in a particular manner. Khaki pants, plaid wool shirts, and black shoes are very common for them. Generally, they wear their clothes too large with the pants gathered around the waist and dragging on the ground. They also use colors to signify differences in gang philosophy. For example, the Eastside Torrance gang will wear black khaki pants and brown bandanas. The Tortilla Flats gang will wear gray khaki pants and blue bandanas. The Keystone gang wears brown khaki pants and red bandanas.

CHARACTERISTICS OF JUVENILE GANGS

According to Walter Miller, juvenile gangs can be distinguished from other types of youth groups on the basis of the below listed characteristics:

- Leadership: gang leadership is generally better defined and more identifiable than that of other youth groups.

- Formal Organization: gangs tend to have more formal or organized elements within the organization.

Yablonski conducted a study of Los Angeles gangs in the 1960s. (*The Violent Gang*, Chicago: Macmillan, 1962). He concluded that youths who were more likely to join violent gangs were youths from disorganized slum communities who had defective socialization because of sociopathic personalities. He contended that the inability to function in normal social structures, the lack of empathy and guilt for their destructive actions, and the lack of social conscience toward others are dominant characteristics of violent gang members. Although his study was conducted in the 1960s, many researchers contend that his findings regarding youths who are more likely to join gangs are still valid today.

NATURE OF THE GANG PROBLEM

A report by the Office of Juvenile Justice and Delinquency Prevention, United States Department of Justice (OJJDP) concluded that gangs are active in nearly every state, including Alaska and Hawaii, as well as Puerto Rico and other territories. ("Gang Suppression and Intervention: Problem and Response" and "Gang Suppression and Intervention: Community Models," October 1994). The report estimated that there are approximately 1,439 well-organized youth gangs in the United States. The report also noted that approximately 55 percent of the gang members were African-American and about 33 percent were Hispanic, 75 percent of the gang members had prior police records, and 11.3 percent of the FBI index crimes in their jurisdictions were committed by youth gang members. The report also noted that the gang problem is not limited to juveniles, and adults were reported to be involved in about 46 percent of the youth gang incidents. While gang members with arrest records were responsible for a disproportionate amount of violent crime, the proportion of total violent crime committed by gang members is still estimated to be fairly low. It is important to consider, however, that the statistics on violent crimes by gang members depend, to a large measure, on the local definitions of gang incidents.

Gang Behavior

The OJJDP report indicates that the key aspects of gang behavior are its prevalence in violent crimes, such as homicide and aggravated assault, and its concentration in certain types of neighborhoods. Gang homicides have accounted for between 25 and 30 percent of the homicides in Los Angeles in recent years. Chicago, which has a more restrictive definition of gang incidents, considers about 10 percent of its homicides as youth gang incidents. It is evident that there is a close relationship between gangs, violence, and a significant crime problem.

When the criminal records of youth gang members are compared with those youths who are not in gangs, it is clear that young gang membership is associated with significantly higher levels of delinquency and index crimes. The rate of violent offenses for gang members is three times higher than the rate for non-gang members. In addition, gang membership appears to prolong the extent and seriousness of criminal careers.

Evidence indicates that a growing proportion of gang youths use and sell drugs. Many youth gangs or cliques within gangs are heavily engaged in street sales of drugs and in mid-level drug distribution. The existence of a relationship between gang-related violence and drug use and sale is unclear. While competition for drug markets may increase the likelihood of gang conflict, most gang homicides appear to be the result of turf wars.

Trafficking in drugs is more characteristic of African-American gangs than Hispanic gangs. In those cases where drug dealing is regarded as the primary purpose of the youth gang, a higher percentage of index crime in the community is attributed to gangs. Gangs that are affiliated across neighborhoods, cities, or states were also more likely to be connected with adult criminal organizations. Such gangs are more likely to be engaged in both street and higher-level drug trafficking, such as transporting drugs across jurisdictions. The report concludes that it is more likely that drug selling or trafficking opportunities have more to do with the development of a serious criminal youth gang problem than vice versa.

Gang Structure

In general, gangs are still regarded as loosely organized. They are, however, more structured than other delinquent groups. Some gangs base membership on age. Others base membership on geographic areas, such as neighborhoods. Some gangs are part of a larger structure known as a "nation." Gang sizes range from four or five members to thousands. Gangs tend to have different classes of members. These classes include core members (e.g., leaders, associates and regulars) peripheral or fringe members, and recruits (e.g., wannabees). The core members are regarded as the inner clique that determines the basic nature and level of gang activity. The extent to which gang members maintain membership status is unclear. It appears that some members join for only short periods of time and that youths may change membership from one gang to another. Core members are generally more involved in delinquency than fringe members.

In recent years, it has appeared that members remain in gangs longer in order to pursue economic gain through increasingly serious criminal acts. The age range of gang membership has expanded in the past few decades. Incidents of extreme gang violence are concentrated in the older teen and young adult age range. The average age of an arrested gang member is 17. The gang member arrested for homicide tends to be several years older than those gang members arrested for other crimes.

While male gang members outnumber female members by about 20 to 1, at least half of the gangs have female auxiliaries or affiliates. Some gangs have female members. There appear to be only a few unaffiliated female gangs. Generally, females join the gangs at a younger age and leave at a younger age than do males. In addition, females' rate of involvement in gang activities is less substantial than that of males. The OJJDP report concluded that, contrary to myth, female gang members are more likely to play a positive role and temper the behavior of male members rather than incite gang members to violent or criminal activity.

Gang socialization processes apparently vary by age, context, and situation. The report states that the reasons for joining gangs include: a need or wish for recognition, status, safety or security, power, excitement, and new experiences. It was noted that youth raised under conditions of social deprivation are particularly drawn to gangs. Many youth view joining a gang as normal and respectable, even when the consequence results in a series of delinquent acts. In certain communities, gang affiliation is a part of an expected socialization process. Often, the gang is an extension of the family. Some youths join gangs as a result of a rational calculation in which the objectives are to achieve security or financial benefits. For others, gangs provide sanction, contacts, and experience that leads to adult criminal activities.

Social Contexts of Gang Membership

According to the research report, community disintegration, increasing relative poverty, social isolation, and the rapid urban population change have contributed to the failure of our social institutions and to the resulting development of youth gangs. The interplay of social disorganization and lack of access to legitimate resources is considered by many to be the reason for the development of seriously deviant groups such as youth gangs.

Family disorganization (as indicated by single-parent families) and conflict between parents appear to be contributing factors to gang membership. In addition, some families condone, or implicitly approve, gang membership.

Although gang violence usually does not erupt in schools, gang recruitment and activity planning appear to take place at schools. A student who does poorly in school and has little identification with the school staff is more likely to become a gang member. The poor student generally does not like school and uses school more often for gang planning purposes or recruitment than for academic or social learning processes.

Organized crime appears to be more involved with youth gangs than it was in the 1950s or 1960s. Many researchers suggest that in the 1990s there is a closer relationship between members of youth gangs and adults involved in organized crime. These researchers suggest that youth gangs are often subunits of organized crime for purposes of drug distribution, car thefts, extortion, and burglary.

Emerging Gang Problems

The OJJDP research report concluded that there were differences between emerging and chronic gang problems, particularly since the 1980s. The research noted that the beginning of gang problems in various cities seems to show a pattern.

The emergence of gang problems is indicated by youth congregating or hanging out at certain locations. The lines of membership of these small groups are unclear. There is a general absence of distinctive features of the traditional youth gangs such as names, colors, symbols, graffiti, turf, and drive-by shootings. However, with the passage of time, characteristic youth gang behavior surfaces. The youth gangs clash. Vandalism and graffiti in and around the schools and local area increases. Tension between the youth groups results in an increase in the recruiting of new members. Assaults become more frequent at shopping and recreation centers and other areas favored by youth groups. These activities result in stabbings, shootings, and homicides, thus the media focuses greater attention on gangs. The youth gang problem crystallizes as it assumes crisis proportions. The police, politicians, schools, and other agencies begin to take more action.

Often, the community leaders will argue that the problem is imported from outside, from gangs in other cities. The OJJDP report concluded, however, that most new gangs are not franchises nor are they developed as part of a calculated expansion for status or purposes of economic gain. The emigration of gangs to communities that have been free of them appears to result from the movement of low-income families into communities with improved housing, employment opportunities, and a better life for their children. Youth in these families have been or are prone to gang membership. The newcomers seek the protection of status and gang membership in the new communities, often at school. Often, newcomers move into gang membership because indigenous youth are hostile to them.

Other community leaders argue that the local youth were ready to participate in gangs without the need for outsiders because of deteriorating family, school, social, and economic conditions. Usually within two or three years after the city has recognized that a gang problem exists, a serious drug trade problem develops. According to the research study, the relationship of youth gang members to drug trafficking and other more organized criminal activities is more difficult to detect.

In cities with chronic problems where gangs are established, cycles of organized gang activity, including retaliatory killings, are often followed by periods of relative tranquility as older, more serious offenders are imprisoned. Later, the offenders may return to their gangs where many resume patterns of gang violence, or they may stimulate the development of new gangs and in turn recruit younger gang members. Youth gangs often serve as a basis for recruitment and even a potential infrastructure for the development of adult criminal enterprises.

Succeeding generations of youths may create different patterns of gang-related behavior. For some youth gangs, drug use, vandalism, and satanism may become popular. Generally, however, the youth involved in these activities shift and integrate into the traditional forms of youth gang violence.

According to the OJJDP report, drug trafficking and other adult criminal patterns are most readily developed in areas of chronic poverty and in minority ghettos. The adult criminal system in those areas tends to reinforce youth gang patterns. The reinforcement is more often indirect rather than direct.

Reasons for Leaving Gangs

Several factors are credited with motivating youths to leave gangs. Those factors include:

- Growing up and getting smarter
- Fear of injury for oneself and others

- Prison experience
- A girlfriend or marriage
- A job
- Drug dealing
- Concern for youth
- Interests in politics
- Religious experience
- The assistance and interest of a helping adult

Often, the transition out of the gang results in a complete break with gang peers or leaving the neighborhoods. In other cases, it means simply desisting from gang violence and criminality, but not restricting relationships with former gang buddies. There appears to be a stronger tie to the gang culture for African-American youths than for Hispanic youths. The opportunities for leaving the gang for legitimate life-styles seems more available to Hispanic youths than to African-American youths.

RESPONSES TO YOUTH GANGS

As noted in the OJJDP report, there are five basic strategies for dealing with youth gangs:

1. Neighborhood mobilization
2. Social intervention (notably youth outreach and work with street gangs)
3. Provision for social and economic opportunities (special school and job programs)
4. Gang suppression and incarceration
5. An organizational development strategy (police gang and specialized probation units)

The report noted that these strategies are often mixed.

Neighborhood mobilization evolved in the 1920s and was an early attempt to bind together local citizens, social institutions, and the criminal justice system in a variety of informal and formal ways. Neighborhood agencies worked to socialize youth in general and did not specifically target delinquent or gang youth. These early efforts developed into the social intervention approach, a more sophisticated outreach program to street gangs in the 1950s. Under this latter approach, youth gangs were viewed as relatively normal phenomena for socially deprived neighborhoods. This approach assumed that the youths could be redirected through social intervention steps. Such steps included counseling, recreation programs, work groups, and social service referrals.

The social and economic opportunities approach developed in the 1960s. This approach was not specifically targeted to the youth gang problem. In the late 1950s, there was rising concern regarding the increasing rates of juvenile delinquency, unemployment, and school failures of intercity youths. As part of the "Great Society," a series of innovative programs designed to change institutional structures and reduce poverty were started. The programs included Head Start and Job Corps. There was considerable debate regarding the effectiveness of these programs, especially since some evidence indicated that there was a rise in the scope and seriousness of the gang problem in the late 1960s and early 1970s.

The suppression and incarceration approach emerged in the late 1970s and early 1980s. It is probably the prevailing approach used today. Its development is related to several factors: the decline in local community and youth outreach programs, insufficient opportunity provisions to target or modify gang structures, the changing labor market that can no longer adequately absorb unskilled young workers, and the increasing criminalization and sophistication of youth gangs. The 1980s witnessed an increasing reliance on the law enforcement-dominated suppression approach. Youth gangs were increasingly viewed as dangerous and criminal. Community protection became the key goal, the final approach includes the use of organizational development strategies which continue to evolve in the 1990s. Focusing on the goal of community protection, specialized units were developed to combat juvenile crime and to remove gang leaders and serious youth offenders from society. Often this involved the establishment of specialized police units and specialized probation units to deal with youth gangs.

Institutional Responses to Gang Problems

Police: Law enforcement agencies are using increasingly sophisticated suppression techniques to deal with juvenile gangs. These techniques include surveillance, stakeouts, aggressive patrol and arrest, follow-up investigations, and intelligence-gathering. In addition, the police are using complex data and information systems to monitor youth gang activities. There have been no systematic evaluations of the varied police approaches to determine their effectiveness. The OJJDP report concludes that suppression efforts may be effective in smaller cities or those with emerging gang problems. There is little evidence, however, that the efforts have reduced the gang problems in large cities like Los Angeles or Chicago.

Some police departments have used community-oriented strategies that focus on community collaboration, social intervention, and opportunity enhancements. Officers assigned to the gang problem in these communities have provided counseling, job development, referral, and tutoring. The officers, also, have engaged in extensive community relations and development activities. There is some evidence that the youth gang problem has declined in cities that have used these complex approaches. It is not clear, however, whether the decline is due to changed police strategies or unrelated structural changes in the community environment, such as more legitimate jobs becoming available or greater access to income-producing drug trafficking.

Prosecution: Prosecutors have used vertical prosecution to focus on serious gang offenders. Under vertical prosecution, one prosecutor or team of prosecutors handles the case from start to finish. In addition, added emphasis is placed on those cases in which the individual has been identified as a serious delinquent or youth gang leader.

Courts: The judiciary has emphasized a get-tough strategy and the removal of serious juvenile gang offenders from the jurisdiction of juvenile courts in favor of adult criminal courts. While judges generally use a broad social rehabilitation approach with respect to juvenile offenders, little consideration is given to using such approaches for juvenile gang offenders.

Corrections: Most probation and parole departments have not given any special attention to the gang problem. However, innovative approaches such as specialized programs emphasizing suppression in collaboration with law enforcement are being used in major California cities. These programs often involve vertical case management and intensive supervision. The California Youth Authority has used former gang members and a strong community involvement strategy in an attempt to reduce gang activity. Traditional suppression approaches still predominate in most of our prisons. A few youth institutions are using comprehensive community-based approaches to reduce gang problems.

Schools: Gang problems in schools often originate in the streets. Students who are gang members bring with them destructive gang attitudes and behaviors. They claim the schools as their turf. Most gang members are bored with school and feel inadequate in class. The peak recruitment period for gang members appears to be between the fifth and eighth grades. It is at this time that students are more in danger of dropping out because of poor grades. There has been a tendency for schools to ignore the problem because of other concerns. However, schools may be the best community resource for the prevention of and the early intervention into youth gang problems. Youth services are being used in some communities to establish gang prevention programs. These programs often target the high-risk gang youth for special supervision and remedial education. In addition, many schools are now establishing special anti-gang curriculums for children in the early elementary grades. There is a lack of clear evidence as to the effectiveness of these programs.

According to the OJJDP research, there are at least three components to a school's effective control or suppression strategy.

1. The development of a school gang code, with guidelines specifying an appropriate response by teachers and staff to different kinds of gang behavior, including a mechanism for dealing with serious gang delinquency.

2. The application of these rules and regulations within a context of positive relationships and open communication by school personnel with parents, community agencies, and students.

3. A clear distinction between gang and non-gang related activity so as not to exaggerate the scope of the problem.

ANTI-GANG PROGRAMS

In this section, we will review some of the more popular support programs designed to diminish the hold of gangs on their members or to lessen the chance that young people will join a gang. Despite the fact that juvenile gangs are the subject of many research efforts, it appears that none of the programs discussed below have been systematically evaluated.

■ In-school anti-gang education programs — alert grade school youths to the consequences of gang membership and encourage their participation in positive alternative activities.

■ Social agency crisis intervention teams — mediate disagreements between the gangs. The teams are designed to work closely with police and probation officers to identify potential trouble spots, prevent gang retaliations, and resolve gang problems without violence.

- Alternative education programs — teach young people basic skills, which they may not have mastered while in school and prepare dropouts for GED tests.

- Vocational training and job placement assistance — supports former gang members in their efforts to hold jobs.

- Pairing of gang members with local businessmen — provides the gang member with support, guidance, and a positive role model, and channels energy into positive activities.

- Parent education classes and similar programs — help promote the family as a strong unit capable of providing youths with emotional support and supervision as well as food, clothing, and shelter.

- Instructional classes — provided to school personnel, community residents, and agency staff members on gang activities and their impact, signs and symbols, and methods to counter gang influence.

National Youth Gang Survey: Executive Summary

The youth gang problem in the United States has become an important public policy issue in recent years, largely because of the growth of youth gang violence and apparent proliferation of youth gangs throughout the United States. In order to measure the extent of the problem, the U.S. Dept. of Justice, Office of Justice Programs, Office of Juvenile Justice and Delinquency Prevention's 1996 National Youth Gang Survey was conducted by the National Youth Gang Center. This survey was the largest of its type, and the results are fully representative of the nation as a whole. Almost 5,000 law enforcement agencies were surveyed, and more than 80 percent of the survey recipients responded. Survey recipients were asked about youth gangs in their jurisdiction in 1996, including questions about the number of gangs and gang members, gang member demographics, gang drug distribution, gang migration, and the level of crime in which gang members were involved. A *gang* was defined as "a group of youths or young adults in (the respondent's) jurisdiction that (the respondent) or other responsible persons in (the respondent's) agency or community are willing to identify or classify as a 'gang'."

The 1996 National Youth Gang Survey was sent to two groups: a statistically representative sample of 3,024 law enforcement agencies and a sample of 1,956 law enforcement agencies that were surveyed in the 1995 National Youth Gang Survey, but not selected for the 1996 representative sample. Information and analyses included in this report were limited to the survey responses for the statistically representative sample, as the data were more comprehensive and allowed for a more complete nationwide perspective.

This statistically representative sample was composed of jurisdictions in four area types: all large cities with populations greater than 25,000; a random sample of small cities with populations between 2,500 and 25,000; all suburban counties; and a random sample of rural counties.

When the number of gang members reported in each jurisdiction was accounted for, the number of gang members nationwide was evenly split between juveniles and adults. The vast majority of gang members (71 percent) were reported to be from 15 to 24 years of age. Adult gang members were most prevalent in suburban counties (58 percent) and large cities (51 percent). Males were reported to be substantially more involved in gang activity than their female counterparts. When the number of gang members reported in each jurisdiction was controlled, females constituted only 10 percent of gang members throughout the country. This contrasts with several recent self-report studies in which females represented approximately one-fourth to one-third of all gang members in urban adolescent samples.

Results of the survey also revealed that the racial/ethnic composition of gangs has changed compared with earlier national surveys and research involving smaller samples. When the number of gang members reported in each jurisdiction was controlled. Caucasians accounted for 14 percent of all gang members nationwide. In addition, the proportion of Caucasian gang members was more than twice the national average in rural counties (32 percent) and small cities (31 percent). However, Hispanic and African-American gang members continued to constitute the majority of gang members, especially in large cities and suburban counties. Respondents estimated that 47 percent of the gangs in their jurisdictions were multiethnic/ multiracial when the results were weighted for the number of gangs reported in each jurisdiction.

Most respondents (84 percent) indicated that they had experienced some migration of gang members into their jurisdictions. After the number of gang members reported in each jurisdiction was controlled for, it was estimated that 21 percent of all gang members in jurisdictions that experienced some migration had migrated to the jurisdiction in which they were residing. The average proportion of gang migrants reported by survey respondents decreased as the population of jurisdictions increased.

Youth gang members were estimated to have been involved in 2,364 homicides in large cities and 561 homicides in suburban counties. Regarding other crimes, respondents indicated that youth gang members were more involved in larceny/theft, followed fairly closely (in the order of degree of involvement) by aggravated assault, burglary, and motor vehicle theft. Youth gang members were not extensively involved in robbery—almost half the respondents reported a high level of gang control of drug distribution.

The results of this survey indicate that the youth gang problem in this country is substantial and affects communities of all sizes. Almost three-fourths of the cities surveyed with populations greater than 25,000 reported youth gangs in 1996. Furthermore, a majority of suburban counties had gangs, as did a significant percentage of small cities and rural counties. Caucasians were found to be more involved in gang activity than previous studies and surveys had indicated, and their predominance in rural counties and small cities was especially high. Gang members were involved in a significant amount of crime, but the degree of involvement and type of crime varied by area type, region, and population. Examination of these data by the National Youth Gang Center will continue, and subsequent surveys will help to gather more information about gangs and gang members.

DISCUSSION QUESTIONS

1. Define *juvenile gangs*, and explain how they are different from other groups.

2. Why do youths join gangs?

3. Why do youths leave gangs?

4. Compare the Crips and the Bloods.

5. Diagram the development of the Bloods.

6. Explain the importance of colors to gangs.

7. Explain how Walter Miller distinguishes gangs from other types of youth groups.

8. Evaluate the conclusions of Yablonski regarding the Los Angeles gangs in the 1960s.

9. Explain the key aspects of gang behavior according to the OJJDP report.

10. Diagram the general structure of youth gangs.

11. Explain the social contexts of youth gang membership.

Chapter 5

Abused and Neglected Juveniles

"America would rather build prisons than invest in a child."

U.S. Attorney General Janet Reno

Until recently, child abuse and neglect were an insignificant part of the business of our court system. Today, they are considered a major court activity. This chapter will cover abused and neglected juveniles. This discussion will include the handling of dependent youths, runaways, status offenders, abused, homeless and victimized youths, self-perpetuating violence theories, levels of child abuse, and child abuse laws.

Child abuse and neglect are normally divided into categories of neglect, physical abuse, emotional abuse, and sexual abuse. Each of these has profound effect on the behaviors and attitudes of children.

NATURE OF THE PROBLEMS

Neglect is defined as the disregarding of the physical, emotional, and moral needs of children or adolescents. The most serious forms of neglect include the failure to feed, the failure to provide adequate shelter, the failure to keep clean, and the failure to provide adequate medical care. Reports of neglect occur about twice as often as reports of abuse. In 1993, approximately three million children were reported abused or neglected. This number represents a 132 percent increase in the past decade. ("Family Violence: Interventions for the Justice System," *Bureau of Justice Assistance Report,* Washington D.C.: U.S. Dept. of Health and Human Services, 1988).

Physical abuse is behavior directed toward the child that is likely to cause or intend to cause pain, injury, or death. It is estimated that approximately 1.8 million children are physically abused each year. It is also estimated that over 2,000 young

As the primary provider of child care, females were the perpetrators in most maltreatment

| | Percent of perpetrators | | | |
	Male only	Female only	Mixed: male and female	All
Victim age				
0–17	22%	54%	24%	100%
Less than 1	5	70	25	100
1–5	16	58	25	100
6–11	25	52	24	100
12–17	35	42	23	100
Maltreatment type				
All	22%	54%	24%	100%
Physical abuse	33	41	26	100
Neglect	10	64	25	100
Medical neglect	5	70	25	100
Sexual abuse	62	9	29	100
Psychological abuse	26	37	37	100

- In 1996, over one-half (54%) of maltreatment cases involved only female perpetrators, and about one-quarter (24%) involved both male and female perpetrators. As a result, at least one female was identified as a perpetrator in more than 3 in 4 maltreatment cases (78%). In contrast, at least one male was identified as a perpetrator in about 1 in 2 cases (46%).

- Male perpetrators were more common in maltreatment cases involving older victims. For example, at least one male was identified as the perpetrator in 30% of cases involving victims under the age of 1, compared to 58% of cases involving victims ages 12–17.

- For most maltreatment types, females were more likely than males to be identified as a perpetrator. The one exception is sexual abuse. At least one male was identified in 91% of these reports. In contrast, at least one female was identified in 38% of cases involving sexual abuse.

Note: Detail may not total 100% because of rounding. The male proportion includes cases with at least one male perpetrator and no females. The female proportion includes cases with at least one female perpetrator and no males. The mixed proportion includes cases with at least one male and one female perpetrator. It should be noted that cases identifying multiple perpetrators do not imply equal involvement of each perpetrator.

Source: Authors' analysis of unpublished data from the U.S. Department of Health and Human Services, Children's Bureau, on the detailed case component of the *National Child Abuse and Neglect Data System.*

Juvenile Offenders and Victims: 1999 National Report

children are murdered each year. (Leroy H. Pelton, *The Social Context of Child Abuse and Neglect*, NewYork: Human Services Press, 1981).

Sexual abuse refers to any sexual activity that involves physical contact or sexual arousal of a child. Included are stimulation of erogenous areas of the body, masturbation, oral-genital relations, and intercourse. The most frequent form of incest is brother-sister. It takes place far more often than father-daughter incest, but father-daughter is normally a more devastating experience for the child and often has long term consequences. Mother-son incest appears to be rare.

The consequences of child abuse and neglect are considerable for the young victims. The victims often have low self-esteem, suffer from depression, have poor social relationships and high anxiety. Adult criminals frequently blame their conduct on their backgrounds of abuse. Female prostitutes often claim that they were sexually abused as children.

It appears that boys who witness their fathers' violence are ten times more likely to engage in spousal abuse and or child abuse in later adulthood than boys from nonviolent homes. In houses where spousal abuse occurs, children are abused at a rate 1,500 percent higher than the national average.

USA Today reported that there are four million American children presently growing up in deeply troubled neighborhoods where poverty, unemployment and dropping out of school are a way of life. The paper also states that one in five children in the United States lives in poverty. According to the report, American children fall into three groups: top one-third that is doing well, the middle group that is doing okay and the bottom group which is suffering. About one-half of the troubled kids live in troubled communities in six states: California, Illinois, Michigan, New York, Ohio, and Texas.

FAMILY INFLUENCES

As discussed in the *OJJDP Summary*, "Comprehensive Strategy for Serious, Violent and Chronic Juvenile Offenders," June, 1994, the family is the most important influence in the lives of children and the first line of defense against delinquency. Programs that strengthen the family and foster healthy growth and development of children from prenatal care through adolescence should be widely available. These programs should encourage the maintenance of a viable family unit and bonding between parent and child, and they should provide support for families in crisis. Such programs should involve other major spheres of influence such as religious institutions, schools, and community-based organizations. By working together, these organizations will have a pronounced impact on preserving the family and preventing delinquency.

To have the greatest impact, assistance must reach families before significant problems develop. Therefore, the concept of earliest point of impact should guide the development and implementation of prevention programs involving the family. Researchers in the area of juvenile delinquency and the family have found that the following negative family involvement factors are predictors of delinquency:

➢ Inadequate prenatal care

➢ Parental rejection

➢ Inadequate supervision and inconsistent discipline by parents

➢ Family conflict, marital discord, and physical violence

➢ Child abuse

The following programs directly address negative family involvement factors and explain how to establish protective factors:

➢ Teen abstinence and pregnancy prevention

➢ Parent effectiveness and family skills training

➢ Parent support groups

➢ Family crisis intervention services

➢ Family life education for teens and parents

➢ Runaway and homeless youth services

Relationship Between Child Abuse and Delinquency

One of the strongest positions on the relationship between child abuse and delinquency is taken by Mark Fleisher in his study of the Crips and the Bloods. Based on his interviews with gang members, Fleisher stated that almost without exception the gang members grew up in homes with "dangerous family environments." He concludes that youths leave home and join gangs to escape the violence or drift away because they are abandoned or neglected by their parents and there is "no comfort, protection, security, or emotional warmth in the home." Fleisher also concludes that gang members develop a "defensive world view." This view is characterized by six attributes:

1. A feeling of vulnerability and a need to protect oneself

2. A belief that no one can be trusted

3. A need to maintain social distance

4. A willingness to use violence and intimidation to repel others

5. An attraction to similarly defensive people

6. An expectation that no one will come to their aid

Homelessness

According to the United States General Accounting Office, on any given night there are approximately 100,000 children homeless. When a family is homeless, the stress on the parents may result in child neglect or abuse. In addition, homeless children generally experience this stress and are likely to exhibit antisocial behavior (e.g., acting out, restlessness, aggressive behavior, depression, school behavioral problems, learning problems, and regressive behavior. (Michelle Fryt Linehan, "Children Who are Homeless: Educational Strategies for School Personnel," *Phi Delta Kappan*, September 1992). In addition to the above tendencies, the below four conditions generally characterize the homeless experience:

> ➢ Lack of basic resources such as food, clothing and shelter which results in deprivations with long-reaching effects.

> ➢ Frequent changes in school which result in lower or failing grades and an unwillingness to form friendships or to participate in school activities.

> ➢ Constant moving which results in a lack of roots, a lack of stability, and a tendency to view life as temporary.

> ➢ Overcrowded living quarters which results in withdrawal or in aggressiveness.

Many of the homeless children are entirely on their own having been kicked out of their homes. Estimates of the number of runaways or throwaways range from 100,000 to 300,000 yearly.

NEGLECTED CHILDREN

We tend to think of neglected children as those in poverty. While the majority of neglected children are in poor families, neglect is not limited to poor families. Neglected children may be from families who have no set routine for family activities, families where children are allowed to roam the streets at all hours, or where the family unit is in discord and fragmented by death, divorce, or desertion of parents. Many children in these families are being raised in a moral vacuum.

In some families, parents are hesitant to discipline their children in the mistaken belief that discipline may restrict the children's self-expression or unbalance them emotionally. At the opposite extreme are those families who discipline their children injudiciously, excessively, and frequently.

The physical indicators of neglect include frequent hunger, poor hygiene, inappropriate dress, and unattended physical needs that require medical or dental treatment. The behavioral indicators of neglect include begging, stealing food, extending time away from the family by arriving early at school and leaving late, constant fatigue, listlessness, falling asleep in class, alcohol or drug abuse, and statements indicating that no one at home cares about them.

CHILD ABUSE

Throughout history, children have been subjected to physical violence. At one time, society condoned the killing of newborn infants as a form of birth control, to avoid the dishonor of illegitimacy, or as a method of disposing of retarded or deformed children.

Child abuse may be divided into three levels: collective abuse, institutional abuse, and individual abuse. *Collective abuse* refers to the social injustice that many children experience because they were unlucky and were born in poverty. Children suffer collective abuse by being required to eat and drink contaminated food and water, by growing up in slums where they observe constant violence and where they are blocked from any reasonable legitimate opportunity to escape from poverty.

Efforts to correct social injustice are subject to strong political beliefs. As the American people and our political parties debate over what kinds of corrective actions are appropriate, we tend to forget the children who are the victims of collective abuse.

Institutional abuse refers to abuse of children by institutions such as schools and to the denial of rights to children in custody. One movement to prevent institutional abuse was the banning of corporal punishment by such institutions. Presently corporal punishment is banned in 26 states and its use is declining in the other 24 states.

Individual abuse is what we normally think of as child abuse. This is where one or more individuals, often the parents, abuse a child. Individual abuse includes physical, emotional, and sexual abuse.

Fetal Alcohol Syndrome

Fetal alcohol syndrome (FAS) is a form of child abuse that occurs before the child is born. Children who are exposed to excessive amounts of alcohol while in the womb suffer lifelong effects after they are born. FAS children may exhibit impulsivity and poor communication skills and may be unable to predict consequences or use appropriate judgment in their daily lives. Many researchers contend that FAS is the leading cause of mental retardation in the United States. A similar situation occurs with "crack babies." Crack children are children exposed to cocaine while in the womb. These children may overwhelmingly exhibit severe social, emotional, and cognitive problems.

Emotional Abuse

Researchers contend that emotional abuse is as damaging to the child as is physical abuse. Emotional abuse is difficult to define. It includes verbal statements to the child indicating that the child is worthless, not as good as other children; it also includes excessive criticisms of the child, ridicule, making the child the butt of practical jokes and other conduct that destroys the child's feeling of self-value.

Physical indicators of emotional abuse include speech disorders, lags in physical development, and a general failure to thrive. Behavioral indicators include habit disorders such as thumb sucking, biting, and rocking back and forth, in addition to antisocial behavior. Other indicators include sleep disorders, inhibitions to play, compulsion, phobias, behavioral extremes, and often attempted suicide.

Emotional abuse and neglect increased more than other forms of maltreatment between 1986 and 1993			
	Number of victims of maltreatment		
Maltreatment type	1986	1993	Percent change
Total	1,424,400	2,815,600	98%
Abuse	590,800	1,221,800	107
Physical	311,500	614,100	97
Sexual	133,600	300,200	125
Emotional	188,100	532,200	183
Neglect	917,200	1,961,300	114
Physical	507,700	1,335,100	163
Emotional	203,000	584,100	188
Educational	284,800	397,300	40*

*Indicates that increase did not reach statistical significance.

Note: Victims were counted more than once when more than one type of abuse or neglect had occurred.

Source: Authors' adaptation of the National Center on Child Abuse and Neglect's *The third National Incidence Study of Child Abuse and Neglect (NIS–3)*.

Juvenile Offenders and Victims: 1999 National Report

Battered Child Syndrome

The advances in diagnostic X-ray technology permitted doctors to detect patterns of healed fractures in young children. In 1946, John Caffey, a pediatric radiologist, concluded that multiple fractures in the long bones of young children had "traumatic origin" and perhaps were inflicted by their parents. In the 1960s, C.H. Kempe coined the phrase "battered child syndrome" based on clinical evidence of maltreatment. By 1964, states began enacting mandatory child abuse laws using Dr. Kempe's definition of a battered child. By 1966, all but one state had adopted the "battered child syndrome" concept in their statutes.

Sexual Abuse

Over 100,000 child sexual abuse cases are reported each year. It is estimated that less than 10 percent of sexual abuse cases are reported. Some researchers estimate that at least 40 percent of females have been sexually abused prior to their eighteenth birthday. Approximately 50 percent of female rape victims are under the age of 18. Eighty to 90 percent of all incest victims are girls. Men constitute 97 percent of child sexual abusers. (B. Kay Shafer, "Child Sexual Abuse and the Law," *Los Angeles Lawyer*, September 1989).

Sexual abuse is classified as either "intrafamilial" or "extrafamilial." Intrafamilial sexual abuse is abuse by a parent or other family member; extrafamilial sexual abuse is abuse by a stranger or friend. According to several research reports, in about 85 percent of child abuse cases the offender was a relative or friend of the child. The home is no "safe haven" for child abuse victims since most of the abuses occur in or near the home.

With the exceptions of pregnancy or venereal disease, physical indicators of sexual abuse are rarely noticed. Behavioral indicators, however, are more apparent. Behavioral indicators of sexual abuse include an unwillingness to change clothes for or to participate in physical education classes, withdrawal, infantile behavior, bizarre sexual behavior, sexual sophistication beyond one's age, unusual knowledge of sex, poor peer relationships, delinquency or runaway behaviors, and an unexplained decrease in school grades. In some cases, the behavior of the parents may provide indicators of sexual abuse. Behavioral indicators in the parents may include jealously and overprotectiveness of the abused child.

Sexual abuse may begin when the perpetrator is under some form of stress with which he feels unable to cope. The stress may be caused by difficulties arising out of employment, finances or feelings of inadequacy in his relationship with adult females. The stress that precipitates the initial sexual contact with the child is usually blatant. The first act of sexual abuse may be committed on impulse and facilitated by the consumption of alcohol. The offender, feeling inadequate, fantasizes the young girl is an adult, willing to adore and satisfy him so he can regain his sense of power and control.

Although the first act may be impulsive, the sexual conduct becomes premeditated and often grows into a long-lasting activity. The abuser generally abuses his victim multiple times and often renews his activities with other younger females when the first female has grown too old. The behavior becomes addictive. To hide the crime, the offender convinces the victim that her disclosure will only disrupt the family and cause pain to its members. Often, the offender is able to convince the victim that the wrongdoing is her fault.

A second category of child sexual abusers involves the offender— a man who forms few or no close relationships, especially those of an intimate or sexual nature, with adults. This type of child sexual abuse constitutes the minority of cases. This offender identifies with children and exhibits a sexual preference for them which arises in adolescence. Most of these offenders choose prepubescent boys as their victims and tend to prey on strangers or develop relationships solely for purposes of sexual abuse. This group of offenders often possess child pornography. They generally exhibit arrested emotional development and often were victims of sexual abuse as children.

The increased awareness of the nature and the scope of the child sexual abuse problem has resulted in an increased reporting of incidents of sexual abuse. One reaction to the increased number of reports has been denial and disbelief. An organization was formed which claims to defend innocent adult victims of child abuse hysteria. The organization is known as VOCAL (Victims of Child Abuse Laws). Numerous studies, however, reveal that less than 10 percent of child sexual abuse reports were false. The majority of false child sexual abuse reports were made by parents involved in child custody disputes.

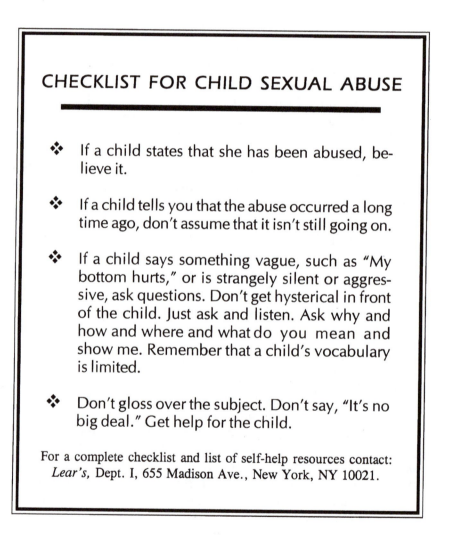

CHECKLIST FOR CHILD SEXUAL ABUSE

❖ If a child states that she has been abused, believe it.

❖ If a child tells you that the abuse occurred a long time ago, don't assume that it isn't still going on.

❖ If a child says something vague, such as "My bottom hurts," or is strangely silent or aggressive, ask questions. Don't get hysterical in front of the child. Just ask and listen. Ask why and how and where and what do you mean and show me. Remember that a child's vocabulary is limited.

❖ Don't gloss over the subject. Don't say, "It's no big deal." Get help for the child.

For a complete checklist and list of self-help resources contact: *Lear's*, Dept. I, 655 Madison Ave., New York, NY 10021.

Child sexual abuse victims who *don't* tell are frequently asked:

"Why didn't you tell sooner?"

The answers are:

➢ I didn't know anything was wrong.
➢ I didn't know it was illegal.
➢ I didn't know who to tell.
➢ I did tell and no one believed me.
➢ I was ashamed.
➢ I was scared.

The abuser keeps the abuse secret through threats:

➢ If you tell, I will kill you.
➢ If you tell, you will be sent away.
➢ If you tell, I'll kill your little sister.
➢ If you tell, I'll molest your little brother.
➢ If you tell, I'll kill your dog.
➢ If you tell, it will kill your mother.
➢ If you tell, no one will believe you.
➢ If you tell, you will go to hell.
➢ If you tell, then you will go to the insane asylum.
➢ If you tell, I'll go to jail and you'll starve.

Source: Heidi Vanderbilt, *Lears*, February 1992, p.42.

Cycles of Violence

Susan Paisner contends that violence is learned behavior and that children who are victims or who have witnessed spousal abuse are 1,000 times more likely to grow up to be a child or spousal abuser. ("Domestic Violence: Breaking the Cycle," *Police Chief*, February 1991). Donna Halvorsen notes that many American homes are not safe havens for children but are instead training grounds for criminals. That children are harmed by the sight and sounds of violence in addition to the physical blows that may strike them. ("Children Who Witness Abuse Bear Scars," *Minneapolis/ St. Paul Star Tribune*, November 8, 1993, p.7A.)

Texas Penal Code 22.041.
Abandoning or Endangering Child

(a) In this section, "abandon" means to leave a child in any place without providing reasonable and necessary care for the child, under circumstances under which no reasonable, similarly situated adult would leave a child of that age and ability.

(b) A person commits an offense if, having custody, care, or control of a child younger than 15 years, he intentionally abandons the child in any place under circumstances that expose the child to an unreasonable risk of harm.

(c) A person commits an offense if he intentionally, knowingly, recklessly, or with criminal negligence, by act or omission, engages in conduct that places a child younger than 15 years in imminent danger of death, bodily injury, or physical or mental impairment.

MISSING CHILDREN

In 1984, the federal government, concerned about missing and abducted children in the United States, passed the Missing Children's Act. To comply with the mandate of this act, the National Incidence Studies of Missing, Abducted, Runaway, and Thrownaway Children (NISMART) was developed. Its stated objective was to collect data to estimate the incidence of five categories of children who were: abducted by family members, abducted by non-family members, runaways, thrownaways, and missing because they had gotten lost or injured. After a five-year study, completed in 1990, the major conclusions reached included:

- Many of the children in at least four of the categories were not literally missing. Caretakers did know where they were. The problem was in recovering them.

- Family abduction was a substantially larger problem than previously thought.

- The runaway problem did not appear to be larger in 1988 than from the last national survey in 1975.

- About one-fifth of the children who had been considered runaways should actually be considered thrownaways.

- There was a large group of literally missing children who have not been adequately recognized by previous research and policy concerning missing children. These were children who were missing because they were injured, they got lost, or because they miscommunicated with caretakers about where they would be or when they would be home.

From the Household Survey portion of NISMART, the researchers concluded that there were 354,100 family abductions annually. This estimate is three times higher than the official estimates. The researchers also estimated that there were less than 5,000 non-family abductions and kidnappings a year. They also estimated that there were from 43 to 147 stranger abduction homicides annually between 1976 and 1987. Their analysis of FBI homicide data indicated no discernible change in the rate of stranger abduction homicides over the 12-year period. The survey indicated an estimated 114,600 cases of attempted stranger abductions yearly. The majority of these attempts consisted of passing motorists attempting to lure children into their cars. In a majority of cases, the police were not contacted. In addition, children seem to have a fairly large number of encounters with strangers where an abduction seems to have been threatened.

There are an estimated 450,000 runaways from households yearly. In addition, an estimated 12,800 children ran away from juvenile facilities.

There are an estimated 127,000 thrownaways a year. Compared to runaways, thrownaways tend to experience more violence and conflict with their families and are more likely to still be gone from their homes. To qualify as a "thrownaway," one of four situations must exist:

1. The child has been told directly to leave.

2. The child has been away from home, and a caretaker has refused to allow the child back.

3. The child has run away but the caretaker has made no effort to recover the child or does not care whether or not the child returns.

4. The child has been abandoned or deserted.

A mixed group of children missing from their caretakers did not fit into the other categories. Most of the episodes or periods missing were short, about one-third lasting less than six hours. Only two percent were missing for more than one day. About half the episodes occurred during the summer months. In about 21 percent of the cases, the children experienced physical harm during their absence. In about 14 percent of the cases, the children were abused or assaulted during the episodes.

The report concluded that increased attention needs to be given to the problem of family abductions. In addition, the report recommended that public policy more clearly differentiate regarding each of the separate social problems included under the "missing children" umbrella.

Texas Penal Code 25.06.
Harboring Runaway Child

(a)   A person commits an offense if he knowingly harbors a child and he is criminally negligent about whether the child:
(1)   is younger than 18 years; and
(2)   has escaped from the custody of a peace officer, a probation officer, the Texas Youth Council, or a detention facility for children, or is voluntarily absent from the child's home without the consent of the child's parent or guardian for a substantial length of time or without the intent to return.

[Sections (b) and (c) omitted.]

(d)   An offense under this section is a Class A misdemeanor.

(e)   On the receipt of a report from a peace officer, probation officer, the Texas Youth Council, a foster home, or a detention facility for children that a child has escaped its custody or upon receipt of a report from a parent, guardian, conservator, or legal custodian that a child is missing, a law enforcement agency shall immediately enter a record of the child into the National Crime Information Center.

CHILD PROTECTIVE SERVICES

The first child protective service organization was formed in 1875. Prior to that, in 1871, the Society for the Prevention of Cruelty to Children was formed. The forming of the society occurred when church workers removed a child by the name of Mary Ellen from her home, where she had been badly beaten and neglected. The child was removed under laws designed to prevent cruelty to animals.

Child protective services of one form or another are used in all 50 states as a method of providing protective services to child victims of abuse and neglect. The cost of these services helps illustrate the high cost of child abuse and neglect. In 1993, for example, it cost approximately $10,000 for each child protective service case opened. Long-term costs for psychological or medical care for sexually abused children can be much higher. Temporary foster care costs about $12,500 per child per year. Home based services average about $75 per visit and 40 visits per year are not uncommon. The total annual cost in the United States for child protective services is estimated to be approximately $10 billion a year.

Child Abuse Reporting

In every state, certain professional workers are required to report expected physical or sexual child abuse. Generally, workers required to report include child-care workers, medical and health care persons, and public school employees. Others can report suspected abuse but may not be required to. In a few states, like Texas, all persons must report suspected child abuse. In most jurisdictions, a toll-free hot line has been established for the reporting of child abuse. If the abuse is discovered by a physician or mental health professional, the rules protecting privileged communications do not apply and the professional is required to report the abuse.

In those cases where a person is under a legal duty to report, the reporting person is immune from both criminal and civil liability as long as the report is made in good faith. In those cases where the reporting person was not required to report the child abuse, the reporting person will be immune as long as any false report was not made either knowingly or with reckless disregard for the truth or falsity of the report. All reports filed are confidential and the name of the reporting person may not be released except under court order.

The report must be forwarded immediately to a law enforcement agency, child protective services, county welfare, or a probation department. In most states, the person required to report child abuse must transmit a written report within 36 to 48 hours. The agency that receives the report is generally under a duty to report the information to other agencies.

California Penal Code 11166

(a) Except as provided in subdivision (b), any child care custodian, health practitioner, employee of a child protective agency, child visitation monitor, firefighter, animal control officer, or humane society officer who has knowledge of or observes a child, in his or her professional capacity or within the scope of his or her employment, whom he or she knows or reasonably suspects has been the victim of child abuse, shall report the known or suspected instance of child abuse to a child protective agency immediately or as soon as practically possible by telephone and shall prepare and send a written report thereof within 36 hours of receiving the information concerning the incident. A child protective agency shall be notified and a report shall be prepared and sent even if the child has expired, regardless of whether or not the possible abuse was a factor contributing to the death, and even if suspected child abuse was discovered during an autopsy. For the purposes of this article, "reasonable suspicion" means that it is objectively reasonable for a person to entertain a suspicion, based upon facts that could cause a reasonable person in a like position, drawing when appropriate on his or her training and experience, to suspect child abuse. For the purpose of this article, the pregnancy of a minor does not, in and of itself, constitute a basis of reasonable suspicion of sexual abuse.

(b) Any child care custodian, health practitioner, employee of a child protective agency, child visitation monitor, firefighter, animal control officer, or humane society officer who has knowledge of or who reasonably suspects that mental suffering has been inflicted upon a child or that his or her emotional well-being is endangered in any other way, may report the known or suspected instance of child abuse to a child protective agency.

(c) Any commercial film and photographic print processor who has knowledge of or observes, within the scope of his or her professional capacity or employment, any film, photograph, videotape, negative, or slide depicting a child under the age of 14 years engaged in an act of sexual conduct, shall report the instance of suspected child abuse to the law enforcement agency having jurisdiction over the case immediately, or as soon as practically possible, by telephone, and shall prepare and send a written report of it with a copy of the film, photograph, videotape, negative, or slide attached.

Protective Actions

If it appears that a child has been abused and there is a risk of further abuse, law enforcement or child protective services may temporarily remove the child from the home. The official removing the child should then petition to juvenile court for a judicial determination as to the disposition of the child. Unless the safety of the child is in danger, the agency removing the child must normally notify the parents within a short period of time after taking custody of the child. In most states, the child has a right to establish telephone contact with the parents within a few hours after having been taken into custody. In most cases, the child is taken to a hospital for examination. Many states, like California, have a protocol for emergency room persons who examine victims of sexual assault. In addition, many major hospitals have established SCAN (Suspected Child Abuse and Neglect) teams.

Typically, a hearing must be held by the juvenile court within 48 hours or the next court day. At that hearing, an attorney is required to be appointed for parents who cannot afford one. If the minor wants an attorney and the judge believes that there is a conflict between the rights of the parents and the rights of the juvenile, the court will appoint another attorney for the juvenile. An attorney from the district or county attorney's office normally represents child protective services and in some cases the juvenile.

As will be discussed in later chapters, juvenile courts are not generally open to the public. After the filing of a petition and the detention hearing, unless that hearing is waived, a hearing is held to determine whether the child has been physically abused. If the court makes a determination that the child is a person in need of protection, the child becomes a ward of the court. This hearing is frequently referred to as the jurisdictional hearing in that the court must find that the child is in need of protection before the court has jurisdiction to proceed in the case. Usually, jurisdictional hearings must take place within a few days after detention. For example, in California, the jurisdictional hearing must take place within ten days after the child is placed in detention.

If the child is determined to be a victim of physical or sexual abuse and there is no reasonable method to prevent its reoccurrence, the child is declared to be a ward of the court, and the child will be permanently removed from the home. In most states, family reunification is a stated legislative goal. Accordingly, children are placed with relatives when possible. In some cases, the child may be turned over to the non-abusing parent. If this is not a reasonable option they are generally placed in foster homes. In many cases, the children are placed in foster homes with the goal of family reunification within 18 months. If that goal is not possible or not met, generally steps are taken to terminate parental rights over the child. The parent may return to court at a later time to have the court orders modified or set aside and parental control reinstated. The average stays in foster homes are from about six months to two and one-half years.

Most law enforcement departments have special units to investigate child abuse. Officers assigned to those units will interview the child, the parents, friends, etc., in an attempt to determine if the abuse is of a nature to warrant criminal prosecution.

Child Witnesses

Many states, like California, have taken special steps to prosecute child abusers. For example, in California, criminal cases involving child abuse are given priority in the court calendar over other criminal cases. The jury may be instructed that a child's testimony is not to be disbelieved solely because the child is immature (ten years old or younger).

Most states provide that a child witness is unavailable to testify if expert testimony establishes that the trauma engendered by the crime alleged has made that testimony impossible without additional traumatization. In these cases, the court may permit the use of videotaped testimony of the child victim. Another alternative is to permit the child to testify by the use of remote closed-circuit testimony. Other protections for the child include the right of the child to have a friend or relative close to the child during testimony. Questions may be required to be phrased in a manner that is not misleading or challenging to the child. The judges are generally given latitude to take steps to make the child's testifying less threatening.

Child Abuse Protection Programs

The majority of states have enacted legislation to establish child abuser prosecution programs and legislative stated policies regarding the prosecution of child abusers. The following California statutes are typical examples of the legislation in this area.

California Penal Code 868.8.
Child Witnesses
In Criminal Proceedings
Involving Certain Crimes

Notwithstanding any other provision of law, in any criminal proceeding in which the defendant is charged with a violation of Section 243.4, 261, 273a, 273d, 285, 286, 288, 288a, 288.5, or 289, subdivision (1) of Section 314, Section 647.6, or former Section 647a, committed with or upon a minor under the age of 11, the court shall take special precautions to provide for the comfort and support of the minor and to protect the minor from coercion, intimidation, or undue influence as a witness, including, but not limited to, any of the following:

(a)   In the court's discretion, the witness may be allowed reasonable periods of relief from examination and cross-examination during which he or she may retire from the courtroom. The judge may also allow other witnesses in the proceeding to be examined when the child witness retires from the courtroom.

(b)   Notwithstanding Section 68110 of the Government Code, in his or her discretion, the judge may remove his or her robe if the judge believes that this formal attire intimidates the minor.

(c)   In the court's discretion the judge, parties, witnesses, support persons, and court personnel may be relocated within the courtroom to facilitate a more comfortable and personal environment for the child witness.

California Penal Code 999r.
Child Abuser Prosecution Program

(a)   There is hereby established in the Office of Criminal Justice Planning, a program of financial and technical assistance for district attorneys' offices, designated the Child Abuser Prosecution Program. All funds appropriated to the Office of Criminal Justice Planning for the purposes of this chapter shall be administered and disbursed by the executive director of such office, and shall to the greatest extent feasible, be coordinated or consolidated with any federal or local funds that may be made available for these purposes. The Office of Criminal Justice Planning shall establish guidelines for the provision of grant awards to proposed and existing programs prior to the allocation of funds under this chapter. These guidelines shall contain the criteria for the selection of agencies to receive funding and the terms and conditions upon which the Office of Criminal Justice Planning is prepared to offer grants pursuant to statutory authority. The guidelines shall not constitute rules, regulations, orders, or standards of general application. The guidelines shall be submitted to the appropriate policy committees of the Legislature prior to their adoption.

(b)   The executive director is authorized to allocate and award funds to counties in which child abuser offender prosecution units are established or are proposed to be established in substantial compliance with the policies and criteria set forth in Sections 999s, 999t, and 999u.

(c) The allocation and award of funds shall be made upon application executed by the county's district attorney and approved by its board of supervisors. Funds disbursed under this chapter shall not supplant local funds that would, in the absence of the California Child Abuser Prosecution Program, be made available to support the prosecution of child abuser felony cases. Local grant awards made under this program shall not be subject to review as specified in Section 14780 of the Government Code.

California Penal Code 999s.
Enhanced Prosecution Efforts and Resources

Child abuser prosecution units receiving funds under this chapter shall concentrate enhanced prosecution efforts and resources upon individuals identified under selection criteria set forth in Section 999t. Enhanced prosecution efforts and resources shall include, but not be limited to:

(a) Vertical prosecutorial representation, whereby the prosecutor who, or prosecution unit which, makes the initial filing or appearance in a case performs all subsequent court appearances on that particular case through its conclusion, including the sentencing phase.

(b) The assignment of highly qualified investigators and prosecutors to child abuser cases. "Highly qualified" for the purposes of this chapter means: (1) individuals with one year of experience in the investigation and prosecution of felonies or specifically the felonies listed in subdivision (a) of

Section 999l or 999t; or (2) individuals whom the district attorney has selected to receive training as set forth in Section 13836; or (3) individuals who have attended a program providing equivalent training as approved by the Office of Criminal Justice Planning.

(c) A significant reduction of caseloads for investigators and prosecutors assigned to child abuser cases.

(d) Coordination with local rape victim counseling centers, child abuse services programs, and victim witness assistance programs. That coordination shall include, but not be limited to: referrals of individuals to receive client services; participation in local training programs; membership and participation in local task forces established to improve communication between criminal justice system agencies and community service agencies; and cooperating with individuals serving as liaison representatives of child abuse and child sexual abuse programs, local rape victim counseling centers and victim witness assistance programs.

California Criminal Code 999u. Policies for Child Abuser Cases

Each district attorney's office establishing a child abuser prosecution unit and receiving state support under this chapter shall adopt and pursue the following policies for child abuser cases:

(a) Except as provided in subdivision (b), all reasonable prosecutorial efforts will be made to resist the pretrial release of a charged defendant meeting child abuser selection criteria.

(b) Nothing in this chapter shall be construed to limit the application of diversion programs authorized by law. All reasonable efforts shall be made to utilize diversion alternatives in appropriate cases.

(c) All reasonable prosecutorial efforts will be made to reduce the time between arrest and disposition of charge against an individual meeting child abuser criteria.

DISCUSSION QUESTIONS

1. Explain the term *thrownaway*.
2. What are the various types of child abuse?
3. Explain the effects of emotional abuse.
4. Explain the concerns regarding FAS.
5. Discuss how many sexual abuse cases get started.
6. What is meant by the "cycle of violence"?
7. Name the various classes of sexual abuse.
8. What are some of the steps that states are taking to make it easier to convict child abusers?
9. Explain some of the tactics that a sexual abuser may use to keep the victim from telling.
10. Summarize the findings of the NISMART project.

PART III

THE
JUSTICE
SYSTEM

Chapter 6

Police
and
Juveniles

This chapter discusses the relationships between po lice and juveniles. The discussion will focus on top ics involving specialized police units, police discretion when dealing with juveniles, curfew laws, the police use of violence, and problem-oriented policing.

Often, we expect the police to solve the problems that youths have caused. The police are required to handle a variety of juvenile-caused problems ranging from status offences to murders. For the most part, our expectations of the police, like our expectations of the entire juvenile justice system, are unrealistic.

An additional problem is that many youths consider the police their enemy. It is amazing how little has changed in the last 100 years regarding police involvement with juveniles. The biggest challenge of the police is how to maintain order in a constantly changing urbanized environment. The questions that are unresolved in this area are:

➢ What is the proper role of the police when dealing with juveniles?

➢ If the police are to be engaged in delinquency prevention, what is their role in that regard?

In the 1830s, as full-time police forces were created in larger cities in the United States, the police emerged as a coercive force to keep delinquents in line. While the police have the power to arrest, informal social control methods have traditionally been preferred when dealing with juveniles. In the first part of the twentieth century, the police began to look at preventing delinquency rather than focusing on arresting delinquents. Women were hired to work with delinquents and runaways. These police women patrolled the amusement parks and other places where the juveniles congregated. These officers were tasked with the duty of dissuading youths from engaging in criminal or other delinquent activities.

By 1930, over 90 percent of the police departments had instituted some form of juvenile delinquency prevention programs. One of the most famous is the Police Athletic League (PAL) which was started in the 1920s. Most large police departments assigned welfare officers to troubled areas and established employment assistance bureaus to help the youths. Many departments set up special police units to deal with juveniles.

August Vollmer, who was Chief of Police in Berkeley, California, is credited with establishing the first youth bureau. The concept quickly spread to other police forces. The officers assigned to these youth bureaus were the forerunners to today's juvenile officers.

In 1955, the Central States Juvenile Officers Association was formed. Two years later, the International Juvenile Officers Association was formed. These two associations held international, national, and regional meetings regarding the responsibilities, standards, and procedures to be used in cases involving juvenile offenders. The associations also helped create an awareness of the necessity of training officers to deal with juveniles. The general theme of the associations was to help youths stay crime free.

The preventive concept in dealing with juveniles continued through the 1960s. Police officers worked with schools, speaking to students from elementary to high school in an attempt to prevent delinquency. Many police departments developed speaker's bureaus which provided police officers to address youth groups. The Police Athletic League expanded its athletic programs and established youth leadership programs. Police agencies developed numerous programs to fight drug abuse and to reduce driving under the influence and truancy.

The severe budget cuts in the 1970s and 1980s forced many police departments to cut their youth programs. In addition, the national conservative movement, which was discussed in Chapter 2, also impacted the police departments. Some departments even eliminated their juvenile units. Other departments, faced with decreasing budgets and an increased awareness of neglect and abuse problems, reduced the activities of their juvenile units to that of handling neglect and abuse cases. In some departments, detectives assumed the responsibilities involving juvenile delinquents. The increased publicity of juvenile crime in the 1990s caused many police departments to redirect their limited resources and once again concentrate on juvenile crime. Rather than stressing prevention of juvenile crime, however, most of the departments directed their attention to law enforcement functions involving the handling of young criminals.

ORGANIZATION AND FUNCTIONS

The organization of police departments is similar to that of military organizations. The departments are ranked in a hierarchical structure— from the chief to the private. Management is normally divided into the executive level (whose job it is to make policy decisions), mid-level management (whose job it is to implement the policy decisions), and operational level (whose job it is to supervise the carrying out of the directives, policies, etc., of higher management).

The executive level is the top line of management within any police department. It includes the chief of police and the heads of the key functional units. At this level, policy decisions and strategic planning involving long range objectives are determined. In addition, executive level management is responsible for ensuring that the department is operating within the bounds of society. Mid-level management has two essential tasks: managing operational functions and serving as liaison between the executive level and the operational level. The operational level of management is often referred to as first-line management. This is the core of the department, and the managerial task at this level is to develop the best allocation of resources to accomplish the objectives set by higher management.

Police departments have two major inputs—human and nonhuman resources. Human inputs are the individuals who work for the police department. All other resources are considered nonhuman. Managers at all levels have the duty of coordinating the activities of the human inputs and the expenditures of nonhuman resources.

The major objectives of a police department include maintaining order, keeping the peace, catching criminals and preventing crime. In most departments, the majority of an officer's time is spent maintaining order and keeping the peace. To do this, officers endeavor to keep the streets free from crime and the people in the community safe. In performing their duties, the police are involved with investigating all types of crime from curfew violations to murder.

Police functions are frequently divided into proactive and reactive functions. The proactive role includes crime prevention. The reactive function includes trying to solve crimes and arrest criminals. The police have contact with juveniles in both types of functions: proactive by trying to prevent youths from getting into trouble and reactive by arresting youths who have violated the law. The structure of a police department determines how the police will respond to the various juvenile problems that the community faces.

In the following sections, we will compare police departments that function with special juvenile divisions or officers and those departments that do not.

Departments With Juvenile Units

Major police departments usually have officers trained in handling juvenile cases or gang control problems. Often the officers assigned to work solely with juveniles are pulled from the ranks of patrol officers. Many of these assignments are considered by other officers to be low status assignments. Thus, many officers so assigned would prefer to be back in the patrol division. Often, as in smaller departments, the officers are assigned without the specialized training considered necessary to deal with juveniles.

Departments with the resources often hire specialists to deal with juveniles. These specialists may or may not be commissioned police officers. Generally, their backgrounds include training in social work, sociology, psychology, and counseling. These specialists should understand child development, the nature of juvenile-parent relationships, the problems of adolescence, identity formation problems, drug or alcohol abuse, and the dynamics of living in poverty.

Juvenile units in the larger departments have the normal crime-fighting duties of detecting and investigating crime as the patrol units within the department. They also must hunt and arrest the juvenile offenders for crimes ranging from vandalism to serious felony crimes. In addition, juvenile units are charged with the responsibility of investigating reports of child abuse or neglect, hunting for runaway youths, referring youths to appropriate social service units, and supervising youth activities. Other responsibilities include keeping an eye on youths in high-crime areas, developing and running juvenile delinquency programs, and counseling both parents and youths. To efficiently perform these broad duties, juvenile specialists must be highly trained.

Since the 1960s, gang control units have been formed in many large police departments to help combat youth gang problems. In some departments, these units are called "Youth Service Programs," are temporary in nature, and were formed to deal with a specific gang problem. Often, the officers, while assigned to a gang control unit, are still required to perform their regular duties and are not exclusively concerned with the juvenile problem.

In another type of gang control unit, the "gang detail," traditional police officers are assigned to the gang detail. These officers do not typically assist other officers of the detail on non-gang problems. A third type of unit is called the "gang unit" which is established to work solely on gang problems. Often gang units will develop extensive intelligence networks involving gangs.

Gang control activities generally include the four types noted below:

> ➢ Gathering intelligence regarding the gang, its members, and its activities

> ➢ Delinquency prevention activities and anti-gang programs

> ➢ Investigating possible illegal gang activities and determining the identity of the offenders

> ➢ Taking gang members into custody

Departments Without Juvenile Units

The majority of police departments in the United States have fewer than ten officers. In such small departments, it is not feasible to have specialized officers or units to deal with juveniles. Accordingly, all officers must be involved in dealing with the special needs of juveniles. Few, if any, police officers in small departments have any special training in handling youths. Officers who deal with adult criminals often consider runaways and dependent or neglected children as a nuisance. There is also the tendency to treat juvenile crime as "kiddie crime." It is far more satisfying to make a major drug bust or arrest a murderer than to detain a kid for missing school. In addition, serious juvenile offenders are often treated as adult criminals.

It is important in the small departments that all officers be indoctrinated on the special problems of dealing with juveniles and that officers are aware that truancy cases must be treated differently from serious juvenile crime cases. Officers need to be aware that their handling of a juvenile may be the deciding factor as to whether that juvenile reforms or continues in delinquent and/or criminal conduct.

CONSEQUENCES OF ARREST

The police play an important part in the identification of a youth as a delinquent. While the police are centrally involved in the detection of delinquent activity, even more important are the decisions made by the police on whether to arrest or to handle the matter informally. Approximately 200,000 juveniles are arrested each year. When a juvenile is found to have been engaged in criminal activity, the police are charged with the decision to either release the child, detain him or her temporarily, or to detain the youth and refer to juvenile court. Since most criminal conduct does not result in an arrest, few, if any, persons are aware of the youth's conduct until he or she is arrested. Once the youth is arrested, the youth may be viewed as a delinquent by the community. The youth now has a police record. Teachers who formerly viewed the youth as a "good kid" may now see the youth as a "bad kid"— an undesirable. Other parents may encourage their children to stay away from the youth.

The importance of police behavior is illustrated by William Chambliss in his research describing the legal treatment of two groups of youths: the "Saints" and the "Roughnecks" (*Society*, Vol. 11. 1973, 24-31). The Saints were youths from stable, upper-middle class families. The Roughnecks were youths from less affluent families who lived on the wrong side of the railroad tracks. While both youth groups were engaged in similar amounts of delinquent activities, the Roughnecks were consistently in trouble with the police. The Saints were involved in reckless and drunken driving incidents, vandalism, and similar types of misconduct, but their delinquency was not highly visible because they were not as closely watched by the police as the Roughnecks and because they had automobiles which enabled them to leave town and commit their delinquent acts in other locations. The Roughnecks, however, primarily hung out on street corners in the lower-class neighborhoods. Their delinquency consisted primarily of petty theft, drinking, and fighting. Their infractions, occurring on the streets in the local neighborhoods, were far more visible to the police. The research concluded that although youths in both groups committed many offenses for which they could have been arrested, the evaluation and treatment of the two groups were quite different.

The Roughnecks all had records of multiple arrests. Their encounters with the police were characterized by hostility. The Roughnecks were not inclined to use a "yes sir, no sir" posture with the police. The police considered them bad youths who deserved to have the book thrown at them whenever they were caught. The Saints, on the other hand, when stopped by the police tended to be polite, respectful, and deferential. In general, the Saints received much more lenient treatment. The researcher concluded that the better treatment was in part traceable to accumulated police experiences with their respectable and influential parents. The police accepted the parents' statements that the delinquency of their sons was just youthful pranks and sowing wild oats. The police tended to consider these youths good boys just out on a lark.

The above research project illustrates the considerable discretion that is vested in our police. Police decisions are commonly based on their perception of the situation. While serious crimes almost always meet with arrest, the vast majority of police interventions involve the exercise of police discretion. The police are expected to use common sense in exercising discretion. As demonstrated by the above research, police decisions are influenced by their preconceptions regarding whether the juvenile on first impression is a good or bad kid.

After juveniles are taken into custody, an additional decision must be made about handling the case. In small departments, the dispositional decision may be made by the arresting officer. In larger departments, the dispositional decision is generally made by a juvenile officer. Nationally, approximately one-third of the youths arrested are released by the police without referral to juvenile court or other agencies. Accordingly, considerable discretion remains with the police even after the youth is arrested. The below chart reflects a national average and does not account for different patterns in the cities. For example, it appears that approximately 70 percent of the youths arrested in Syracuse, New York were released without referral to juvenile or adult court.

Police officers have neither unlimited time nor unlimited information when making decisions on the street in juvenile encounters. The officer is required to quickly size up the situation and the parties and then make a decision as to the appropriate course of action to take. Officers generally develop a set of clues which they use in sizing up the youths they face during street encounters. The clues serve as a picture of the type of person they are dealing with. The manner in which the person dresses, the demeanor of the person, and the location where the encounter is taking place are all considered clues by experienced officers.

Donald J. Black and Albert J. Reiss conducted a large-scale study of police handling of juvenile delinquency cases in the cities of Boston, Chicago, and Washington ("Police Control of Juveniles," *American Sociological Review*, vol. 35, 1970). The researchers observed that police encounters with juveniles are generally initiated by citizen complaints. Observational research regarding police discretion indicates that there are certain situational factors which influence the police decisions as to whether the youth should be arrested. Those factors are:

1. The seriousness of the offense

2. Who is present at the scene of the arrest

3. Whether victims or witnesses provide information or lobby for an arrest

4. The youth's demeanor

A fundamental concept is that legal treatment should be based on the crime, not on his or her race or gender. The problem arises that discretionary latitude in police decisions may result in possible discrimination. Many researchers conclude that, in addition to the four factors listed above, the race of the youth bears importantly on whether the juvenile is arrested. For example, Black and Reiss concluded that during an observation period of a research project a strong majority of police officers expressed anti-African-American attitudes in the presence of observers. The researchers indicated that there is a general agreement among researchers that prejudice is common within the police, but not all agree that the prejudice is translated into discriminatory actions.

Several researchers have noted that police encounters with African-American youths occur more often when complainants are present and that generally the complainants are also African-American. These researchers concluded that more African-American complainants, in general, lobby for the arrest of the juvenile than do white complainants. In other words, according to researchers, the African-American youths are arrested at a higher rate because of the actions of African-American complainants. Accepting that this thesis is correct does not justify any unequal treatment of African-American youths. If, as the researchers argue, African-American complainants lobby for arrest of the youth more than complainants of other races, the police should be aware of this and consider this fact when making the dispositional decision.

JUVENILES' ATTITUDES
TOWARD THE POLICE

The attitudes of juveniles toward the police have been the subject of numerous research reports. Several of the most prominent studies will be discussed in this section. Robert Portune conducted a study of 1,000 youths in Cincinnati junior high schools. (*Changing Adolescent Attitudes Toward Police*, Cincinnati: Anderson, 1971). He concluded that juveniles' attitudes toward the police vary by age, race, sex, academic performance in school, and socioeconomic class. The hostility of youths toward police increases as the youths grow older. African-American youths generally have a more hostile attitude toward the police than do other youths. Girls generally have a more favorable attitude toward police than do boys. The students with higher grade point averages generally have a more favorable attitude toward the police than youths with lower grade point averages. In addition, the higher the socioeconomic status of the family, the more favorable views the youths generally have of the police.

Donald Bouma conducted a more detailed study of Michigan school children in ten cities. The students were in grades seven through nine. Bouma agreed with all of the major findings of Portune. In addition, Bouma concluded that while hostility toward the police significantly increased as the students moved to higher grades, the majority of students indicated that they would still cooperate with the police if they saw someone other than a close friend commit a crime. Most youths perceived their friends as more hostile toward the police than they. The youths also perceived that their parents' attitudes toward the police were very similar to their own. Despite these findings, Bouma indicated that over one-half of the students felt that the police were criticized too often and generally that the police are "good guys." While most students felt that more police officers are needed, less than 10 percent indicated that they wanted to be police officers. Both researchers found that juveniles whohad hadcontact with the police tended to have more negative attitudes toward the police than juveniles who had no previous contact with the police.

The nature of the juvenile's contact with the police also appears to affect the juvenile's attitudes. Thomas Winfree and Curtis Griffiths concluded that negative contacts with the police shaped the juveniles' attitudes more than background factors of race, social class, sex, or location of residence. ("Adolescents' Attitudes Toward the Police," *Juvenile Delinquency: Little*

Brother Grows Up, Beverly Hills, CA: Sage, 1977, 79-99). It appears that negative contacts are more important than positive contacts in shaping a juvenile's attitude.

PROBLEM-ORIENTED POLICING

Many police departments are using the problem-oriented policing approach to deal with juvenile crime. Under this approach, police respond to the circumstances that create juvenile problems rather than to the incidents that result from the cause. The general approach to using problem-oriented policing is to examine the data on all juvenile crime known to the police in that jurisdiction and group all similar incidents together. The incidents are then examined to determine if any share common underlying features. Next, the police analyze the problem, collect information from a variety of sources, analyze the basic character of the problem, try to determine the causes of it, and develop a range of possible solutions. A plan of action is then developed to solve the problem. The plan is then put into action. Finally, the police evaluate the results to determine if their plan is working and if any modifications to the plan are needed.

DISCUSSION QUESTIONS

1. Differentiate the treatments by the police between the Saints and the Roughnecks.

2. Explain the factors involved in shaping juveniles' attitudes toward the police.

3. Compare and contrast departments with specialized juvenile units from those departments without the specialized units.

4. What are the factors used by a police officer in determining whether to arrest the youth during a street encounter?

Chapter 7

Juvenile Courts

This chapter examines the philosophy, jurisdiction, and structure of juvenile courts, as well as the roles of juvenile court personnel. When asked as to the philosophy behind juvenile court, many people will state that it is based on the concept of rehabilitation. Clearly that was the philosophy behind the now "old" juvenile court system. As will be discussed in this chapter, the "new" court's philosophy is focusing on crime control.

PHILOSOPHY

The philosophical underpinnings of the juvenile court have always been problematic. American society has been schizophrenic in its attitudes toward the juvenile offender as well as toward the juvenile court. Feelings of compassion and humanitarianism for juveniles in trouble (particularly those who have caused trouble) have been tinged with fear and vengeance.

Martin L. Forst

Traditionally, the purpose of juvenile court was to "save the children." As noted in *Commonwealth v. Fisher,* a 1905 court decision, juvenile court "is not for the punishment of offenders but for the salvation of children...whose salvation may become the duty of the state." During the early years, juvenile courts acted in an informal manner in an attempt to rehabilitate children, however a series of United States Supreme Court decisions between 1965 and 1975, however, changed the court from an informal proceeding to a more formal legalistic court.

As discussed in Chapter 2, one of the driving forces behind the creation of juvenile courts was the dissatisfaction with the treatment of juveniles and the penal system. Reformers viewed methods of treating juveniles as cruel and inhumane. The reformers were also interested in developing more effective means of controlling urban lower-class youths. Based on these concerns, juvenile court developed a dual orientation of more humane treatment of the youth and youth control. The dual orientation, however, gave rise to a set of procedures and a legal framework that was entirely different from those of adult criminal courts.

Using the doctrine of *parens patriae*, juvenile courts were considered a special class of civil courts rather than criminal courts. While the essence of criminal court was in determining guilt and assessing punishment, the juvenile courts originally were tasked with the responsibility of saving the youth. As one juvenile court judge wrote in 1909:

> The problem for determination...is not, has this boy or girl committed a specific wrong, but what is he, how has he become what he is, and what had best be done in his interest and in the interest of the state to save him from a downward career?

In the 1980s and 1990s, many states amended their juvenile codes in an attempt to change the philosophy of the courts from one of treating youths to one of crime control. For example, in 1995, Texas enacted a new juvenile code *(Texas Family Code, Title 3, section 51.01)*. The new code provides that the purposes of juvenile courts are to:

- Provide for the protection of the public and public safety

- Consistent with the protection of the public and public safety:

√ To promote the concept of punishment for criminal acts

√ To remove, where appropriate, the taint of criminality from children committing certain unlawful acts

√ To provide treatment, training and rehabilitation that emphasizes the accountability and responsibility of both the parent and the child for the child's conduct

- To provide for the care, protection, and the wholesome moral, mental, and physical development of children coming within its provisions

- To protect the welfare of the community and to control the commission of unlawful acts by children

- To achieve the foregoing in a family environment whenever possible. . . .

- To provide a simple judicial procedure...in which the parties are assured a fair hearing and their constitutional and other legal rights. . . .

In its Juvenile Justice Act (Washington Revised Statutes, Section 13.40.010, the state of Washington had stated earlier that the legislature declares:

The following to be equally important purposes of this chapter (on juvenile court):

(a) Protect the citizenry from criminal behavior

(b) Provide for determining whether the accused juveniles have committed offenses. . .

(c) Make the juvenile offender accountable for his or her criminal behavior

(d) Provide for punishment commensurate with the age, crime, and criminal history of the juvenile offender

(e) Provide for due process for juveniles. . .

(f) Provide for necessary treatment, supervision, and custody for juvenile offenders. . .

(h) Provide for restitution to victims of crime. [Note: sections (g), (i), and (j) omitted.]

The Texas and Washington state statutes are similar to those in many other states. Accordingly, it is clear that the present philosophy of the juvenile courts has changed from that of saving children to that of crime control.

In re Michael D.
188 C.A. 2d 1392 (1987)

The minor contends that the juvenile court judge abused his discretion by committing the minor to the California Youth Authority for reasons based on punishment and public safety. The minor contends that his commitment to CYA was an abuse of discretion by the juvenile court in that (1) the minor was improperly committed to CYA for purposes of retribution rather than rehabilitation; (2) the juvenile court did not properly consider less restrictive alternatives; and (3) the minor could not benefit from the commitment.

Minor had admitted to one count of sexual battery. He was caught in the act of rape. Evidence indicated that during the rape, the youth had been choking the victim. After the incident the minor showed no remorse or concern for the victim. The probation officer in her report to the court stated that "The magnitude and outrageousness of the conduct alone warrants a commitment to the California Youth Authority." The judge stated in his findings that he found the youth to be a threat and a danger to society.

The appellate court noted that at the core of the dispute is a fundamental disagreement over the purposes of the juvenile court law. Prior to a 1984 amendment to the Welfare and Institutions Code, section 202, California courts consistently held that juvenile commitment proceedings were designed for the purposes of rehabilitation and treatment, not for punishment. In 1984, that section was amended and now emphasized different priorities for the juvenile justice system. The present provisions recognize punishment as a rehabilitative tool. The amendment also resulted in greater emphasis on protecting public safety. Commitment to CYA, however, cannot be based solely on retribution grounds and that there must be some evidence to demonstrate probable benefits to the youth... [The appeals court upheld the commitment to CYA and stated that the minor would benefit from an environment providing firm, strict discipline for his "out of control" behavior.]

For dependency cases, it is the stated intent of most state legislatures to provide maximum protection for children who are currently being physically, sexually, or emotionally abused, neglected, or exploited, and to protect children who are at risk of that harm. This protection includes provision of a full array of social and health services to help the child and family and to prevent re-abuse of children. That protection shall focus on the preservation of the family whenever possible. Nothing is intended to permit the state to disrupt the family unnecessarily or to intrude inappropriately into family life, to prohibit the use of reasonable methods of parental discipline, or to prescribe a particular method of parenting. Further, nothing is intended to limit the offering of voluntary services to those families in need of assistance.

JURISDICTION

Delinquency and status offenses represent only a fraction of the work of juvenile court. Most juvenile courts also decide matters involving abuse, neglect, and other matters pertaining to the welfare of children. The jurisdiction of juvenile court depends in part on whether the juvenile is before the court on a delinquency or dependency matter. Each of these will be discussed separately in the sections below. Delinquency cases are those cases where the juvenile is alleged to have committed a criminal act. Dependency cases are those cases where the child is in need of supervision or protection.

In determining the age of the child for jurisdiction purposes, the courts generally look at the age of the child at the time of the proceedings and not at the time that the act occurred.

Whitaker v. Estelle, 509 F.2d 194

Offense occurred prior to accused's 17th birthday and juvenile court never formally waived jurisdiction where accused was neither indicted nor tried until after his 17th birthday.

Trial of accused before criminal court was proper. Age at the date of the trial not when offense occurred is used to determine if juvenile court has primary jurisdiction.

State v. Casanova, 494 S.W.2d 812

Where juvenile became 17 years of age before the appeals court reversed delinquency judgment, there could be no remand for a new trial in juvenile court because there was no jurisdiction in the juvenile courts. Note: juvenile could then be tried in adult criminal court.

Delinquency

In delinquency cases, juvenile courts generally have jurisdiction over any person who is under 18 years of age and who has violated any law of the state or any ordinance of any city or county of the state defining crime other than an ordinance establishing a curfew based solely on age. In these cases, the juvenile is within the jurisdiction of the juvenile court, which may adjudge the juvenile to be a ward of the court.

What are the stages of delinquency case processing in the juvenile justice system?

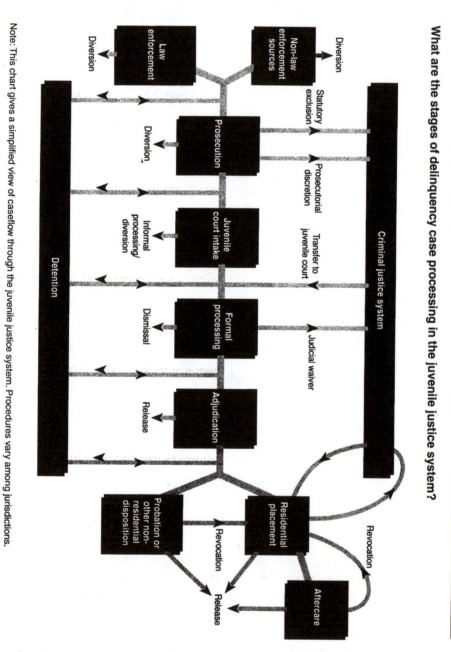

Note: This chart gives a simplified view of caseflow through the juvenile justice system. Procedures vary among jurisdictions.

Juvenile Offenders and Victims: 1999 National Report

In most states, the juvenile court has primary jurisdiction over juveniles. Accordingly, other courts generally do not have jurisdiction to conduct a preliminary examination or to try the case of any person charged with the commission of a crime when such person was under 18 years of age at the time of the proceedings unless the matter has first been submitted to juvenile court, and juvenile court has made an order directing that such person be prosecuted under the general law. In some states, juvenile court has concurrent jurisdiction with other courts when the juvenile has committed certain serious felonies. Concurrent jurisdiction refers to the ability of an adult criminal court to try the juvenile without first obtaining a waiver from juvenile court.

Dependency

Most juvenile courts provide that any minor who comes within any of the following descriptions is within the jurisdiction of the juvenile court which may adjudge that person to be a dependent child of the court:

(a) The minor has suffered, or there is a substantial risk that the minor will suffer, serious physical harm inflicted nonaccidentally upon the minor by the minor's parent or guardian.

(b) The minor has suffered, or there is a substantial risk that the minor will suffer, serious physical harm or illness, as a result of the failure or inability of his or her parent or guardian to adequately supervise or protect the minor, or the willful or negligent failure of the minor's parent or guardian to adequately supervise or protect the minor from the conduct of the custodian with whom the minor has been left, or by the willful or negligent failure of the parent or guardian to provide the minor with adequate food, clothing, shelter, or medical treatment, or by the inability of the parent or guardian to provide regular care for the minor due to the parent's or guardian's mental illness, developmental disability, or substance abuse.

(c) The minor is suffering serious emotional damage, or is at substantial risk of suffering serious emotional damage, evidenced by severe anxiety, depression, withdrawal, or untoward aggressive behavior toward self or others, as a result of the conduct of the parent or guardian or who has no parent or guardian capable of providing appropriate care.

(d) The minor has been sexually abused, or there is a substantial risk that the minor will be sexually abused by his or her parent or guardian or a member of his or her household, or the parent or guardian has failed to adequately protect the minor from sexual abuse when the parent or guardian knew or reasonably should have known that the minor was in danger of sexual abuse.

(e) The minor is under the age of five and has suffered severe physical abuse by a parent, or by any person known by the parent, if the parent knew or reasonably should have known that the person was physically abusing the minor.

(f) The minor's parent or guardian has been convicted of causing the death of another child through abuse or neglect.

(g) The minor has been left without any provision for support; the minor's parent has been incarcerated or institutionalized and cannot arrange for the care of the minor; or a relative or other adult custodian with whom the child resides or has been left is unwilling or unable to provide care or support for the child, the whereabouts of the parent is unknown, and reasonable efforts to locate the parent have been unsuccessful.

(h) The minor has been freed for adoption from one or both parents for 12 months by either relinquishment or termination of parental rights or an adoption petition has not been granted.

(i) The minor has been subjected to an act or acts of cruelty by the parent or guardian or a member of his or her household, or the parent or guardian has failed to adequately protect the minor from an act or acts of cruelty when the parent or guardian knew or reasonably should have known that the minor was in danger of being subjected to an act or acts of cruelty.

(j) The minor's sibling has been abused or neglected and there is a substantial risk that the minor will be abused or neglected. The court shall consider the circumstances surrounding the abuse or neglect of the sibling, the age and gender of each child, the nature of the abuse or neglect of the sibling, the mental condition of the parent or guardian, and any other factors the court considers probative in determining whether there is a substantial risk to the minor.

The juvenile court may retain jurisdiction over any person who is found to be a dependent child of the juvenile court until the ward or dependent child attains the age of 21 years in most states. A juvenile court may assume jurisdiction over a child under the conditions noted above regardless of whether the child was in the physical custody of both parents or was in the sole legal or physical custody of only one parent at the time that the events or conditions occurred that brought the child within the jurisdiction of the court.

STRUCTURE

The structure of juvenile court varies from state to state. In addition, within the states the structure varies from larger cities to rural communities. In many smaller jurisdictions, juvenile cases are handled by judges on a part-time basis. In more urban areas, there are separate courts that exclusively handle juvenile cases. In some jurisdictions, juvenile courts are handled entirely by family court judges. In others, they are handled by judges who perform general trial court duties. Typically, juvenile courts are part of the district or superior court system of the judicial district. In some states, there is a movement to unify all trial courts into single multipurpose courts. In these states, it appears that eventually juvenile courts will be incorporated into those multipurpose courts.

Many states use the approach that is set forth in Sections 245 and 246 of California's Welfare & Institutions Code.

Section 245. Jurisdiction

Each superior court shall exercise the jurisdiction conferred by this chapter [for juvenile courts], and while sitting in the exercise of such jurisdiction, shall be known and referred to as the juvenile court.

Section 246. Designation of Judge

In counties having more than one judge of the superior court, the presiding judge of such court or the senior judge if there is no presiding judge shall annually, in the month of January, designate one or more judges of the superior court to hear all cases under this chapter during the ensuing year, and he shall, from time to time, designate such additional judges as may be necessary for the prompt disposition of the judicial business before the juvenile court.

In all counties where more than one judge is designated as a judge of the juvenile court, the presiding judge of the superior court shall also designate one such judge as presiding judge of the juvenile court.

ACTORS IN JUVENILE COURT

The group of courthouse persons who perform key courtroom roles in the juvenile justice system include: the defense counsel, the judge, the prosecutor, referees, and the juvenile probation officer. One of the problems in defining these various roles is that often the roles of the prosecutor and the juvenile probation officer are interwoven.

The Judge

Generally, juvenile court judges attempt to balance efforts to help and rehabilitate the youthful offenders with concerns of society for punishment and deterrence. The judge is both a helper and a punisher. Different judges may emphasize one of these roles more than another. This dual orientation may account for the different judicial attitudes and styles that have developed.

Referees

To handle the caseload in juvenile courts, many states permit the appointment of referees. The rules regarding the use of referees are very similar in most states. Accordingly, set forth below are the California rules which are representative of most state laws allowing the use of referees.

In California, the judge of the juvenile court, or the presiding judge of the juvenile court or the senior judge if there is no presiding judge, may appoint one or more referees to serve on a full-time or part-time basis. A referee shall serve at the pleasure of the appointing judge. Referees must be licensed to practice law in the state for a period of not less than five years or a combination not less than ten years in the state and any other state.

A referee shall hear such cases as are assigned to him or her by the presiding judge of the juvenile court, with the same powers as a judge of the juvenile court, except that a referee shall not conduct any hearing to which the state or federal constitutional prohibitions against double jeopardy apply unless all of the parties thereto stipulate in writing that the referee may act in the capacity of a temporary judge.

A referee shall promptly furnish to the presiding judge of the juvenile court and the minor, if the minor is 14 or more years of age or if younger has so requested, and shall serve upon the minor's attorney of record and the minor's parent or guardian or adult relative, and the attorney of record for the minor's parent or guardian or adult relative a written copy of his or her findings and order and shall also furnish to the minor, if the minor is 14 or more years of age or if younger has so requested, and to the parent or guardian or adult relative, with the findings and order, a written explanation of the right of such persons to seek review of the order by juvenile court.

Generally, orders of a referee shall become immediately effective, subject also to the right of review, and shall continue in full force and effect until vacated or modified upon rehearing by order of the judge of the juvenile court. In a case in which an order of a referee becomes effective without approval of a judge of the juvenile court, it becomes final on the expiration of the time allowed for application for rehearing. If the application is not made within this time frame and if the judge of the juvenile court has not within such time ordered a rehearing pursuant, the order stands.

Where a referee sits as a temporary judge, his or her orders become final in the same manner as orders made by a judge. At any time prior to the expiration of 10 days after service of a written copy of the order and findings of a referee, a minor or his parent or guardian may apply to juvenile court for a rehearing. Such application may be directed to all or to any specified part of the order or findings, and shall contain a statement of the reasons such a rehearing is requested. If all of the proceedings before the referee have been taken down by an official reporter, the judge of the juvenile court may, after reading the transcript of such proceedings, grant or deny such application. If proceedings before the referee have not been taken down by an official reporter, a rehearing shall be granted as a matter of right.

If an application for a rehearing is not granted, denied, or extended within 20 days following the date of its receipt, it shall be deemed granted. A judge of the juvenile court may, on his own motion made within 20 judicial days of the hearing before a referee, order a rehearing of any matter heard before a referee.

The Prosecutor

Under our system of justice, the final decision as to whether or not a criminal case goes to court rests with the prosecutor. This applies also to juvenile court, except that in many juvenile cases the decision as to whether the court will conduct a hearing is delegated to the probation officer.

Cases may be referred by many types of individuals—police, teachers, social workers, etc. These individuals are believed to refer cases to juvenile court. That is incorrect. The cases are referred to the prosecutor's office. After the case is referred to the prosecutor, he or she must then file the case with the juvenile court. Until the prosecutor takes action, no further actions are taken on the case.

Probation Officer

Probation officers in any county shall be nominated by the juvenile justice commission or regional juvenile justice commission of such county in such manner as the judge of the juvenile court in that county shall direct, and shall then be appointed by such judge.

The probation officer may appoint as many deputies or assistant probation officers as desired, but such deputies or assistant probation officers shall not have authority to act until their appointments have been approved by the judge of the juvenile court. Probation officers may at any time be removed by the judge of the juvenile court for good cause.

Except where waived by the probation officer, judge, or referee and the minor, the probation officer shall be present in court to represent the interests of each person who is the subject of a petition to declare that person to be a ward or dependent child upon all hearings or rehearings of his or her case, and furnish to the court such information and assistance as the court may require. If so ordered, the probation officer will take charge of that person before and after any hearing or rehearing.

It is the duty of the probation officer to prepare for the hearing on the disposition of a case, as is appropriate for the specific hearing, a social study of the minor, containing such matters as may be relevant to a proper disposition of the case. The social study shall include a recommendation for the disposition of the case.

The probation officer, upon order of any court in any matter involving the custody, status, or welfare of a minor or minors, makes an investigation of appropriate facts and circumstances and prepares and files with the court written reports and written recommendations in reference to such matters. The court is authorized to receive and consider the reports and recommendations of the probation officer in determining any such matter. In some cases the duties, concerning dependent children, of a probation officer for juvenile court may be delegated to the county welfare department.

Probation officers generally have the right to state summary criminal history as is considered necessary. The information typically includes:

- Any current incarceration

- The location of any current probation or parole

- Any current requirement that the individual register

- Any history of offenses involving abuse or neglect of, or violence against, a child

- Convictions of any offenses involving violence, sexual offenses, the abuse or illegal possession, manufacture, or sale of alcohol or controlled substances

- Any arrest for which the person is released on bail or on his or her own recognizance

Generally, a probation officer may employ such psychiatrists, psychologists, and other clinical experts as are required to assist in determining appropriate treatment of minors within the jurisdiction of the juvenile court and in the implementation of such treatment. If a probation officer determines that a minor should be removed from the physical custody of his parent or guardian, the probation officer shall give primary consideration to recommending that the minor be placed with a relative of the minor, if such placement is in the best interests of the minor and will be conducive to reunification of the family.

At any time, the judge of the juvenile court may require the probation officer to examine into and report to the court upon the qualifications and management of any society, association, or corporation, other than a state institution, which applies for or receives custody of any ward or dependent child of the juvenile court. Probation officers, however, do not have the authority to enter any institution without its consent. If such consent is refused, juvenile commitments are normally not made to that institution.

In any case in which a probation officer, after investigation, determines that a minor is within the jurisdiction of the juvenile court or will probably soon be within that jurisdiction, the probation officer may, in lieu of filing a petition or subsequent to dismissal of a petition already filed, and with consent of the minor's parent or guardian, undertake a program of supervision of the minor. If a program of supervision is undertaken, the probation officer will attempt to ameliorate the situation which brings the minor within, or creates the probability that the minor will be within, the jurisdiction by providing or arranging to contract for all appropriate child welfare services.

If a family refuses to cooperate with the services being provided, the probation officer may file a petition with the juvenile court. The program of supervision of the minor undertaken pursuant to this section may call for the minor to obtain care and treatment for the misuse of, or addiction to, controlled substances from a county mental health service or other appropriate community agency.

Defense Counsel

The American Bar Association outlines the role of the defense counsel in juvenile court in its *Standards Relating to Counsel for Private Parties*. According to the ABA, the defense counsel's duties include providing legal representation in all proceedings arising from or related to delinquency; in-need-of supervision actions including mental competency, transfer, and disciplinary or other actions related to any treatment program; post-disposition proceedings; probation revocation; and any other proceedings that may substantially affect a juvenile's custody, status, or course of treatment.

Unlike the early court reformer's concept of juvenile court, juvenile court proceedings are now generally considered adversarial in nature. Presently, most juveniles are represented by counsel in court. In many cases, the parents are also represented by counsel. Where possible conflicts of interest may exist, separate counsel must be appointed for the parents and the juvenile.

The two major categories of defense counsel are the retained counsel and the appointed counsel. A retained counsel is a private attorney that has been retained or hired by the juvenile and/or the juvenile's family. In most cases, the juvenile is represented by an appointed counsel. An appointed counsel is one appointed by the judge. The appointed counsel may be from the public defender's office or a private counsel who is appointed by the judge and paid a minimal amount by the county to represent the juvenile.

Public defender's offices have heavy caseloads and limited investigative resources. Accordingly, a public defender spends the majority of time negotiating pleas and little time investigating cases. While there are many public defenders who pursue their clients' interests with all possible vigor, frequently public defenders do not use every possible legal strategy to defend their clients. For example, a public defender is generally less likely to object to minor legal errors made by the judge or the prosecutor. On the whole, it appears that juveniles who are represented by private counsel fare better than those represented by appointed counsel. Accordingly, public defenders generally have a less favorable image among their clients than do retained attorneys.

The duties of the defense counsel are the same whether they are appointed or retained. The duties include seeing that the client is properly represented at all stages of the system, seeing that the client's rights are not violated, and that evidence favorable to the defendant is presented to the judge. The defense counsel should ensure that the case is presented in the light most favorable to the juvenile. To accomplish these duties, the defense counsel is at least, in theory, the adversary of the prosecutor.

Guardian Ad Litem

The court may also appoint a *guardian ad litem* to protect the juvenile's interests. A *guardian ad litem* is a person appointed by the court to promote and protect the interests of the juvenile. The guardian is normally not an attorney. In some cases, the guardian is an employee of the county's child protective services. Generally, a *guardian ad litem* is appointed in cases involving child abuse, neglect, or other dependency cases where the courts have questions regarding the ability or desire of the parents to protect the child's interests.

RIGHTS OF JUVENILES AND PARENTS

Unless their parental rights have been terminated, both parents are required to be notified of all proceedings involving the child. In any case where the probation officer is required to provide a parent or guardian with notice of a proceeding at which the probation officer intends to present a report, the probation officer shall also provide both parents, whether custodial or noncustodial, or any guardian, or the counsel for the parent or guardian, a copy of the report prior to the hearing, either personally or by first-class mail.

When a minor is adjudged a dependent of the juvenile court, any issues regarding custodial rights between his or her parents shall be determined solely by the juvenile court so long as the minor remains a dependent of the juvenile court. No minor shall be found to be dependent of the court if the willful failure of the parent or guardian to provide adequate mental health treatment is based on a sincerely held religious belief and if a less intrusive judicial intervention is available.

When a peace officer or social worker takes a minor into custody, immediate steps must be made to notify the minor's parent, guardian, or a responsible relative that the minor is in custody and inform them of the place where he or she is being held, except when, upon order of the juvenile court, the parent or guardian shall not be notified of the exact whereabouts of the minor.

Immediately after being taken to a place of confinement, except where physically impossible, no later than one hour after he or she has been taken into custody, a minor ten years of age or older shall be advised that he or she has the right to make at least two telephone calls from the place where he or she is being held, one call completed to his or her parent, guardian, or a responsible relative, and another call completed to an attorney. The calls shall be at public expense, if the calls are completed to telephone numbers within the local calling area, and in the presence of a public officer or employee. Any public officer or employee who willfully deprives a minor taken into custody of his or her right to make these telephone calls is guilty of a misdemeanor.

As a condition for the release of such a minor, the probation officer may require the minor or his parent, guardian, or relative, or both, to sign a written promise that either or both of them will appear before the probation officer at a suitable place and time designated by the probation officer.

DISCUSSION QUESTIONS

1. What were the two major forces behind the creation of juvenile court?

2. In dependency cases, what is the stated intent of most state legislatures?

3. Explain the jurisdiction of juvenile court in dependency cases.

   In delinquency cases.

4. Define the role of the probation officer in juvenile court.

Chapter 8

Juvenile
Court
Procedures

DELINQUENCY CASES

Generally a petition of the commencement of proceedings in juvenile court to declare a minor a ward of the court is by a verified petition (signed under oath) and contains the following:

a. The name of the court to which it is addressed.

b. The title of the proceeding.

c. The code section and subdivision under which the proceedings are instituted. Any petition alleging that the minor has committed a crime shall state as to each count whether the crime charged is a felony or a misdemeanor.

d. The name, age, and address, if any, of the minor upon whose behalf the petition is brought.

e. The names and residence addresses, if known to petitioner, of both of the parents and any guardian of the minor. If there is no parent or guardian residing within the state, or if his or her place of residence is not known to the petitioner, the petition shall also contain the name and residence address, if known, of any adult relative residing within the county, or, if there are none, the adult relative residing nearest to the location of the court.

f. A concise statement of facts, separately stated, to support the conclusion that the minor, upon whose behalf the petition is being brought, is a person within the definition of each of the sections and subdivisions under which the proceedings are being instituted.

g. The fact that the minor upon whose behalf the petition is brought is detained in custody or is not detained in custody, and if he or she is detained in custody, the date and the precise time the minor was taken into custody.

h. A notice to the father, mother, spouse, or other person liable for support of the minor child, that: (1) state law may make that person, the estate of that person, and the estate of the minor child, liable for the cost of the care, support, and maintenance of the minor child in any county institution or any other place in which the child is placed, detained, or committed pursuant to an order of the juvenile court; (2) that the person, the estate of that person, and the estate of the minor child may be liable for the cost to the county of legal services rendered to the minor by a private attorney or a public defender appointed pursuant to the order of the juvenile court; (3) state law may make that person, the estate of that person, and the estate of the minor child liable for the cost to the county of the probation supervision of the minor child by the probation officer pursuant to the order of the juvenile court; and (4) that the above liabilities are joint and several (the costs or expenses may be added together).

If a proceeding is pending against a minor child for a violation of the Penal Code, a notice to the parent or legal guardian of the minor that if the minor is found to have violated either or both of these provisions:

1. Any community service which may be required of the minor may be performed in the presence, and under the direct supervision, of the parent or legal guardian pursuant to either or both of these provisions; and

2. If the minor is personally unable to pay any fine levied for the violation of either or both of these provisions, the parent or legal guardian of the minor shall be liable

for payment of the fine pursuant to those sections. If the minor is ordered to make restitution to the victim, the parent or guardian may be liable for the payment of restitution.

Juvenile courts handled more than four times as many delinquency cases in 1996 as in 1960

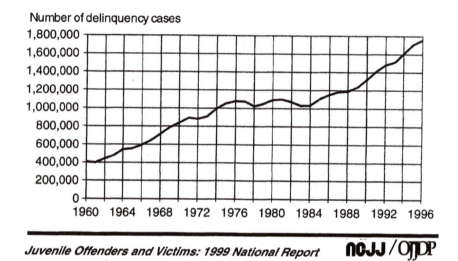

Number of delinquency cases

Juvenile Offenders and Victims: 1999 National Report   **ncJJ/OJJDP**

Detention Hearings

Whenever a minor is taken into custody by a peace officer or probation officer that minor must be released within 48 hours excluding nonjudicial days. Exceptions to this rule occur when a minor willfully misrepresents himself as 18 years of age or older or when a petition to declare that minor a dependent child or ward of the court has been filed.

A proceeding in the juvenile court to declare a minor a dependent child of the court is commenced by the filing with the court, by the probation officer, of a petition. A petition to declare the minor a ward of the court or a criminal complaint is generally filed by the prosecutor, county attorney or district attorney.

In many states, whenever a minor who has been held in custody for more than six hours by the probation officer is subsequently released and no petition is filed, the probation officer must prepare a written explanation of why the minor was held in custody for more than six hours. The written explanation is generally required to be prepared within 72 hours after the minor is released from custody and filed in the record of the case. A copy of the written explanation is also sent to the parents, guardian, or other person having care or custody of the minor.

When a minor willfully misrepresents himself to be 18 or more years of age when taken into custody by a peace officer or probation officer, and this misrepresentation effects a material delay in investigation which prevents the filing of a petition, such petition or complaint shall be filed within 48 hours from the time his true age is determined, excluding nonjudicial days. If, in such cases, the petition is not filed within the time prescribed, the minor should be immediately released from custody.

If a minor has been taken into custody and not released to a parent or guardian, the juvenile court shall hold a hearing (which shall be referred to as a "detention hearing") to determine whether the minor shall be further detained. This hearing shall be held as soon as possible, but, in any event, before the expiration of the next judicial day after a petition to declare the minor a dependent child or ward of the court has been filed. If the hearing is not held within the period prescribed, the minor is required to be released from custody.

If a probation officer or prosecutor determines that a minor shall be retained in custody, he or she shall immediately file a petition pursuant with the clerk of the juvenile court who shall set the matter for hearing on the detention hearing calendar. The probation officer or prosecutor will then notify each parent or guardian of the minor of the time and place of the hearing if the whereabouts of each parent or guardian can be ascertained by due diligence. Each person will be served with a copy of the petition and notified of the time and place of the detention hearing. In some cases, this notice may be given orally if it appears that the parent does not read.

Upon his or her appearance before the court at the detention hearing, each parent or guardian and the minor, if present, shall first be informed of the reasons why the minor was taken into custody, the nature of the juvenile court proceedings, and the right of each parent or guardian and any minor to be represented at every stage of the proceedings by counsel.

In the hearing, the minor, parents or guardians have a privilege against self-incrimination and have a right to confrontation by, and cross-examination of, any person examined by the court. Upon reasonable notification by counsel representing the minor, his parents or guardian, the clerk of the court shall notify such counsel of the hearings.

Citation

If an officer who takes a minor into temporary custody for a criminal offense determines that the minor should be brought to the attention of the juvenile court, he or she may release the minor after preparing a written notice to appear before the probation officer. The notice shall also contain a concise statement of the reasons the minor was taken into custody. The officer then delivers one copy of the notice to the minor or to a parent, guardian, or responsible relative of the minor and may require the minor or his or her parent, guardian, or relative, or both, to sign a written promise that either or both will appear at the time and place designated in the notice. Upon the execution of the promise to appear, the officer has the discretion to release the minor. The officer then forwards a copy of the notice to the probation officer.

In determining whether to hold or to release the minor with a citation (written promise to appear), the officer should use the alternative which least restricts the minor's freedom of movement, provided that alternative is compatible with the best interests of the minor and the community.

Venue

Venue refers to the geographical location of the court in which the proceedings will be conducted. Under the United

States Constitution, an accused in an adult criminal trial has the right to be tried in the county and judicial district where the crime occurred. In juvenile cases, most state statutes provide that in any proceedings involving a juvenile, the proceedings will be held in the county in which the juvenile resides. If the proceedings begin in a different county, the proceedings at the request of the juvenile may be transferred to the county of residence. If a juvenile changes residence during the proceedings, the court may transfer the proceedings to the county of the new residence of the juvenile. For most purposes, a juvenile is considered to reside in the county in which his or her parents or guardian reside.

Intake

The "intake" phase of the juvenile justice case has several purposes. It is used to screen cases in determining whether the juvenile needs the help of the court and to help control the use of detention. It also is used to screen out cases in an effort to reduce the court's caseload. Unlike dependency cases, intake has different functions in different states. In general, intake persons exercise a great deal of discretion during this phase of the proceedings.

One of the first decisions that must be made during intake is whether the case comes under juvenile court jurisdiction. Next, the decision must be made on whether to assume jurisdiction, dismiss the case, or refer the youth to another agency. During this phase, the court may also use informal methods, such as informal probation, to handle the case. If the youth is in detention and the case is not dismissed or referred, the decision must also be made as to whether the detention should continue until the adjudicatory hearing is held.

During this phase, an intake officer generally reviews the case and makes the preliminary decisions noted above. Typically, the intake officer's recommendations are followed by the judge. In many states, the intake officer's duties are performed by a probation officer. The intake officer will normally recommend dismissal or informal probation for first-time offenders unless the youth has committed a serious crime.

Under informal probation, the youth is released if he or she agrees to accept certain conditions imposed by the court. Normally if the youth stays out of trouble for a specified period of time, the case is dismissed. If the youth violates the terms of the agreement or gets involved in other delinquent acts, the court may recall the case and hold the youth for further adjudication.

Consent decrees are also used in delinquency cases. These decrees are court orders agreed to by the youth and accepted by the court. A consent decree removes the need for an adjudicatory hearing. It is similar to a plea bargain in adult criminal court.

Adjudicatory Hearings

After the intake proceedings, the adjudicatory hearing is used in those cases not dismissed, referred to other agencies, or subject to consent decrees. The adjudicatory hearing is equivalent to a trial in adult court.

Caseloads steadily increased between 1987 and 1996 across all four general categories

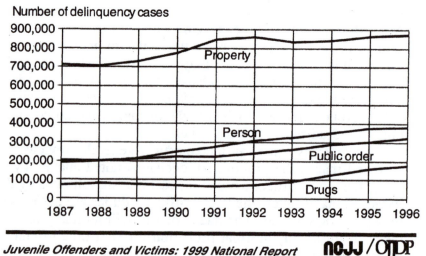

Number of delinquency cases

Juvenile Offenders and Victims: 1999 National Report **ncJJ/OJDP**

Procedural Rights Contained
in the Indiana Juvenile Statutes
(Indiana Juvenile Statutes, 31-6-4-13)

Sec. 13.

(a) This section applies only to a child alleged to be a delinquent child.

(b) The juvenile court shall hold an initial hearing on each petition.

(c) The juvenile court shall first determine whether counsel has been waived... or whether counsel should be appointed...

(d) The court shall next determine whether the prosecutor intends to seek a waiver of jurisdiction [for purposes of referral to adult criminal court]....If waiver is sought, the court may not accept an admission or denial of the allegations from the child...and shall schedule a waiver hearing and advise the child....

(e) The juvenile court shall inform the child and his parents, guardians, or custodian, if that person is present, of:

 (1) the nature of the allegations against the child;

 (2) the child's right to:
 (A) be represented by counsel;
 (B) have a speedy trial;
 (C) confront witnesses against him;
 (D) cross-examine witnesses against him;
 (E) obtain witnesses or tangible evidence by compulsory process;
 (F) introduce evidence on his own behalf;
 (G) refrain from testifying against himself; and
 (H) have the state prove that he committed the delinquent act charged beyond a reasonable doubt.

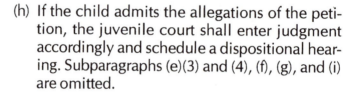

(h) If the child admits the allegations of the petition, the juvenile court shall enter judgment accordingly and schedule a dispositional hearing. Subparagraphs (e)(3) and (4), (f), (g), and (i) are omitted.

While the adjudicatory hearings are less formal that adult trials (as will be discussed in the next chapter) the juvenile has certain due process rights that must be provided during this hearing. Unlike adult trials, the trials are closed to the public, and in most states there are no rights to a jury trial.

The order of proceedings during the adjudicatory hearing is generally very similar to that of adult criminal cases. The prosecutor puts on the case in chief, followed by the defense, and then any rebuttal by the prosecutor.

Rules of evidence are required to be used in the adjudicatory hearings and the proof as to whether the juvenile committed the crime in question must be established beyond a reasonable doubt.

Disposition Hearing

The disposition hearing is similar to the sentencing phase of an adult criminal trial. In most states, after the court determines that the juvenile has committed the offense, the judge sets a date for the disposition hearing. At the disposition hearing, the rules of evidence are relaxed and the judge is permitted to receive a wide range of evidence regarding the youth. In most states, the probation officer is required to present a predisposition report to the court. This report generally contains a written description of the incident, the youth's prior conduct record, information on the youth's family, the employment record of the youth and any other information that may assist the judge in making the disposition decision.

VICTIMS' RIGHTS

In any case in which a minor is alleged to have committed an act which would have been a felony if committed by an adult, the probation officer should obtain a statement from the victim (the parent or guardian of the victim if the victim is a minor, or if the victim has died, the victim's next of kin) concerning the offense which is included in the predisposition report made by the probation officer and submitted to the court and advises the above person(s) as to the time and place of the disposition hearing.

The probation officer also provides the victim with information concerning the victim's right to an action for civil damages against the minor and his or her guardians and the victim's opportunity to be compensated from the restitution fund. The information is in the form of written material prepared by the Judicial Council and provided to each victim for whom the probation officer has a current mailing address.

Finally, the persons from whom the probation officer is required to obtain a statement have the right to attend the disposition hearing and, subject to the court's discretion, to express their views concerning the offense and disposition of the case.

DEPENDENCY, ABUSE, AND NEGLECT CASES

In all cases in which a petition is filed based upon alleged neglect or abuse of the minor, or in which a prosecution is initiated under the Penal Code arising from neglect or abuse of the minor, the probation officer or a social worker who files a petition shall be the *guardian ad litem* to represent the interests of the minor, unless the court appoints another adult as *guardian ad litem*. However, the *guardian ad litem* shall not be the attorney responsible for presenting evidence alleging child abuse or neglect in judicial proceedings. Courts generally waive any bond requirements for a *guardian ad litem* who is an employee of the county probation or child protective services offices.

The proper court to commence proceedings is either the juvenile court in the county in which a minor resides, or in the county where the minor is found, or in the county in which the acts took place or the circumstances exist.

Whenever the probation officer has cause to believe that a child is being abused within the jurisdiction of that officer, immediately an investigation should take place to determine whether child welfare services should be offered to the family and whether proceedings in the juvenile court should be commenced.

If the probation officer determines that it is appropriate to offer child welfare services to the family, referral is made for these services. Whenever any person applies to the probation office to commence proceedings in the juvenile court, that application is in the form of an affidavit alleging that there was or is within the county, or residing therein, a minor in danger of abuse. The affidavit must be supported by facts.

The probation officer immediately initiates an investigation as deemed necessary to determine whether proceedings in the juvenile court should be commenced. If the probation officer does not take action and does not file a petition in the juvenile court, the affidavit of the applicant is endorsed with the decision not to proceed further and the reasons stated. Immediate notification is given to the applicant as to the action taken or the decision rendered. The probation officer is generally required to retain the affidavit and subsequent endorsement for a period of about 30 days after such notice to the applicant.

When any person has applied to the probation officer to commence juvenile court proceedings and the probation officer fails to file a petition within the specified time period after such application, that person may apply to the juvenile court to review the decision of the probation officer. The court may either affirm the decision or order the commencement of juvenile court proceedings.

When it appears to the court that a parent or guardian of the minor desires counsel but is presently financially unable to afford and cannot for that reason employ counsel, the court may appoint counsel. When it appears to the court that a parent or guardian of the minor is presently financially unable to afford and cannot for that reason employ counsel, and the minor has been placed in out-of-home care, or the petitioning agency is recommending that the minor be placed in out-of-home care, the court appoints counsel, unless the court finds that the parent or guardian has made a knowing and intelligent waiver of counsel.

In any case in which it appears to the court that the minor would benefit from the appointment of counsel, the court appoints counsel for the minor. Counsel for the minor may be a county counsel, district attorney, public defender, or other member of the bar, provided that the counsel does not represent another party or county agency whose interests conflict with those of the minor's. The fact that the district attorney represents the minor in a proceeding as well as conducts a criminal investigation or files against another person a criminal complaint or information arising from the same or reasonably related set of facts as the proceeding is not in and of itself a conflict of interest. The court shall determine if representation of both the petitioning agency and the minor constitutes a conflict of interest. If the court finds there is a conflict of interest, separate counsel is appointed for the minor.

The court may fix the compensation to be paid by the county for the services of appointed counsel, if counsel is not a county counsel, district attorney, public defender or other public attorney. The counsel appointed by the court represents the parent, guardian, or minor at the detention hearing and at all subsequent proceedings before the juvenile court. Counsel continues to represent the parent or minor unless relieved by the court upon the substitution of other counsel or for cause. The representation includes representing the parent or the minor in termination proceedings and in those proceedings relating to the institution or setting aside of a legal guardianship.

The counsel for the minor is charged, in general, with the representation of the minor's interests. To that end, the counsel makes or causes to have made any further investigations deemed in good faith to be reasonably necessary to ascertain the facts. This includes the interviewing of witnesses, examining and cross-examining of witnesses in both the adjudicatory and dispositional hearings. Counsel may also introduce and examine their own witnesses, make recommendations to the court concerning the minor's welfare, and participate further in the proceedings to the degree necessary to adequately represent the minor. Generally, in any case in which the minor is four years of age or older, counsel shall interview the minor to determine the minor's wishes and to assess the his or her's well-being. In addition, counsel should investigate the interests of the minor beyond the scope of the juvenile proceeding and report to the court other interests of the minor that may need to be protected by the institution by other administrative or judicial proceedings. The court then takes whatever appropriate action is necessary to fully protect the interests of the minor.

The juvenile's counsel is given access to all records relevant to the case which are maintained by state or local public agencies. Counsel is also given access to records maintained by hospitals and/or by other medical or nonmedical practitioners and by child care custodians.

If a district attorney has represented a minor in a dependency proceeding, there is obviously a conflict of interest and that district attorney will not appear on behalf of the State. All records kept by the district attorney in the course of representation of a minor are confidential. These records cannot be inspected by members of the district attorney's office not directly involved in the representation of that minor. A district attorney who represents or who has represented a minor cannot discuss the substance of that case with a district attorney representing the people in a proceeding brought in which that same minor is the subject of the petition.

In a juvenile court hearing, where the parent or guardian is represented by counsel, the county counsel or district attorney may, at the request of the juvenile court judge, appear and participate in the hearing to represent the petitioner.

At the initial petition hearing, the court examines the minor's parents, guardians, or other persons having relevant knowledge and hears relevant evidence as the minor, the minor's parents or guardians, the petitioner, or their counsel desires to present. The probation officer reports to the court on the reasons why the minor has been removed from the parent's custody; the need, if any, for continued detention; on the available services and the referral methods to those services which could facilitate the return of the minor to the custody of the minor's parents or guardians; and whether there are any relatives who are able and willing to take temporary custody of the minor. The court usually orders the release of the minor from custody unless a *prima facie* showing has been made that any of the following circumstances exist:

➤ There is a substantial danger to the physical health of the minor or the minor is suffering severe emotional damage, and there are no reasonable means by which the minor's physical or emotional health may be protected without removing the minor from the parents' or guardians' physical custody.

➢ There is substantial evidence that a parent, guardian, or custodian of the minor is likely to flee the jurisdiction of the court.

➢ The minor has left a placement in which he or she was placed by the juvenile court.

➢ The minor indicates an unwillingness to return home, if the minor has been physically or sexually abused by a person residing in the home.

The court also makes a determination on the record as to whether reasonable efforts were made to prevent or eliminate the need for removal of the minor from his or her home and whether there are available services which would prevent the need for further detention. Services to be considered for purposes of making this determination are case management, counseling, emergency shelter care, emergency in-home caretakers, out-of-home respite care, teaching and demonstrating homemakers, parenting training, transportation, and any other child welfare services authorized by the State Department of Social Services. Also, the court reviews whether the social worker has considered whether a referral to public assistance services could eliminate the need to take temporary custody of the minor or would prevent the need for further detention.

If the minor can be returned to the custody of his or her parent or guardian through the provision of those services, the court typically orders those services.

If the minor cannot be returned to the custody of his or her parent or guardian, the court determines if there is a relative who is able and willing to care for the child. Where the first contact with the family has occurred during an emergency situation in which the child could not safely remain at home, even with reasonable services being provided, the court may make a finding that the lack of preplacement preventive efforts were reasonable. Whenever a court orders a minor detained, the court shall state the facts on which the decision is based and specify why the initial removal was necessary, and order services to be provided as soon as possible to reunify the minor and his or her family, if appropriate.

When the minor is not released from custody, the court may order that the minor be placed in the suitable home of a relative or in an emergency shelter or other suitable place.

Relative generally means an adult who is related to the minor by blood or affinity, including all relatives whose status is preceded by the words "step," "great," "great-great," or "grand." However, only the following relatives shall be given preferential treatment for placement of the minor: an adult who is a grandparent, aunt, uncle, or a sibling of the minor.

When a hearing is held and no parent or guardian of the minor is present or has had actual notice of the hearing, a parent or guardian of the minor may file an affidavit stating such with the clerk of the juvenile court and the clerk may set the matter for rehearing. Upon the rehearing, the court then proceeds in the same manner as upon the original hearing.

If the minor, a parent or guardian, or the minor's attorney or *guardian ad litem* requests evidence of the *prima facie* case, a rehearing shall be held within a reasonable time to consider evidence of the *prima facie* case. If the *prima facie* case is not established, the minor is then released from detention. In lieu of a requested rehearing, the court may set the matter for trial within a few days. Upon motion of the minor or a parent or guardian, the court may continue any hearing or rehearing for one day, excluding Sundays and nonjudicial days.

Any peace officer, probation officer, or social worker who takes a minor into temporary custody should immediately inform, through the most efficient means available, the parent, guardian, or responsible relative, that the minor has been taken into protective custody. A written statement is then made available which explains the parent's or guardian's procedural rights and the preliminary stages of the dependency investigation and hearing.

Generally, the written statement is made available for distribution through all public schools, probation offices, and appropriate welfare offices. It should include, but is not limited to, the following information:

➤ The conditions under which the minor will be released, hearings which may be required, and the means whereby further specific information about the minor's case and conditions of confinement may be obtained.

➤ The rights to counsel, privileges against self-incrimination, and rights to appeal possessed by the minor, and his or her parents, guardians, or responsible relative.

If a good faith attempt was made at notification, the failure on the part of the peace officer, probation officer, or social worker to notify the parent or guardian shall be considered to be due to circumstances beyond their control. Furthermore, it shall not permit a new defense to any juvenile or judicial proceeding or interfere with any rights, procedures, or investigations accorded under any other law.

COURT ORDERS

In most states, all written findings and orders of the court are served by the clerk of the court personally or by first-class mail on the petitioner, the minor or the minor's counsel, the parent or the parent's counsel, and the guardian or the guardian's counsel. No order of a referee removing a minor from his home shall become effective until expressly approved by a judge of the juvenile court.

A court may also find there is a substantial risk of serious future injury based on the manner in which a less serious injury was inflicted. A history of repeated inflictions of injuries on the minor or the minor's siblings, or a combination of these and other actions by the parent or guardian may indicate the child is at risk of serious physical harm. *Serious physical harm* does not include reasonable and age-appropriate spanking to the buttocks where there is no evidence of serious physical injury. *Severe physical abuse* means any of the following:

➤ Any single act of abuse which causes physical trauma of sufficient severity that, if left untreated, would cause permanent physical disfigurement, permanent physical disability, or death.

> ➤ Any single act of sexual abuse which causes significant bleeding, deep bruising, or significant external or internal swelling.

> ➤ More than one act of physical abuse, each of which causes bleeding, deep bruising, significant external or internal swelling, bone fracture, or unconsciousness.

> ➤ The willful, prolonged failure to provide adequate food.

Typically, a minor may not be removed from the physical custody of his or her parent or guardian on the basis of a finding of severe physical abuse unless a probation officer has made an allegation of severe physical abuse.

Across all ages in 1996, property offense case rates were highest, but drug offense case rates had the sharpest increase with age

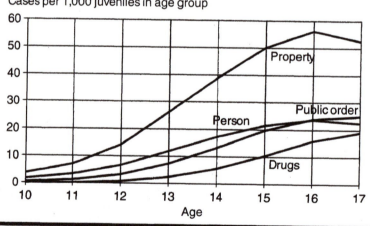

Cases per 1,000 juveniles in age group

Juvenile Offenders and Victims: 1999 National Report

DISCUSSION QUESTIONS

1. What rights does a minor have at the adjudicatory hearing?

2. Explain the safeguards present to protect a minor when the minor has been taken into custody.

3. What are the functions of intake? Why is it considered one of the most important proceedings in the process?

4. What are the functions of the adjudicatory hearings?

5. What may a judge consider in determining the proper disposition of a youth who has committed a crime?

6. Differentiate between disposition hearings and adjudicatory hearings.

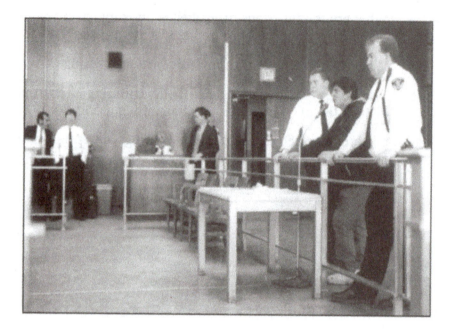

Chapter 9

Juvenile
Case Law

The key Supreme Court decisions that have impacted the juvenile justice system are discussed in this chapter: decisions in due process rights, search and seizure issues, and interrogation and confession problems. The leading United States Supreme Court cases involving the legal rights of juveniles will be highlighted. The decisions have been edited or rephrased to make them shorter and more readable.

DELINQUENCY DETERMINATION CASES

Kent v. United States

Kent v. United States (383 U.S.541 1966) set forth the procedural guidelines to be used in the waiver of a delinquent from juvenile to adult courts. Morris Kent was a 16-year-old with a police record. He was arrested and charged with housebreaking, robbery, and rape. He admitted committing the crimes. After being held in a juvenile detention center for about six days, the juvenile court judge transferred jurisdiction to the adult criminal court without holding a hearing.

This case was decided on the narrow issue of whether juveniles have a right to a hearing before being transferred to adult criminal court. The impact of the decision, however, went far beyond its narrow issue. It was a warning to juvenile courts that their traditional laxity toward procedural and evidentiary standards would be subject to scrutiny by the Supreme Court. The Supreme Court had indicated its concern regarding juveniles as early as 1948 in *Haley v. Ohio* (322 U.S. 596 1948). The *Haley* case involved a juvenile tried in adult criminal court for first-degree murder. The Court held that the due process

A series of U.S. Supreme Court decisions made juvenile courts more like criminal courts but maintained some important differences

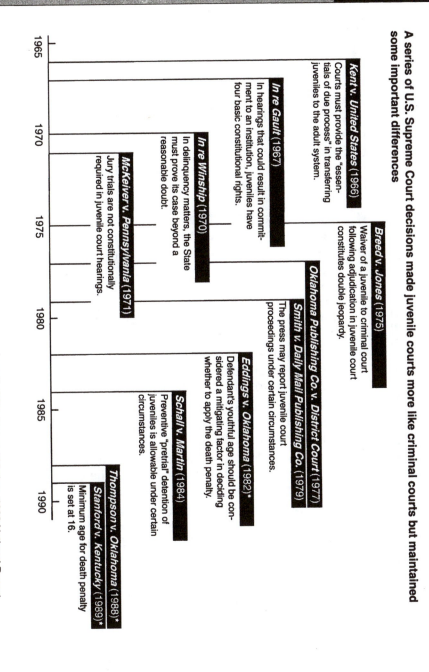

Kent v. United States (1966)
Courts must provide the "essentials of due process" in transferring juveniles to the adult system.

In re Gault (1967)
In hearings that could result in commitment to an institution, juveniles have four basic constitutional rights.

In re Winship (1970)
In delinquency matters, the State must prove its case beyond a reasonable doubt.

McKeiver v. Pennsylvania (1971)
Jury trials are not constitutionally required in juvenile court hearings.

Breed v. Jones (1975)
Waiver of a juvenile to criminal court following adjudication in juvenile court constitutes double jeopardy.

Oklahoma Publishing Co. v. District Court (1977)
The press may report juvenile court proceedings under certain circumstances.

Smith v. Daily Mail Publishing Co. (1979)

Eddings v. Oklahoma (1982)*
Defendant's youthful age should be considered a mitigating factor in deciding whether to apply the death penalty.

Schall v. Martin (1984)
Preventive "pretrial" detention of juveniles is allowable under certain circumstances.

Thompson v. Oklahoma (1988)*

Stanford v. Kentucky (1989)*
Minimum age for death penalty is set at 16.

1965 1970 1975 1980 1985 1990

Juveniles Prosecuted in State Criminal Courts

A 1997 publication by the Bureau of Justice Statistics (BJS), *Juveniles Prosecuted in State Criminal Courts*, presents data from their 1994 National Survey of Prosecutors and other BJS statiticians, as well as data from the National Center for Juvenile Justice. Following are the highlights of that publication:

- Nationwide, 94% of state court prosecutors offices had responsibility for handling juvenile cases.

- Among prosecutors' offices handling juvenile cases, almost two-thirds transferred at least one juvenile case to criminal court in 1994. Of these offices, 37% transferred at least one aggravated assault case, 34% at least one robbery case, and 32% at least one murder case.

- 19% of prosecutors' offices handling juvenile cases had a specialized unit that dealt with juvenile cases transferred to criminal court.

- 16% of prosecutors' offices handling juvenile cases had written guidelines about the transfer of juveniles to criminal court.

- States have developed several mechanisms to permit proceeding against alleged juvenile offenders as adults in criminal court jurisdiction.

- The percentage of petitioned cases judicially waived to criminal court has remained relatively constant at about 1.4% since 1985. In 1994, 12,300 juvenile cases were judicially waived.

- From 1985-91 property offenses comprised the largest number of cases judicially waived. Since 1991 violent offenses have outnumbered property offenses as the most serious charge.

- Currently no national data describe the number of juvenile cases processed in criminal court under concurrent jurisdiction or statutory exclusion provisions.

clause barred the use of a confession obtained by force by juvenile authorities.

The *Kent* case was the first case directly involving the juvenile court. In an appendix to the Court's decision, the Court set forth the criteria to be used by juvenile courts in determining whether to waive jurisdiction of juveniles. The criteria are discussed in more detail in Chapter 10.

In re Gault

Any examination of legal rights of juveniles must include a study of the *In re Gault* (387 U.S. 1 1967) case. Gerald Francis Gault was 15 years old at the time he was committed to the State Industrial School by the Juvenile Court of Gila County, Arizona.

On June 8, 1964, Gault and a friend were taken into custody by the local sheriff as the result of a verbal complaint of a neighbor, Mrs. Cook. The neighbor alleged that Gerald had made a telephone call to her that contained lewd and indecent remarks. At the time Gerald was on six month's probation from a February 25, 1964 court order as the results of his having been in the company of another boy who had stolen a wallet from a lady's purse.

When Gault was taken into custody, his parents were at work. No notice that Gault was taken into custody was served on his parents nor left at their residence. No steps were taken to advise them of the location of their son. When Gault's mother arrived home and found Gault was not present, she sent his oldest brother to look for him. Later that evening, they learned that Gault was in custody at the Children's Detention Home. When his mother contacted the home, she was informed by a deputy probation officer that Gerald was in custody and that a hearing in his case would be held in juvenile court at 3:00 P.M. the following day, June 9, 1964.

The arresting officer, Flagg, filed a petition with the court on the day of the hearing. No copy was served on the parents or on Gault. They did not see the petition until August 17, 1964, at a *habeas corpus* hearing to set aside the commitment. The petition was stated in formal language with no supporting factual statements regarding the basis for the judicial action. The petition alleged only: "...said minor is under the age of eighteen years, and is in need of the protection of this Honorable Court." The petition prayed (requested) that "... a hearing be held and that an order be issued regarding the care and custody of the said minor."

Gault, his mother, his older brother, the probation officer, and Officer Flagg appeared before the juvenile court judge on June 9, 1964. Mrs. Cook, the complainant, was not present. No one was sworn. No witnesses were called. No transcript of the proceeding nor memorandum of the substance of the hearing was made. There was a conflict over what occurred at the hearing. According to Gault's mother, Gault admitted dialing the telephone, but claimed that he gave the telephone to his friend who made the remarks. Officer Flagg recalled that Gault admitted making the lewd remarks. After the hearing, Gault was taken back to the detention home. He was released from custody on either June 11 or 12. There is no explanation as to why he was released. When he was released, the mother received a letter signed by Officer Flagg. The entire text of the letter was as follows:

Mrs. Gault:

Judge McGhee has set Monday June 15, 1964, at 11:00 A.M. as the date and time for further Hearing on Gerald's delinquency.

/s/ Flagg

At the June 15 hearing, a probation report was filed with the court. The contents of the report were neither disclosed to Gault nor his parents. The report listed the charge against Gault as "lewd phone calls." Gault's mother requested that Mrs. Cook be called so that she could identify which youth made the remarks. The judge refused her request. After the hearing, the judge committed Gault as a delinquent to the State Industrial School for the period of his minority (until he was 21) unless sooner discharged by due process of law. Had Gault been tried in adult criminal court, the maximum jail term would have been six months. At that time, no appeal was permitted from juvenile court by Arizona law. This case went to the U.S. Supreme Court by *writ of habeas corpus*.

The Court noted that the state was proceeding as *parens patriae*. This Latin phrase proved to be a great help to those who sought to rationalize the exclusion of juveniles from the constitutional scheme, but its meaning is murky and its historic credentials are of dubious relevance. The Court also noted that there was no trace of the doctrine of *parens patriae* in criminal jurisprudence.

The Supreme Court in its opinion noted that from the inception of the juvenile court system, wide differences have been tolerated between the procedural rights accorded to adults and those accorded to juveniles. From the start, the idea of crime and punishment was to be abandoned. The child was to be treated and rehabilitated. The right of the state, as *parens patriae*, to deny to the child the procedural rights available to his elders was elaborated by the assertion that a child, unlike an adult, has a right not to liberty but to custody. He can be made to heed his parents, go to school, etc. If his parents default in effectively performing their custodial functions— that is, if the child is delinquent— the state may intervene. In doing so, it does not deprive the child of any rights because he has none. It merely provides the custody to which the child is entitled. On this basis, proceedings involving juveniles were described as civil, not criminal, and therefore not subject to the requirements which restrict the State when it seeks to deprive a person of liberty.

The Court reasoned that the initial hearing in the case was a hearing on the merits, notice was not timely, and if there was a conceivable purpose served by the deferral proposed by the justice court, it would have to yield to the requirements that the child and his parents or guardian be notified, in writing, of the specific charge of factual allegations to be considered at the hearing, and that such written notice be given at the earliest practicable time.

The Court decided that the concept of fundamental fairness must be made applicable to juvenile delinquency proceedings. Accordingly, the Court held that the due process clause of the

Fourteenth Amendment required that certain procedural guarantees were essential to the adjudication of delinquency. Juveniles who have violated a criminal statute and who may be committed to an institution in which their freedom may be curtailed are entitled to:

➢ Fair notice of the charges against them.

➢ The right to be represented by counsel.

➢ The right to confrontation and cross-examination of witnesses against them.

➢ The right to the privilege against self-incrimination.

The Court, however, did not hold that juvenile offenders were entitled to all the procedural guarantees applicable to adults charged in criminal cases. In addition, the decision was not clear as to what rights should apply to nondelinquent children before the juvenile court. The practical effects of the *Gault* decision was that juvenile courts could no longer deal with children in a benign and paternalistic fashion (that the courts must process juvenile offenders within the framework of appropriate constitutional procedures). Due to this case, today, the right to counsel, the privilege against self-incrimination, and the right to fair notice are applied at all stages of the juvenile justice process.

Fare v. Michael C.

A difficult question associated with juvenile rights has to do with the juvenile's ability to waive *Miranda* rights. Under what circumstances are children mature enough to waive their right to be silent? In *Fare v. Michael C.* (442 U.S. 707 1979) the Court ruled that a juvenile's request to speak to his probation officer was not a request to remain silent nor was it tantamount to a request to speak to an attorney.

Michael was implicated in the murder of Robert Yeager. The murder occurred during a robbery of the victim's home on January 19, 1976. A truck registered to Michael's mother was seen near the scene of the crime at the time of the killing. A youth answering Michael's description was identified as having been near the Yeager home a short time before the killing. Based on this information, Michael was taken into custody. At the time, he was 16 years old and on probation to the juvenile court. He had been on probation since he was 12. Approximately one year earlier, he had served a term in a youth correction camp. He had a record of several previous offenses, including burglary of guns and purse snatching, stretching back over several years.

When Michael arrived at the police station, two police officers began to interrogate him. The officers and Michael were the only persons present in the room. Michael was advised of his *Miranda* rights. During the advisement, he asked if his probation officer could be present. One officer informed him that the officers were not going to telephone the probation officer because it was too late. Next Michael was asked if he understood the right to have an attorney present. He indicated that he did. He was then asked if he would talk to the officers without an attorney present. He stated he would. Michael then talked to the officers and drew sketches that incriminated him in the murder.

Based on Michael's incriminating statements, probation authorities filed a petition in juvenile court alleging that Michael had killed Yeager. Michael's counsel moved to suppress the statements based on the fact that when Michael requested to speak with his probation officer, that request should have been treated as a request for an attorney.

The Court noted that the rule in *Miranda* was based on the fact that a lawyer occupies a critical position in our legal system because of his unique ability to protect the Fifth Amendment rights of a client undergoing custodial interrogation. A probation officer, however, is not in the same posture with regard to either the accused or the system of justice as a whole. Often he is not trained in the law, and so is not in a position to advise the accused as to his legal rights. Neither is he a trained advocate, skilled in the representation of the interests of his client. He does not assume the power to act on behalf of his client by virtue of his status as adviser, nor are the communications of the accused to the probation officer shielded by the lawyer-client privilege.

In addition, the probation officer is an employee of the State which seeks to prosecute the alleged offender. He is a peace officer, and as such is allied to a greater or lessor extent, with his fellow peace officers.

The Court held that the request for his probation officer was not an invocation of his Fifth Amendment rights under *Miranda*. Accordingly, the juvenile court's finding that the respondent voluntarily and knowingly waived his rights and that the statement was voluntarily given was correct.

Schall v. Martin

In *Schall v. Martin* (467 U.S. 253 1984), the Supreme Court established the right of juvenile court judges to deny youths pretrial release if they perceive the youths to be dangerous. The case also establishes due process standards for detention hearings that include notice and statement of substantial reasons for continued detention.

The youth, Gregory Martin, was arrested on December 13, 1977, and charged with first-degree robbery, second-degree assault, and criminal possession of a weapon under New York law. He, with two others, allegedly hit a youth on the head with a loaded gun and stole the victim's jacket and sneakers. He was 14 years of age at the time of the crime and subsequent detention. He was taken into custody at about 11:30 P.M. on December 13 and detained overnight.

On December 14, a petition of delinquency was filed and he made his initial appearance in family court that same day. The judge, citing the possession of the loaded weapon, the false address given to the police, and the lateness of the hour of the incident as evidence of a lack of supervision, ordered Martin detained. On December 19, a probable cause hearing was held and probable cause was found to exist for all the crimes charged. At a fact-finding hearing on December 27, 28, and 29, Martin was determined to have committed the offenses of robbery and criminal possession. He was adjudicated a delinquent and placed on two years probation. At that time, he had been detained a total of 15 days.

On December 21, while still in detention, Martin's attorney filed a *habeas corpus* class action on behalf of those persons who are, or during the pendency of this action will be, preventively detained. The Court stated that there was no doubt that the due process clause is applicable to juvenile proceedings. One of the questions before the Court was whether preventive detention of juveniles is compatible with the fundamental fairness required by due process. To answer this question, the Court looked at whether preventive detention under the New York statutes serve a legitimate state objective and what procedural safeguards are required regarding pretrial detention of youths.

The Court held that the preventive detention was designed to protect the child and society from the potential consequences of his criminal acts and therefore was permissible. The Court concluded that the state has a legitimate and compelling interest in protecting the community from crime. The Court then indicated that the juvenile and his parent should be provided with adequate notice, given a right to a hearing, to counsel, and to a statement of reasons for the necessity of continuing detention.

Breed v. Jones

In *Breed v. Jones* (421 U.S. 519 1975), the Supreme Court provided answers to several questions involving transfer proceedings. First, the case prohibits trying a juvenile in adult court after there has been a prior adjudicatory juvenile hearing involving the same misconduct. Second, while probable cause to hold the youth may be established at the transfer hearing, this does not violate subsequent jeopardy if the child is transferred to adult criminal court. Third, since the same evidence is often used in both the transfer hearing and the subsequent trial in either adult or juvenile court, a different judge is required at trial from the judge that was involved in the transfer hearing.

This case involved a youth who was alleged to have committed armed robbery with a deadly weapon. An adjudicatory hearing was held. After the hearing, a transfer hearing was then held and the youth was transferred to adult court. The youth's attorney filed a petition raising the claim of violation of the constitutional protection against double jeopardy.

Prior to this case, many states would hold an adjudicatory hearing to determine if the youth was involved in misconduct and then, if appropriate, hold a transfer hearing to determine if the youth should be tried in adult court or be subject to juvenile sanctions. The Court held that a trial on the merits of the charge after the youth has been subjected to an adjudicatory hearing was double jeopardy. As a result of this case, a transfer hearing, if held, must be held prior to a determination as to whether the juvenile committed the misconduct in question.

In re Winship

In the case of *In re Winship* (397 U.S. 358 1970), the Supreme Court held that due process requires proof beyond a reasonable doubt as a standard for juvenile adjudication proceedings. The New York Family Act defined a juvenile delinquent as any person over the age of seven and less than 16 years of age who does any act which, if done by an adult, would constitute a crime. The Family Court found that the youth had entered a locker and stolen $112 from a woman's pocketbook. The family court judge noted that proof of guilt might not be established beyond a reasonable doubt, but that the New York Family Act required that any determination at the conclusion of an adjudicatory hearing must be based on a preponderance of evidence. The New York Court of Appeals affirmed the decision, and it was appealed to the U.S. Supreme Court.

The Court noted that the requirement that guilt of a criminal charge be established by proof beyond a reasonable doubt dates at least from our early years as a nation. The Court then stated that the observance of the standard of proof beyond a reasonable doubt will not compel the States to abandon or displace any of the substantive benefits of the juvenile justice process. The Court also held that the constitutional safeguard of proof beyond a reasonable doubt is as much required during the adjudicatory stage of a delinquency proceeding as are those safeguards applied in *Gault*.

McKeiver v. Pennsylvania

McKeiver v. Pennsylvania (403 U.S. 528 1971), decided in 1971, marked a shift in the Supreme Court's thinking. Not only did this case deny juveniles the constitutional right to a jury trial, but it also retreated from the previously standard practice of judicial equalization of procedure in adult and juvenile courts. In deciding for the State, the Court recognized that while recent constitutional cases focused on the issue of fundamental fairness in fact finding procedures, juries are not actually an essential part of juvenile justice due process.

Joseph McKeiver, then age 16, was charged with robbery, larceny, and receiving stolen goods as acts of delinquency. At the adjudication hearing, his counsel requested a jury trial. His request was denied based on Pennsylvania law. This case was consolidated on appeal with the case of *Terry v. Pennsylvania*. Both cases involved the same issue— the right of juveniles to a jury trial. Edward Terry, then age 15, was charged with assault and battery on a police officer and conspiracy. At the adjudication hearing, Terry's counsel also requested a jury trial and was denied. Both youths were adjudged to be delinquents.

The Court noted that the right to an impartial jury in all federal criminal prosecutions is guaranteed by the Sixth Amendment. The Court also noted that it had held that trial by jury in criminal cases is fundamental to the American scheme of justice. The Court noted that, in spite of all the disappointments and shortcomings, trial by jury in juvenile court's adjudicative stage is not a constitutional requirement for state juvenile justice systems. The Court stated that if the formalities of the criminal adjudicative process are to be superimposed upon juvenile courts, there is little need for its separate existence.

SEARCH AND SEIZURE

New Jersey v. T.L.O.

The *New Jersey v. T.L.O.* case involved the question of whether school officials may search students in order to determine whether they are in possession of contraband. In 1980, a teacher discovered two girls smoking in a lavatory. One of the

What is the minimum age authorized for the death penalty?

Younger than 18	Age 18	None specified
South Dakota (10) [a]	California	Arizona
Arkansas (14) [b]	Colorado	Delaware
Utah (14)	Connecticut [e]	Florida
Virginia (15)	Illinois	Idaho
Alabama (16)	Maryland	Montana
Indiana (16)	Nebraska	Pennsylvania
Kentucky (16)	New Jersey	South Carolina
Louisiana (16)	New Mexico	Washington
Mississippi (16) [d]	Ohio	
Nevada (16)	Tennessee	
Oklahoma (16)	Federal System	
Wyoming (16)		
Georgia (17)		
New Hampshire (17)		
North Carolina (17) [e]		
Texas (17)		

Note: Ages at the time of the capital offense were indicated by the offices of the State Attorneys General.

a. Only after a transfer hearing to try a juvenile as an adult.

b. See Arkansas code Ann. 9-27-318(b)(1)

c. See Conn. Gen. State 53a-46a-(g)(1)

d. Minimum age defined by statute is 13, but effective age is 16 based on an interpretation of the U.S. Supreme Court decisions by the state attorney general's office.

e. Age required is 17 unless the murderer was incarcerated for murder when a subsequent murder occurred; the age may then be 14.

two girls was T.L.O., who at the time was a 14-year-old high school freshman. Because smoking in the lavatory was in violation of a school rule, the teacher took the two girls to the principal's office. In re sponse to questioning by the assistant principal, Mr. Choplick, T.L.O. denied that she had been smoking in the lavatory and claimed that she did not smoke at all.

Mr. Choplick asked T.L.O. to come into his private office and demanded to see her purse. Opening the purse, he found a pack of cigarettes, which he removed from the purse and held before T.L.O. as he accused her of having lied to him. He also noticed a package of rolling papers in the purse. He then conducted a full search of the purse and discovered a small amount of marijuana, a pipe, a number of empty plastic bags, a substantial quantity of money in one-dollar bills, an index card that appeared to be a list of students who owed T.L.O. money, and two letters that implicated T.L.O. in marijuana dealing.

The State brought delinquency charges against T.L.O. Her counsel moved to suppress the evidence as a violation of her rights against unreasonable searches and seizures under the Fourth Amendment. The Supreme Court first found that the Fourth Amendment's prohibition against unreasonable searches and seizures also applies to searches conducted by public school officials. However, it held that the search in question was neither unreasonable nor unlawful. The Court stated that the need to maintain an orderly educational environment modified the usual requirements of warrants and probable cause. The Court declared that the school's right to maintain discipline on school grounds allowed it to search a student and his or her possessions as a safety precaution based only on the lessor standard of "reasonable suspicion."

DEATH PENALTY

Thompson v. Oklahoma

The *Thompson v. Oklahoma* (108 S.CT. 2687 1988) case, decided by the U.S. Supreme Court on June 29, 1988, examined the question of whether an individual could be executed for a crime committed while a juvenile. Thompson, in concert with three older persons, committed a brutal murder of his former brother-in-law. The evidence indicated that the victim had been shot twice and that his throat, chest, and abdomen had been cut. The victim also had multiple bruises and a broken leg. His body was chained to a concrete block and dumped into a river. Each of the four participants were tried separately and each was sentenced to death.

At the time of the crime, Thompson was 15 years old. He was tried as an adult. At the penalty phase of the trial, the prosecutor asked for the death penalty based on the fact that the

Most States that specify a minimum age for the death penalty set the minimum at age 16 or 18

None specified	Age 16 (or less)	Age 17	Age 18
Arizona	Alabama	Georgia	California
Idaho	Arkansas (14)[b]	New Hampshire	Colorado
Louisiana	Delaware	N. Carolina[e]	Connecticut[f]
Montana	Florida	Texas	Federal system
Pennsylvania	Indiana		Illinois
S. Carolina	Kentucky		Kansas
S. Dakota[a]	Mississippi (13)[c]		Maryland
Utah	Missouri		Nebraska
	Nevada		New Jersey
	Oklahoma		New Mexico
	Virginia (14)[d]		New York
	Wyoming		Ohio
			Oregon
			Tennessee
			Washington

[a] Juveniles may be transferred to criminal court. Age can be a mitigating factor.
[b] See Arkansas Code Ann. 9–27–318(b)(2)(Repl.1991).
[c] The minimum age defined by statute is 13, but the effective age is 16 based on interpretation of U.S. Supreme Court decisions by the State attorney general's office.
[d] The minimum age for transfer to criminal court is 14 by statute, but the effective age for a capital sentence is 16 based on interpretation of U.S. Supreme Court decisions by the State attorney general's office.
[e] The age required is 17 unless the murderer was incarcerated for murder when a subsequent murder occurred; then the age may be 14.
[f] See Conn. Gen. Stat. 53a–46a(g)(1).

Note: Minimum ages (at the time of the capital offense) reflect interpretation by State attorney general offices. States not listed do not have the death penalty.

Source: Authors' adaptation of Snell's Capital punishment 1997, *BJS Bulletin.*

murder was especially heinous, atrocious, or cruel and that there was a high probability that Thompson would commit future criminal acts of violence and thus constitute a continuing threat to society. The Court granted his writ to consider whether a sentence of death is cruel and unusual for a crime committed by a 15 year old.

The Court stated that the authors of the Eighth Amendment drafted a categorical prohibition against the infliction of cruel and unusual punishments, but they made no attempt to define the contours of that category. They delegated that task to future generations of judges who have been guided by the "evolving standards of decency that mark the progress of a maturing society." The Court noted that they were reminded of the importance of "the experience of mankind, as well as the long history of our law, recognizing that there are differences which must be accommodated in determining the rights and duties of children as compared with those of adults." The Court also noted that there are distinctions between the treatment of children and adults in contracts, in torts, in criminal law and procedure, in criminal sanctions and rehabilitation, and in the right to vote and hold political office. Oklahoma also recognizes these differences in a number of its statutes. The Court noted that in Oklahoma a person under the age of 18 could not vote or purchase alcohol or cigarettes. The Court stated that it could not find any Oklahoma statutes that treated a person under the age of 16 as anything but a "child" except the certification procedures used to authorize a petitioner's trial in this case.

The Court's opinion pointed out that the line between childhood and adulthood is drawn in different ways by various states. However, there is complete or near unanimity among all fifty states in treating a person under 16 years of age as a minor. All states have enacted legislation designating the maximum age for juvenile court jurisdiction at no less than 16. The Court then concluded that it would offend civilized standards of decency to execute a person who was less than 16 years old at the time of the offense. The Court stated that the Eighth and Fourteenth Amendments prohibit the execution of a person who is under the age of 16 at the time of his or her offense.

In June, 1989, the U.S. Supreme Court in *Stanford v. Kentucky* (109 S.Ct. 2969 1989) decided by a five to four plurality decision that the imposition of the death penalty on persons who murder at 16 to 17 years of age does not violate the Eighth Amendment.

DEPENDENCY CASES

Santosky v. Kramer

In the *Santosky v. Kramer* (455 U.S. 745 1981) case, the Supreme Court decided the question of what standard of proof a state must have before terminating parental rights in dependency proceedings. Under New York law, the state may terminate, over parental objection, the rights of parents over their natural child upon a finding that the child is "permanently neglected."

The statute requires only a "fair preponderance of the evidence" to support the findings. The Court noted that the factual certainty required to extinguish the parent-child relationship is no greater than that necessary to award money damages in an ordinary civil action. The Court held that the due process clause of the Fourteenth Amendment demands more than this—that before a state may sever completely and irrevocably the rights of the parents over their natural child, due process requires that the state support its allegations by at least clear and convincing evidence.

Lassiter v. Department of Social Services

In *Lassiter v. Department of Social Services* (452 U.S. 18 1981), the Supreme Court held by a five-four decision that the Fourteenth Amendment's due process clause does not require the appointment of counsel for indigent parents in every parental status termination proceeding. However, the majority of states do provide for the appointment of counsel. The Court did note that it is not disputed that state intervention to terminate the relationship between a parent and a child must be accompanied by procedures meeting the requisites of the due process clause.

CHILDREN'S RIGHTS

Coy v. Iowa

In the *Coy v. Iowa* (487 U.S. 1012 1988) case, the Supreme Court limited the protections available to child sex abuse witnesses. In this case, two girls were allowed to be cross-examined behind a screen that separated them from the defendant. The Court ruled that the screen violated the defendant's right to confront witnesses and reversed the case. The Court made it clear that their decision ruling out a protective screen did not bar states from using videotapes or closed-circuit television.

In *Maryland v. Craig,* (497 U.S. 1990) the Court decided that alleged child abuse victims could testify by closed-circuit television if face-to-face confrontation with the defendant would cause the victims trauma.

Goss v. Lopez

In *Goss v. Lopez* (419 U.S. 565 1975), the Supreme Court established guidelines for determining the constitutionality of school disciplinary procedures. Ohio law empowered principals of Ohio public schools with the authority to either suspend students for misconduct for a period not in excess of ten days or to expel them. The principals were required to notify the parents within 24 hours and state the reasons for their actions. Either a pupil who is expelled or his parents may appeal the decision to the Board of Education. The Board may reinstate the student after conducting a hearing at a board meeting. The *Goss* case was a class action suit by nine Ohio public school students who had been suspended from school. The class action was based on the denial of due process rights of the students. The school officials argued that no due process rights existed where there was no constitutional right to a public education.

The suspensions arose out of a period of widespread student unrest in the Columbus school district during February and March, 1971. None of the students were given a hearing prior to being suspended. Each, however, with their parents was invited to a conference, subsequent to the effective date of the suspension, to discuss the students' future. A three-judge federal district court declared that there were minimum requirements of notice and a hearing prior to suspension, except in emergency situations. The school officials appealed the district court's decision. The officials contended that because there is no constitutional right to an education at public expense, the due process clause of the Constitution does not protect the students from expulsions from the public school system.

The Supreme Court stated that the school's position misconceives the nature of the issue and is refuted by prior decisions of the Court. The Fourteenth Amendment forbids the State to deprive any person of life, liberty, or property without due process of law. Protected interests in property are normally "not created by the Constitution." Rather they are created and their dimensions are defined by an independent source such as state statutes or rules entitling citizens to certain benefits.

Ohio, having chosen to provide the right to an education to people, cannot withdraw that right based on grounds of misconduct without fundamentally fair procedures to determine whether misconduct has occurred. While Ohio is not required to establish and maintain a public school system, it has nevertheless done so and has required students to attend. These young people do not leave their constitutional rights at the schoolhouse door.

The due process clause also forbids arbitrary deprivations of liberty. Where a person's good name, reputation, honor, or integrity is at stake because of what the government is doing to him, the minimal requirements of the due process clause must be satisfied. The Court then held that at minimum, students facing suspension from school require notice and a right to be heard. The right to be heard, however, includes the right to counsel and the right to confront or cross-examine witnesses. The extent of the due process requirements would be established on a case-by-case basis.

Tinker v. Des Moines School District

The *Tinker v. Des Moines School District* (393 U.S. 503 1969) case is a significant decision of the Supreme Court because it recognizes the child's right to free speech in a public school system. The case involved students who wore black armbands to school to protest the Vietnam War. There was a school policy prohibiting such behavior. The students who wore the armbands were suspended. The suspended students filed a civil rights action against the school district. The Court held that neither "students nor teachers shed their constitutional rights to freedom of speech or expression at the schoolhouse gate." This case established two concepts: (1) a child is entitled to free speech in school under the First Amendment of the Constitution and (2) the test to be used to determine whether the child has gone beyond proper speech is whether he or she materially and substantially interferes with the requirements of appropriate discipline in the operation of the school.

Hazelwood School District v. Kuhlmeier

The *Hazelwood School District v. Kuhlmeier* (108 S.Ct. 562 1988) case involved the extent to which educators may exercise control over the contents of a high school newspaper which was produced as part of the school's journalism curriculum. The students contended that school officials violated their First Amendment rights by deleting two articles from the May 13, 1983, issue of the *Spectrum*. The *Spectrum* was written and edited by the journalism class at Hazelwood High School. The newspaper was published every three weeks and more than 4,500 copies of the paper were distributed that year to students, school personnel, and members of the community.

The Board of Education allocated funds from its annual budget for the printing of the newspaper. The funds were supplemented by proceeds from the sale of the paper. The practice was for the journalism teacher to submit page proofs of each *Spectrum* issue to the principal for his review prior to publication. On May 10, the proofs were delivered to the principal. The principal objected to two articles in the proposed issued. One article described three students' experiences with pregnancy. The other article discussed the impact of divorce on students at the school. Although the article on pregnancy used false names, the principal was concerned that the pregnant students might be identifiable from the text. He also objected to the article's references to sexual activity and birth control.

The article on divorce contained information about one student who was identified by name. The identified student had complained that her father "wasn't spending enough time with my mom, my sister and I" prior to the divorce and that the father was always out of town or out late playing cards. The principal indicated that the student's parents should be given an opportunity to respond to the statements contained in the article prior to publication.

The district court concluded that school officials may impose restraints on students' speech in activities that are an integral part of the school's educational function—including the publication of a school-sponsored newspaper by the journalism class. The Court of Appeals reversed the district court and held that the newspaper was not only a part of the school adopted curriculum, but also a public forum, because the newspaper was intended to reflect and to operate as a conduit for student viewpoint.

The Supreme Court overruled the Court of Appeals. The Supreme Court stated that the First Amendment rights of students are not automatically coextensive with the rights of adults in other settings. That public schools do not possess all the attributes of streets, parks, and other traditional public forums that have been used for purposes of assembly, communicating thoughts between citizens, and discussing public questions. The publication of the paper in this case was a regular school activity. There is insufficient evidence to indicate that the school intended, as found by the Court of Appeals, to create a public forum. Accordingly, school officials are entitled to regulate the contents of the *Spectrum* in any reasonable manner. The Court then concluded that the principal acted reasonably in deleting the two articles in question.

Veronia School District 47J v. Acton

The Supreme Court in *Veronia School District 47J v. Acton* (recently decided on June 26, 1995), held that public schools may randomly test their student athletes for drugs. By a 6-3 ruling, the Court held that the intrusion on student privacy wasn't great when considered in the light of other physical examinations and vaccinations that are generally required of students.

The *Veronia* case began in 1991, when seventh-grader James Acton was barred from playing football because he refused to be tested for drugs. His parents filed suit on his behalf and, after a trial court defeat, persuaded the Federal Court of Appeals to overrule the testing policy. The appellate court had held that the town's interest in cutting drug use and discipline problems was outweighed by Acton's right not to be forced to be tested in the absence of any specific suspicion that he used drugs. The Supreme Court, however, stated that the appellate court had miscalculated the constitutional balance.

Justice Scalia, writing for the majority, stated that student athletes give up their privacy by using communal lockers and showers, by undergoing especially rigorous physical exams—which often involve urine tests having nothing to do with drugs—and by close supervision by coaches. The Court also noted that the school used procedures for collecting urine samples that minimized student embarrassment and took precautions against jumping to conclusions. Positive results for drugs led to retesting. If retesting also showed drug use, the student and his parents were invited to a hearing. The student was given the choice of suspension from sports or undergoing counseling while continuing with athletics. Positive test results were not turned over to the police and were not supposed to have any future criminal consequences.

Justice Sandra Day O'Connor, in a strong dissent, warned that "the greatest threats to our constitutional freedoms come in times of crisis." Even if limited to student athletes, she added, the ruling could force millions of youngsters who have not given school officials any particular reason to suspect that they use illegal drugs to undergo intrusive drug tests.

DISCUSSION QUESTIONS

1. Differentiate the rights that exist in adult criminal courts to those not available to juveniles.

2. Explain the due process rights that a juvenile has at a transfer hearing.

3. Explain free speech rights and restrictions on school students.

4. Should the courts be more active in the juvenile justice area? Explain.

Chapter 10

Transfers
and
Waivers

One of the most controversial debates in crime control policy is the selection of jurisdiction for adjudicating juvenile crime. It reflects our differences in assumptions about the causes of crime and our philosophies of jurisprudence and punishments.

In cases involving violent youths, many critics view the traditional goals of juvenile court and the "best interests of the child" standard as being contrary to the public's concern for retribution and incapacitation of criminals. These critics see the choice as one between the rehabilitative goals of juvenile court and the explicitly punitive goals of adult criminal courts in dealing with a young violent person. They contend that juvenile court sanctions are not only inappropriate and disproportionate for the seriousness of the crime, but also ineffective in deterring subsequent crime.

Supporters of juvenile courts argue that violent juvenile crime is in many cases a transitory behavioral pattern that is unlikely to escalate to more serious or persistent crime. The supporters also argue that adolescent offenders benefit from the treatment services that pose only a minimal threat to public safety while avoiding the lasting stigma of adult criminal justice processing.

Beginning in the late 1970s, over forty states passed statutes that limit the jurisdiction of juvenile court. Some states, like New York, have lowered the age of jurisdiction of adult criminal courts. Other states, such as New Jersey and Ohio, have expanded the basis for transfer of cases from juvenile court jurisdiction to adult criminal court. Still other states, like Florida and Michigan, have established concurrent jurisdiction for selected offenders or offenses giving prosecutors discretion over the choice of court.

New legislation generally indicates that legislatures believe the traditional age boundary of 18 for criminal liability should be modified for specific types of crimes. Legislatures therefore have created an age-behavior gradient for the legal definition of childhood. For example, a 15-year-old youth who commits a violent offense may be held criminally responsible in adult criminal court, while that same youth may remain a juvenile for minor violations of the law.

Some states, such as California, New York, and Colorado, have enacted determinate sentencing and mandatory sentencing laws. These laws have the practical effect of removing the discretion in disposition, placement, and release decisions from the juvenile court judge to the legislatures.

The legislative effort to remove dangerous or violent offenders from juvenile court jurisdiction has occurred in two ways. First, many states have eliminated juvenile court jurisdiction for specific age/offense/offender categories and reduced the age of majority for specified serious, violent, or repeat felony offenders. One practical effect of these statutes is to make the prosecutor's charging decision the determinate factor. For example, if a 15-year-old commits a serious crime, the prosecutor may charge the serious crime to have the youth adjudicated in adult criminal court. The prosecutor, however, may charge a lessor offense, at his or her discretion, and thereby permit the youth to be adjudicated in juvenile court.

The second method to remove dangerous or violent juvenile offenders from juvenile court is to establish concurrent jurisdiction for certain crimes/offenders. This allows the prosecutor to determine if the case is going to be handled in juvenile or adult criminal court. Both methods increase the discretion of the prosecutor and lessen the discretion of the juvenile court judge.

STANDARDS FOR THE ADMINISTRATION OF JUVENILE JUSTICE

The Task Force on Juvenile Justice published standards to be used in making transfer decisions. Portions of those standards are set forth in this section.

Delinquency adjudications grew 64% between 1987 and 1996

Most serious offense	All cases	Percent change 1987–1996			
		Formal cases			
		Total	Waived	Adjudicated	Not adjudicated
Delinquency	49%	78%	47%	64%	104%
Person	100	121	125	112	133
Property	23	44	–2	33	65
Drugs	144	183	124	161	224
Public order	58	104	22	81	148

■ Across all four general offense categories, the relative growth in adjudications was greater than the increase in the overall caseload, but less than the growth in formally processed cases. Therefore, the growth in formally processed cases resulted in a greater proportion of court activity devoted to cases in which the court was not able to find that the youth committed the offense charged (i.e., not adjudicated).

Source: Authors' analysis of Snyder et al.'s *Easy access to juvenile courts statistics: 1987–1996* [data presentation and analysis package].

Juvenile Offenders and Victims: 1999 National Report

3:116 Transfer to Another Court— Delinquency

The family court should have the authority to transfer a juvenile charged with committing a delinquency offense to a court of general criminal jurisdiction if:

a. The juvenile is at least 16 years of age.

b. There is probable cause to believe that the juvenile committed the act alleged in the delinquency petition.

c. There is probable cause to believe that the act alleged in the delinquency petition is of a heinous or aggravated nature, or that the juvenile has committed repeated serious delinquency offenses.

d. There is clear and convincing evidence that the juvenile is not amenable to treatment by the family court because of the seriousness of the alleged conduct, the juvenile's record of prior adjudicated offenses, and the inefficacy of each of the dispositions available to the family court.

This authority should not be exercised unless there has been a full and fair hearing at which the juvenile has been accorded all essential due process safeguards.

Before ordering transfer, the court should state, on the record, the basis for its finding that the juvenile could not be rehabilitated through any of the dispositions available to the family court.

Commentary

The President's Commission on Law Enforcement and the Administration of Justice (*Task Force Report: Juvenile Delinquency and Youth Crime,* 25, 1967) termed transfer of accused delinquents to adult criminal courts, "a necessary evil, imperfect but not substantially more so than its alternatives." Waiver of jurisdiction in cases involving juveniles for whom the specialized services and programs available to the family court are inappropriate, functions as a safety valve to relieve the pressure of reducing the maximum age of family court jurisdiction and facilitates the provision of services to those juveniles who appear more likely to respond.

This standard, following the lead of the *Task Force Report* and *United States v. Kent* (383 U.S. 541 1966), recommends criteria to regulate the operation of this safety valve to assure that those juveniles for whom treatment as an adult offender is appropriate are transferred and that those for whom stigmatization as a convicted felon is unnecessary remain under family court jurisdiction.

The first criterion is that juveniles under 16 years of age should remain under the jurisdiction of the family court. This is in accord with the recommendations of most recent standards and models and is the practice in about a quarter of the states. No matter what age is set, there will always be a juvenile offender for whom transfer may be appropriate. Although many serious crimes are committed by juveniles under 16 years of age, it is anticipated that the number of cases in which transfer of such juveniles would be proper under the other criteria listed in the standard will be minimal.

The standard further recommends that no juvenile be transferred unless it has been determined that there is probable cause to believe that a delinquent act has been committed and that the juvenile committed it. About half the states with statutory provisions on waiver include such a probable cause requirement. A new probable cause determination regarding the juvenile's involvement in the offense is not necessary if such a determination has been made during a detention hearing or on request of the respondent following the filing of a delinquency petition.

However, in most cases, there will still need to be a determination regarding the seriousness of the conduct and the juvenile's prior record of serious felonies. The standard endorses the Task Force provision that a delinquent act must be shown to be of a heinous or aggravating nature or part of a pattern of serious offenses committed by the juvenile. The term "felony" is insufficient to convey the degree of seriousness required for transfer. Although linking a waiver to the classification scheme used for dispositional purposes may be one method of implementing the standard, the mere citation of a particular class of felonies still does not necessarily address the nature and circumstances of the particular act in question. Between a quarter and a third of the states require that the delinquent act be the equivalent of a felony before a juvenile may be transferred. *The Model Act for Family Courts, supra,* recommends consideration of the "nature" of the offense and the juvenile's prior record in determining the "prospects for rehabilitation." The *Uniform Juvenile Court Act, supra,* does not.

The fourth criteria focuses directly on the issue of the juvenile's amenability to treatment. The standard endorses the position adopted by the IJA/ ABA Joint Commission that the family court judge must determine that there is clear and convincing evidence that a juvenile, because of the nature of the alleged offense and his/her response to the dispositions imposed for prior offenses, is unlikely to respond to any of the dispositions available to the family court. In making this decision, the judge should review each of the available types of dispositional alternatives. The Task Force standard does not specify the level of proof, but otherwise agrees in concept with the IJA/ ABA Joint Commission proposal.

Kent instructs that juveniles subject to a transfer proceeding are entitled to a hearing, to counsel, to "access by counsel to the social records and probation or similar reports which presumably are considered by the court, and to a statement of reasons for the juvenile court's decision." This holding was raised to constitutional proportions by *In re Gault,* 387 U.S. 1 (1967). The reference in the standard to all essential due process safeguards is intended to go beyond *Kent* and to be read in conjunction with Standard 3.171, which recommends that accused delinquents should be entitled to notice, to be present at all proceedings, to compel the attendance of witnesses, to present evidence and cross-examine witnesses, to have an impartial decision maker, to the right against self-incrimination, and to have a verbatim record made of the proceeding.

The explicit statement of the facts and reasons underlying the transfer decision, which is called for in the final paragraph, follows *Kent* and is part of the effort throughout these standards to consistently exercise use of discretionary authority. Although the transfer decision can probably never be a "scientific evaluation," the enumeration of specific criteria and the explanation of the basis for the transfer decision in terms of those criteria should facilitate review and promote understanding of and consistency in the transfer process.

CRITERIA FOR TRANSFER

As discussed in Chapter 9, the United States Supreme Court in *Kent v. United States* established the following criteria for the juvenile courts to consider in deciding whether to transfer a juvenile to adult criminal court:

- The seriousness of the alleged offense and whether the protection of the community requires waiver.

- Whether the alleged offense was committed in an aggressive, violent, premeditated, or willful manner.

- Whether the alleged offense was against persons or against property, greater weight being given to offenses against persons, especially if personal injury resulted.

- The prospective merit of the complaint.

- The desirability of trial and disposition of the offenses in one court when the juvenile's associates in the alleged offense are adults who will be charged with crimes in the adult court.

- The sophistication and maturity of the juvenile as determined by consideration of his or her home environmental situation.

- The record and previous history of the juvenile.

What case characteristics affect the transfer decision?

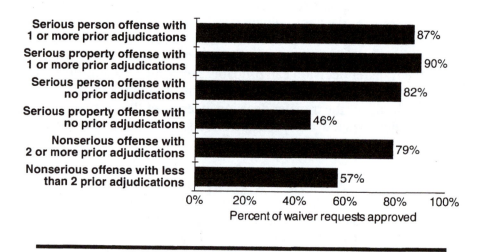

Serious person offense with 1 or more prior adjudications	87%
Serious property offense with 1 or more prior adjudications	90%
Serious person offense with no prior adjudications	82%
Serious property offense with no prior adjudications	46%
Nonserious offense with 2 or more prior adjudications	79%
Nonserious offense with less than 2 prior adjudications	57%

Percent of waiver requests approved

Juvenile Offenders and Victims: 1999 National Report   **ncJJ/OJDP**

CONCURRENT CHARGING

One of the arguments against allowing the prosecutor to bring charges in adult criminal court rather than originally filing in juvenile court is that the juvenile is denied a transfer hearing and the discretion as to whether the juvenile should be treated as a juvenile is left to the prosecutor rather than a judge. When a judge makes the decision, the juvenile has a right to a hearing using the criteria set forth above. When the prosecutor makes the decision, however, no hearing of any type is required on the transfer decision. The following case of *People v. Thorpe* discusses this issue. Note that the decision of the case has been edited to make it easier to understand. In addition, that part of the case dealing with evidentiary issues has been omitted.

People v. Thorpe

The defendant, Gary Thorpe, was convicted by a jury of murder in the first degree, aggravated robbery, and conspiracy to commit aggravated robbery. We affirm the convictions. On October 12, 1978, William Sather, proprietor of Sather Jewelry in Denver, was shot to death during an aggravated robbery of his store. An information was filed against the defendant and Richard Banks on November 14, 1978 charging them with first degree murder. The defendant, who was 16 years of age at the time, was charged in the district court. (Section 19-1-104(4)(b)(1) provides in relevant part: "(b) A child may be charged with the commission of a felony... when the child is: (1) Alleged to have committed a crime of violence defined by section 18 1 105, C.R.S. 1973, as a class 1 felony, and is fourteen years of age or older . . . .)" Separate trials were granted on motion of the defendant.

On November 17, 1978, while the defendant was in custody and after he had been arraigned, he contacted Officer Thomas P. Haney of the Denver Police Department. In response to the call, Haney went to the detention center and spoke with the defendant in the presence of his mother. Haney advised the defendant of his rights and left him alone with his mother to discuss the situation. Thereafter, the defendant indicated that he wished to make a statement and Haney returned and recorded it. In the statement, the defendant described his role in the robbery and claimed that Banks had killed the victim.

At trial, the people presented evidence that the defendant's palm prints had been identified on a display case in the jewelry store and that Banks' fingerprints had been found inside a watch case. Two witnesses identified the defendant as the man they had seen running in the alley behind the jewelry store just before the robbery was discovered. The defendant was seen carrying boxes in a white cloth. Witnesses also saw a green Cadillac driven by a white man whom they identified as Banks.

Patrice Hill testified that on the morning of October 12, 1978, the defendant and Richard Banks entered the house she shared with Banks, John James, and her sister. The defendant was carrying a white bundle and Hill noticed blood on his clothing. She also identified a green Cadillac that she had seen the defendant drive.

John James testified that Richard Banks had earlier asked him to assist with the robbery, but James declined to do so. He stated that on October 12, the defendant had entered his house wearing bloody clothing and carrying a white bundle out of which some jewelry fell. James stated that he gave the police information regarding the robbery hoping to receive consideration on assault charges Patrice Hill had filed against him. He was released and the charges were dropped after he gave the statement.

The defendant raises the following arguments for reversal of his conviction. First, he contends that section 19-1-104(4)(b)(1) is unconstitutional and its application to him denied him due process and equal protection of the law. Second, the defendant asserts that it was prejudicial error to deny his motion to suppress his statement and to admit the statement into evidence. Third, it was error to admit the identification testimony of witnesses Rodney Chavez and Raymond Riggins. Finally, the defendant argues that it was prejudicial error to admit two photographs of the murder victim which he contends were not probative of any issue and served only to inflame the jury. We discuss the issues raised in order.

Defendant's constitutional argument is based on his contention that section 19-1-104(4)(b)(1), C.R.S. 1973 (1978 Repl. Vol. 8) is invalid because it allows a district attorney to charge a child 14 years of age or older, alleged to have committed a crime of violence defined as a class 1 felony, with the commission of a felony and to prosecute the child in a criminal proceeding in the district court rather than as a juvenile in the juvenile court. The defendant reasons that the decision of the prosecutor to charge a juvenile as an adult when there are no statutory guidelines and without a prior hearing cannot be constitutionally justified as a valid exercise of prosecutorial discretion. Since there is no hearing prior to the charging process at which the juvenile may be present, heard, and be represented by counsel, the argument goes, he is denied due process. Furthermore, since the prosecutor may choose to prosecute one 14-year-old violent offender as an adult and another 14-year-old violent offender as a juvenile, and since there are no statutory criteria to guide him in making that decision, the statute denies one in the defendant's position equal protection of the law.

The defendant recognizes that the proposition he urges us to adopt is contrary to this court's decision in *Myers v. District Court,* 184 Colo. 81, 518 P. 2d 836 (1974), which considered a predecessor section of the Juvenile Code, now codified as section 19-1-104(4)(b)(11), C.R.S. 1973 (1978 Repl. Vol. 8). In *Myers* we held:

Petitioners' final argument is that the broad discretion granted to the district attorney by C.R.S. 1963, 22-1-4(b)(iii) denies them due process and equal protection of the laws.

It is well settled that a prosecutor has constitutional power to exercise discretion in deciding which of several possible charges to press in a prosecution... it follows that the district attorney may properly invoke the concurrent jurisdiction of the district court under C.R.S. 1963, 22-1,(b)(iii) and C.R.S. 1963,

22-1-3(17)(b)(iii) in deciding to proceed against a person between the ages of sixteen and eighteen in district rather than juvenile court.

In *People v. District Court,* 191 Colo. 28,549 P.2d 1317 (1976), we again upheld the exercise of prosecutorial discretion. In a juvenile proceeding, the district attorney elected to amend the petition in delinquency to include a more serious felony, thus causing the case to be transferred for trial as a criminal case. We there stated:

It is clear that the design of the statute is to permit the juvenile court, in case of a less serious felony, to determine in a transfer hearing whether, in the best interests of the accused juvenile, the case should be transferred to the criminal side of the court section 19-1-104(4)(a), but in those circumstances where a more serious felony is charged, as set forth in subsections (4)(b)(I). (11), and (III), no such discretion lies in the court to retain the case in the juvenile side of the court when the district attorney elects to have the case transferred for trial as a criminal action. *(People v. District Court, supra).*

The prohibition against judicial intervention in, or control of, the exercise of prosecutorial discretion flows from the doctrine of separation of powers expressly set out in Article III of the Colorado Constitution and inherent in the enumerated powers of the United States Constitution. The defendant acknowledges this firmly established principle and recognizes our many decisions upholding the exercise of discretion by a prosecutor in determining what charges shall be brought.

The defendant, however, would have us overrule *Myers, supra,* and *People v. District Court, supra,* and adopt an exception to the principle of prosecutorial discretion in juvenile cases. He urges that we adopt the view espoused by the dissent in the case of *United States v. Bland,* 472 F.2d 1329 (D.C.Cir. 1972), that since the consequences to the child from his prosecution in a criminal case vary so significantly from those flowing from a juvenile proceeding, the child should be afforded the same protections as he would have were the case filed in the juvenile court and transfer to the criminal division sought.

The defendant cites *Kent v. United States,* 383 U.S. 541, 86 S. Ct. 1045, 16 L.Ed.2d 84 (1966), in support of his argument that a hearing with the assistance of counsel is required before the "critically important" decision is made to put the child through the criminal court process. This case, though instructive, lends no support to his position. There, the Federal Juvenile Court Act required a waiver of jurisdiction by the juvenile court before criminal proceedings could be brought by the United States Attorney. There, the Federal Juvenile Code vested original and exclusive jurisdiction of a child in the juvenile court and contained no provisions for a direct filing in a criminal proceeding, as does our statute, section 19-1-104(4)(b)(I).

We decline to require that a quasi-judicial hearing be held by the district attorney as a precondition to his determination that a child fourteen years of age or older alleged to have committed a crime of violence defined as a class 1 felony shall be prosecuted in a criminal proceeding. The majority opinion in *Bland, supra,* which is consistent with our view, holds that, even though a prosecutor is an officer of the court, he is nevertheless a member of the executive department and acting as such when exercising his discretion in choosing what charges to file and in what court they should be filed. Therefore, while there may be circumstances in which courts would be entitled to review the prosecutorial discretion function, "in the absence of such 'suspect' factors as 'race, religion, or other arbitrary classification,' the exercise of discretion by the United States Attorney [in deciding whether a person shall be charged as a juvenile or an adult] in the case at bar involves no violation of due process or equal protection of the law. Another in his same circumstance could be treated as a juvenile and charged with delinquency. We reiterate that the conscious exercise of selectivity in the enforcement of laws is not in itself a constitutional violation of equal protection of the law, absent a showing that a prosecutor has exercised a policy of selectivity based upon an unjustifiable standard such as "race, religion, or any other arbitrary classification," which was not shown here (*People v. MacFarland,* 189 Colo. 363,540 P.2d 1073 1975).

We also reject the defendant's challenge to the facial constitutionality of this state. As we stated in *People v. McKenzie, supra,* "[W]e must recognize that the legislature is free to adopt any classification it deems appropriate to promote the general welfare, so long as the classification bears a reasonable relation to a proper legislative purpose and is neither arbitrary nor discriminatory and operates equally on all persons within the classification." It is clear that the General Assembly intended to exclude certain offenders from the juvenile court system by defining certain serious offenses as per se criminal and properly within the constitutional jurisdiction of the district court even if committed by a juvenile over the age of 14. This is not unreasonable in light of the apparent legislative decision that certain repeat offenders, or those who have committed serious offenses, should be separated from those juveniles who perpetrate relatively less serious or less violent crimes and who, in the view of the legislature, are more likely candidates for rehabilitation.

We are not persuaded by defendant's arguments that section 19-1-104(4)(b)(1), C,R,S. 1973 (1978 Repl. Vol, 8), is invalid and we hold it to be constitutional on its face and as applied to the defendant.

UNIFORM JUVENILE COURT ACT

The provisions of the Uniform Juvenile Court Act for a waiver of jurisdiction and discretionary transfer to an adult criminal court along with several key court decisions regarding transfer procedures are set forth in this section.

The average maximum prison sentence for transferred juveniles convicted of felonies was 9¼ years

Most serious conviction offense	Mean maximum sentence length for convicted felons sentenced to prison (in months)		
	Transferred juveniles	Adults under age 18	Adults age 18 or older
All felonies	111	87	69
Person offenses	139	128	115
Murder/nonnegligent manslaughter	287	279	258
Rape	200	117	149
Robbery	139	107	112
Aggravated assault	75	102	81
Other person offenses	130	124	70
Property offenses	50	67	56
Burglary	52	68	67
Larceny and motor vehicle theft	45	62	45
Fraud	44	57	51
Drug offenses	80	58	60
Possession	66	42	48
Trafficking	83	62	66
Weapons offenses	66	62	46
Other offenses*	61	68	40

■ Average maximum prison sentences for transferred juveniles were sometimes substantially longer than maximum sentences imposed on felons under 18 who were adults in their State or for adults age 18 or older. Overall, transferred juveniles convicted of felonies and sentenced to prison were sentenced to an average maximum of 9¼ years. In comparison, under-18 adults had an average maximum of 7¼ years, and adults 18 or older an average maximum of 5¾ years.

* Includes nonviolent offenses such as receiving stolen property and vandalism.

Note: Means exclude sentences to death or life in prison. Detail may not add to total because of rounding.

Source: Authors' adaptation of Brown and Langan's *State court sentencing of convicted felons, 1994.*

Juvenile Offenders and Victims: 1999 National Report

Waiver Provisions

The Waiver of Jurisdiction and Discretionary Transfer to Criminal Court is as follows:

(a) The juvenile court may waive its exclusive original jurisdiction and transfer a child to the appropriate district court or criminal district court for criminal proceedings if:

    (1) the child is alleged to have violated a penal law of the grade of felony;

    (2) the child was 15 years of age or older at the time he is alleged to have committed the offense and no adjudication hearing has been conducted concerning that offense; and

    (3) after full investigation and hearing the juvenile court determines that there is probable cause to believe that the child, before the court committed the offense alleged and that because of the seriousness of the offense or the background of the child, the welfare of the community requires criminal proceedings.

(b) The petition and notice requirements of this code must be satisfied, and the summons must state that the hearing is for the purpose of considering discretionary transfer to criminal court.

(c) The juvenile court shall conduct a hearing without a jury to consider transfer of the child for criminal proceedings.

(d) Prior to the hearing, the juvenile court shall order and obtain a complete diagnostic study, social evaluation, and full investigation of the child, his circumstances, and the circumstances of the alleged offense.

(e) At the transfer hearing, the court may consider written reports from probation officers, professional court employees, or professional consultants in addition to the testimony of witnesses. At least one day prior to the transfer hearing, the court shall provide the attorney for the child with access to all written matter to be considered by the court in making the transfer decision. The court may order counsel not to reveal items to the child or his parent, guardian, or *guardian ad litem* if such disclosure would materially harm the treatment and rehabilitation of the child or would substantially decrease the likelihood of receiving information from the same or similar sources in the future.

(f) In making the determination required by Subsection (a) of this section, the court shall consider, among other matters:

    (1) whether the alleged offense was against person or property, with greater weight in favor of transfer given to offenses against the person;

    (2) whether the alleged offense was committed in an aggressive and premeditated manner

    (3) whether there is evidence on which a grand jury may be expected to return an indictment;

    (4) the sophistication and maturity of the child;

    (5) the record and previous history of the child; and

    (6) the prospects of adequate protection of the public and the likelihood of the rehabilitation of the child by use of procedures, services, and facilities currently available to the juvenile court.

(g) If the juvenile court retains jurisdiction, the child is not subject to criminal prosecution at any time for any offense alleged in the petition or for any offense within the knowledge of the juvenile court judge as evidenced by anything in the record of the proceedings.

(h) If the juvenile court waives jurisdiction, it shall state specifically in the order its reasons for waiver and certify its action, including the written order and findings of the court, and shall transfer the child to the appropriate court for criminal proceedings. On transfer of the child for criminal proceedings, he shall be dealt with as an adult and in accordance with the Code of Criminal Procedure. The transfer of custody is an arrest. The court to which the child is transferred shall determine if good cause exists for an examining trial. If there is no good cause for an examining trial, the court shall refer the case to the grand jury. If there is good cause for an examining trial, the court shall conduct an examining trial and may remand the child to the jurisdiction of the juvenile court.

(i) If the child's case is brought to the attention of the grand jury and the grand jury does not indict for the offense charged in the complaint forwarded by the juvenile court, the district court or criminal district court shall certify the grand jury's failure to indict to the juvenile court. On receipt of the certification, the juvenile court may resume jurisdiction of the case.

(j) The juvenile court may waive its exclusive original jurisdiction and transfer a person to the appropriate district court or criminal district court for criminal proceedings if:

(1) the person is 18 years of age or older;

(2) the person was 15 years of age or older and under 17 years of age at the time he is alleged to have committed a felony;

(3) no adjudication concerning the alleged offense has been made or no adjudication hearing concerning the offense has been conducted;

(4) the juvenile court finds from a preponderance of the evidence that after due diligence of the state it was not practicable to proceed in juvenile court before the eighteenth birthday of the person because:

(A) the state did not have probable cause to proceed in juvenile court and new evidence has been found since the eighteenth birthday of the person; or

(B) the person could not be found; and

(5) the juvenile court determines that there is probable cause to believe that the child before the court committed the offense alleged.

(k) The petition and notice requirements of this code must be satisfied, and the summons must state that the hearing is for the purpose of considering waiver of jurisdiction under subsection (j) of this section.

(l) The juvenile court shall conduct a hearing without a jury to consider waiver of jurisdiction under subsection (j) of this section.

Selected Court Decisions

Listed below are some selected court decisions regarding transfer procedures. While these cases are all taken from Texas appellate courts, the rules of law set forth in them are followed by the majority of states.

Matter of Honsaker (Tex. Civ. App.1976) 539 S.W.2d 198: Purpose of discretionary transfer proceedings of juvenile to district court for criminal proceedings is not to determine guilt or innocence of juvenile but to establish whether juvenile's and society's best interests would be served by maintaining juvenile custody of child or by transferring him.

Where juvenile was served with a citation charging he was a child who had committed robbery and escape and that juvenile court should waive its jurisdiction and transfer the case to criminal district court for criminal proceedings, where juvenile's natural mother was appointed his guardian ad litem, and where juvenile was effectively represented by competent counsel, juvenile court did not violate juvenile's due process rights by conducting discretionary transfer proceeding without notifying juvenile's natural father of said proceeding.

Matter of P.A.C. (Tex. Civ. App.1978) 562 S.W.2d 913: A juvenile certification hearing is not a trial on the merits. At a juvenile certification hearing, the court does not consider guilt or innocence, but whether the juvenile's and society's best interests would be served by maintaining custody of the child in the juvenile system or by a transfer to a district court for trial as an adult.

R.E.M. v. State (Civ. App. 1975) 532 S.W.2d 645, appeal after remand 541 S.W.2d 841: Once jurisdiction of juvenile court has been timely invoked by filing of petition for waiver of that court's jurisdiction and transfer of alleged offender to district court for prosecution as an adult, jurisdiction of juvenile court continues until there has been a final disposition of question of waiver of jurisdiction, whatever be the age of such alleged offender at time of final disposition.

Carner v. State (Tex. Cr. App. 1980) 592 S.W.2d 618: Minor criminal defendant was timely notified of discretionary transfer proceeding and absence of defendant's mother at such hearing, after she had been duly summoned, was not fatal.

Matter of E.D.N. (Tex. App.1982) 635 S.W.2d 798: In order to transfer juvenile case to district court for adult criminal proceedings, trial court must conclude that seriousness of the offense or background of child and welfare of the community requires criminal proceedings.

Matter of G.F.O. (Tex. App.1 Dist. 1994) 874 S.W.2d 729: In prosecution of 15-year-old for murder in drive-by shooting, trial court's order waiving jurisdiction and transferring juvenile to district court was supported by police officer's testimony that defendant was member of gang, had trouble with member of rival gang, and that juvenile's house had been shot at in the past, and youth commission psychologist's testimony that juvenile charged with homicide could spend up to two years and nine months at youth facility, and then could go on parole supervision in community, and that it could be more difficult to rehabilitate gang member.

DISCUSSION QUESTIONS

1. What steps may be taken to ensure that the transfer decision is not based on the race, socioeconomic class, or gender of the youth?

2. Should transfer decisions be left entirely to the courts or should the district attorney be given the authority to decide which cases she will refer to juvenile courts and which she will refer to adult criminal courts?

3. What changes should be made in our transfer proceedings?

PART IV

JUVENILE DISPOSITION AND CORRECTIONS

Chapter 11

Juvenile Probation

JUVENILE PROBATION

Juvenile probation refers to a conditional release of a delinquent juvenile. Probation can have several different meanings within our present juvenile justice system. Probation typically refers to a sentence that has been given to a defendant where the youth is placed and maintained in the community under the supervision of an agent of the juvenile court. Probation refers to a status or class (i.e., he or she is on probation and thus is subject to certain rules and conditions that must be followed in order to avoid being institutionalized). Probation also refers to an organization (i.e., the county juvenile probation department).

Once a juvenile is determined to be a delinquent, the most frequently used method of court disposition is probation. It is clear that not every delinquent youth should be institutionalized. Nationwide, over 70 percent of all delinquents who appear at a disposition hearing receive probation.

Probation is a disposition that imposes conditions not involving prolonged confinement or, if any, at most involving only short periods of confinement. Under probation, the juvenile court retains authority over the case to supervise, modify the conditions, and resentence the juvenile if the terms of probation are violated. Probation is a legal status created by the juvenile court. While the classic definition of probation as set forth above indicates that it does not involve commitment, it is being increasingly linked to a short period of commitment at a training school, boot camp, or other local custody facility.

Probation permits the youth to remain in the community under the supervision of the juvenile probation officer. Probation usually involves:

1. A judicial finding that the behavior of the child has been such as to bring him or her within the purview of the court.

2. The imposition of conditions upon the youth's continued freedom.

3. The provisions of means of helping him or her meet these conditions and for determining the degree to which he or she needs them. Probation is more than giving the child another chance. Its central thrust is to give positive assistance in adjusting to the free community.

HISTORY OF PROBATION

John Augustus of Boston is considered the originator of the concept of probation. As early as 1841, Augustus, a private citizen, requested that Boston judges release young defendants under his supervision. It is estimated that over an 18-year period he supervised about 2,000 individuals on probation. Most of these were youths between the ages of 16 and 19. He helped them get jobs and reestablish them in the community. Only a few of the individuals under his supervision became involved in subsequent criminal behavior.

Augustus's work inspired the Massachusetts legislature to authorize the hiring of a paid probation officer for Boston. By 1880, probation was extended to other jurisdictions within the state. Missouri and Vermont soon copied the Massachusetts procedures. The federal government established a probation system in 1925. By that date, most other states had also adopted similar systems.

STATUS OF PROBATION

Juvenile probation is based on the philosophy that the average delinquent is not a violent dangerous criminal, but a youth who needs additional guidance in order to conform to society's demands. Probation generally involves the replacing of the youth's commitment to an institution with a conditional release. Probation is essentially a contract between the youth and the juvenile court. If the youth complies with certain orders of the juvenile court (conditions of probation), the court will not require the youth to be committed to a secure facility. If the youth later violates the terms of the contract, the court is no longer restricted by the contract and may commit the youth to a secure facility.

The characteristics of adjudicated cases ordered to probation changed between 1987 and 1996 as did the profile of those ordered to residential placement

Case characteristics	Percent of residential placement cases		Percent of formal probation cases	
	1987	1996	1987	1996
Most serious offense	100%	100%	100%	100%
Person	18	24	16	21
Property	53	44	60	49
Drugs	7	10	7	11
Public order	22	23	16	18
Sex	100%	100%	100%	100%
Male	88	87	86	81
Female	12	13	14	19
Race	100%	100%	100%	100%
White	63	59	66	66
Black	34	36	31	30
Other	3	5	3	4
Age at referral	100%	100%	100%	100%
13 or younger	12	13	16	17
14	16	17	16	17
15	25	26	24	24
16	28	26	26	24
17 or older	19	18	19	17

■ Compared with 1987, profiles of cases ordered to probation and cases ordered to residential placement showed greater proportions of person offenses, females, and younger juveniles in 1996.

■ Compared with adjudicated cases that resulted in residential placement in 1996, adjudicated delinquency cases that resulted in probation involved a higher percentage of whites (66% vs. 59%), females (19% vs. 13%), and youth charged with a property offense (49% vs. 44%).

Note: Detail may not total 100% due to rounding.

Source: Authors' analysis of Snyder et al.'s *Easy access to juvenile court statistics: 1987–1996* [data presentation and analysis package].

In some states, the youth is informed at the time he or she is placed on probation as to the terms of the commitment being probated. For example, the youth may be committed to a state training school until he or she reaches 21 years of age with the commitment probated for five years. If the youth stays out of trouble for five years, then the commitment is never served. If the youth's probation is revoked, then the youth is committed.

In most states, the youth is placed on probation for a certain period of time. If the probation is revoked, then the youth receives a commitment the length of which is determined at a disposition hearing after the probation is revoked.

Probation is also the most popular sentence given in adult felony cases. In some states, the juries may recommend probation. However, even in those states where the juries may decide the punishment, only the judge may grant probation. Most states have restrictions on the granting of probation for certain serious crimes. In addition, it appears that the death penalty may not be probated. This is based on the fact that the death penalty is limited to those cases where the defendant is beyond rehabilitation.

The length of the probation period may vary. A five-year period appears to be a common one for adult felony cases. In fact, the Federal Criminal Code recommends that federal probation periods last for five years. In juvenile cases, the period of probation is usually until the juvenile reaches the age of majority or the age of 21.

In many adult cases, the judge grants probation only if the defendant agrees to serve a period of local time (jail). For example, one judge, as a matter of policy, will not grant probation in felony cases unless the accused does at least thirty days' time in the local jail. This practice is known as "split sentencing."

Shock probation is frequently used in the case of first-time young offenders. In these cases, the judge grants probation only after the accused has sampled prison life. Shock probation is designed to give defendants a "taste of the bars" before placing them on probation. Evaluations of shock probation have indicated that shock probation's rate of effectiveness may be as high as 78 percent. Critics of shock probation claim that even a brief period of incarceration can reduce the effectiveness of probation which is designed to provide the offender with nonstigmatized community-based treatment. The boot camp form of shock probation is discussed later in this text.

EXTENT OF PROBATION

There are approximately 1,900 probation agencies in the United States. About half are associated with state-level agencies and the remaining with county or city governments. Approximately thirty states have combined probation and parole agencies. While prison populations have been increasing at a rapid rate in the past twenty years, it appears that the number of persons on probation has been increasing at an even faster rate. On any given day, there are approximately 1.8 million individuals in the United States on probation, over 50 percent under the age of 18. One of the reasons for the popularity of probation is its low cost. It costs less than $5 per day to maintain a delinquent on probation.

Criteria for Granting Probation

Listed below are the recommended criteria for granting probation developed by the American Law Institute's Model Penal Code. The criteria are also used in many juvenile cases.

1. The court shall deal with a person who has been convicted of a crime without imposing sentence of imprisonment unless, having regard to the nature and circumstances of the crime and the history, character and condition of the defendant, it is of the opinion that his or her imprisonment is necessary for protection of the public because:

   a. There is undue risk that during the period of a suspended sentence or probation the defendant will commit another crime; or

   b. The defendant is in need of correctional treatment that can be provided most effectively by his or her commitment to an institution; or

   c. A lesser sentence will depreciate the seriousness of the defendant's crime.

2. The following grounds, while not controlling the direction of the court, shall be accorded weight in favor of withholding sentence of imprisonment:

   a. The defendant's criminal conduct neither caused nor threatened serious harm;

   b. The defendant did not contemplate that his or her criminal conduct would cause or threaten serious harm;

   c. The defendant acted under a strong provocation;

   d. There were substantial grounds tending to excuse or justify the defendant's criminal conduct, though failing to establish a defense;

   e. The victim of the defendant's criminal conduct induced or facilitated its commission;

   f. The defendant has compensated or will compensate the victim of his criminal conduct for the damage or injury that he sustained;

   g. The defendant has no history of prior delinquency or criminal activity or has led a law-abiding life for a substantial period of time before the commission of the present crime;

   h. The defendant's criminal conduct was the result of circumstances unlikely to recur;

   i. The character and attitudes of the defendant indicate that he or she is unlikely to commit another crime;

   j. The defendant is particularly likely to respond affirmatively to probationary treatment;

   k. The imprisonment of the defendant would entail excessive hardship to the defendant or his or her dependents.

3. When a person has been convicted of a crime and is not sentenced to imprisonment, the court shall place him or her on probation if he or she is in need of the supervision, guidance, assistance or direction that the probation service can provide.

CONDITIONS OF PROBATION

A probated disposition is an act of clemency on the part of the court. Accordingly, in most states, the court may place conditions that restrict an individual's constitutional rights. For example, a judge may require that the youth voluntarily submit to searches and/or drug testing when requested by the juvenile probation officer. Generally, there are two sets of conditions that are imposed on a probationer: standard conditions that are imposed on every probationer, and special conditions designed for a particular defendant. Set forth below are the standard rules or conditions of probation used in the state of Texas which are very similar to those used in most states.

Texas Code of Criminal Procedure, Article 42.12

1. Commit no offense against the laws of the state of Texas or of any other state or of the United States.

2. Avoid injurious or vicious habits.

3. Avoid persons or places of disreputable or harmful character.

4. Report to the probation officer as directed.

5. Permit the probation officer to visit him at his home.

6. Regularly attend school or work faithfully at suitable employment as far as possible.

7. Remain within the county unless travel outside the county is approved by probation officer.

8. Pay any fines imposed and make restitution or reparation in any sum that the Court deems proper.

9. Support your dependents.

10. Participate in any community-based program as directed by the court or probation officer.

11. Reimburse the county for any compensation paid to appointed defense counsel.

12. Compensate the victim for any property damage or medical expense sustained by the victim as a direct result of the commission of the offense.

From 1987 to 1996, adjudicated cases ordered to probation or residential placement rose more than 50% — other sanctions rose 125%

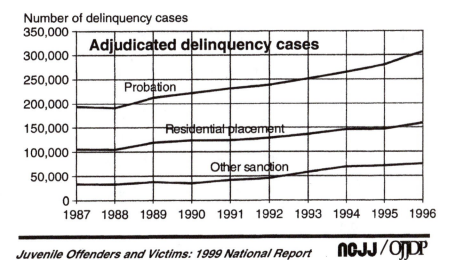

Number of delinquency cases

Juvenile Offenders and Victims: 1999 National Report **ncJJ/OJJDP**

Probationers' Rights

The courts have ruled that probationers (those on probation) have fewer constitutional rights than other citizens. The theory is that probation is an act of mercy by the court, and therefore certain conditions can be placed on individuals accepting probation.

The three major issues in probationers' rights are:

1. Search and seizure

2. Right of confidentiality

3. Revocation rights

Courts have traditionally held that juveniles on probation may be searched by their probation officers without the need for a warrant or probable cause. The basis of the search is that by accepting the conditions of probation the juvenile has consented to waive his rights against unreasonable searches and seizures. Some states, however, limit the right to search without warrant or probable cause to only probation officers and not other law enforcement members. The courts have also held that probationers' homes may be searched without a warrant. The courts have also indicated that probationers may be required to consent to future searches as a condition of probation. The courts have also held that the probation officer-client relationship is not a confidential relationship and therefore, the probation officer may testify as to matters related to him or her in confidence by the probationer.

Before probation may be revoked, the probationer has certain procedural due process rights. Generally, when the probation officer makes the decision to revoke probation, the offender is notified and a formal hearing is scheduled. The rules for revoking probation and parole are the same. There are three major United States Supreme Court decisions in this area that pertain to adult probation, but would presumably apply to juvenile probationers as well.

Mempa v. Rhay, decided by the court in 1967, held that a probationer was constitutionally entitled to counsel in a revocation of probation hearing where the imposition of the sentence had been suspended. Most lower courts interpreted this case to apply only in those situations that involved deferred sentencing and not in those cases where the probationer was sentenced at the time of trial. Accordingly, some jurisdictions provide counsel at revocation hearings and other jurisdictions do not. While this case involved an adult criminal, it also appears to be applicable to juvenile probation revocations.

In *Morrissey v. Brewer,* the Supreme Court required an informal hearing to determine if there is probable cause to believe that an individual on parole had violated the terms of his parole. If the informal hearing establishes probable cause of a parole violation, then a formal hearing needs to be held to determine if parole should be revoked. At the formal hearing, the parolee has procedural due process rights. The lower courts have applied the *Brewer* case to probation revocations.

In *Gagnon v. Scarpelli*, the Supreme Court held that both probationers and parolees have a constitutionally limited right to counsel in revocation proceedings.

FUNCTIONS OF PROBATION

As noted earlier, a juvenile probation department's primary goal is to provide services designed to help youths in overcoming their problems and their environments. For probation to be successful, the reasons that the juvenile came into contact with the justice system must be resolved and the youth reintegrated into the community. Probation is preferred over other forms of disposition for the following reasons:

➤ It allows the juvenile to remain in the community and function at a fairly normal level while providing protection for the community against further law violations.

➤ It helps the juvenile to avoid the negative effects of institutionalization.

➤ Probation decreases the stigma of the labeling process because the description of the crime is usually worded in a less severe manner than in those cases involving other dispositions.

➤ The rehabilitation program is facilitated by keeping the youth in the community and living at home.

➤ It is much less expensive than is institutionalization.

Future of Probation

Many individuals have voiced concerns regarding the placing of criminals on probation. Despite this, it appears that probation will continue as the most popular form of alternative sentencing available to judges. Part of the appeal of probation is based on its low cost and its flexibility. There appears to be a trend to use probation in conjunction with community treatment programs.

JUVENILE PROBATION OFFICE

Generally, there is a probation office for each juvenile court. In large urban areas, the probation offices of several courts may be merged into one office. The individual in charge of a juvenile probation office is normally called the "chief juvenile probation officer" (CJPO). It is the duty of the CJPO to carry out policy and to supervise the probation officers. Juvenile probation officers (JPOs) are generally charged with four primary tasks:

➤ Investigations—usually related to the predisposition investigation that the court uses in deciding on the appropriate disposition.

➤ Intake—refers to the process by which probation officers interview individuals regarding cases that have been scheduled in court for the initial appearance. It is directed toward the possibility that the case may be settled without further court action.

➤ Diagnosis—the juvenile probation officer's analysis of the juvenile's personality and the development of a personality profile of the youth occurs during the diagnosis functions. Diagnosis also involves the formulation of the treatment necessary to rehabilitate the juvenile (i.e., the JPO diagnoses that the youth has a drinking problem).

➤ Treatment supervision—refers to the duties of the JPO after the youth has been placed on probation. During the treatment supervision phase, the JPO should evaluate the effectiveness of the treatment programs ordered by the court.

PREDISPOSITION EVALUATIONS

One important function of a juvenile probation office is the predisposition of juveniles after they have been adjudicated as a delinquent. Samples of the usual requirements regarding predisposition are set forth below:

The probation officer shall upon order of any court in any matter involving the custody, status, or welfare of a minor or minors, make an investigation of appropriate facts and circumstances and prepare and file with the court written reports and written recommendations in reference to such matters. The court is authorized to receive and consider the reports and recommendations of the probation officer in determining any such matter.

Prior to disposition and after considering a recommendation on the issue which shall be made by the probation department, the juvenile court may remand a minor to the custody of the Department of the Youth Authority for a period not to exceed 90 days for the purpose of evaluation and report concerning his or her amenability to training and treatment offered by the Department of the Youth Authority. If the court decides not to remand the minor to the custody of the Department of the Youth Authority, the court shall make a finding on the record that the amenability evaluation is not necessary. However, a juvenile court shall not sentence to the state institution any minor who was under 16 years of age when he or she committed any criminal offense unless he or she has first been remanded to the custody of the Department of the Youth Authority for evaluation and report pursuant to this section. The need to protect society, the nature and seriousness of the offense, the interests of justice, and the needs of the minor shall be the primary considerations in the court's determination of the appropriate disposition for the minor.

Whenever a minor appears to come within jurisdiction of the juvenile court, the county probation department or the county welfare department shall, pursuant to a jointly developed written protocol, initially determine which status will serve the best interests of the minor and the protection of society. The recommendations of both departments shall be presented to the juvenile court with the petition which is filed on behalf of the minor, and the court shall determine which status is appropriate for the minor.

The probation department and the welfare department in each county shall jointly develop a written protocol to ensure appropriate local coordination in the assessment of a minor and the development of recommendations by these departments for consideration by the juvenile court. These protocols shall require, but shall not be limited to, consideration of the nature of the referral, the age of the minor, the prior record of the minor's parents for child abuse, the prior record of the minor for out-of-control or delinquent behavior, the parents' cooperation with the minor's school, the minor's functioning at school, the nature of the minor's home environment, and the records of other agencies which have been involved with the minor and his or her family. The protocols also shall contain provisions for resolution of disagreements between the probation and welfare departments regarding the need for dependency or ward status and provisions for determining the circumstances under which a new petition should be filed to change the minor's status.

Between 1987 and 1996, the volume of nonadjudicated cases order to informal probation rose 35%

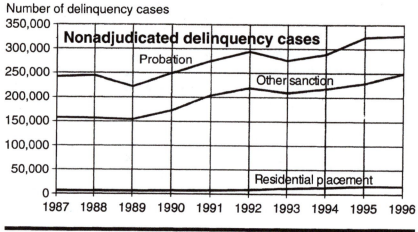

Number of delinquency cases

Juvenile Offenders and Victims: 1999 National Report   NCJJ/OJJDP

DISCUSSION QUESTIONS

1. Describe why probation is the most popular disposition given in juvenile cases.

2. What constitutional rights should an individual on probation have?

3. How can we make probation more effective?

Chapter 12

Juvenile Parole

This chapter begins the discussions regarding juvenile corrections. Research reports on the leading programs dealing with the problems associated with juvenile corrections are included in this section. There are too many programs to discuss each in this text. Accordingly, only those considered the most critical are included here.

No matter how perfect the police and the courts, if we fail in the area of corrections, the system will be unsuccessful in reducing crime and rehabilitating juveniles. Juvenile probation is the most popular disposition currently being used in juvenile corrections.

TYPES OF INSTITUTIONS

Currently, juveniles who have been adjudicated as delinquent and committed may be held in one of six types of facilities. The six types are:

1. Detention centers

2. Shelters

3. Reception/diagnostic centers

4. Training schools

5. Ranches or camps

6. Halfway houses or group homes

Detention centers are short-term, secure facilities that hold juveniles awaiting adjudication, disposition, or placement in an institution. Shelters are also short-term term facilities that are operated like detention centers, but with an unrestricted physical environment. Reception/diagnostic centers are also short-term facilities. They are used to screen youths for assignments to appropriate levels of custody and institution.

Training schools are generally long-term secure facilities that are used only for adjudicated delinquents. Ranches, forestry camps, and farms are long-term nonsecure facilities used for adjudicated juveniles. Halfway houses or group homes are nonsecure facilities that are used to help integrate the youths back into the community. They may be either long- or short-term facilities.

Determinate and Indeterminate Sentencing

A determinate sentence is a sentence with a fixed period of confinement imposed by the judge of the sentencing court. The determinate sentence is based on the concept that each crime should have a price tag. You commit the crime, you pay the price. Its underlying ideology is based on retribution, just deserts, and incapacitation. A form of determinate sentencing now being used by the federal government and many states is the "presumptive" sentence. A presumptive sentence is a sentence suggested by the legislative body based on certain factors regarding the crime and the criminal. The judge is expected to impose the presumptive sentence. If the presumptive sentence is not given, the judge must justify why it was not imposed. Generally, determinate sentencing is used in adult criminal courts.

The indeterminate sentence is based on the concept that the sentence should be tailored to the needs of the defendant. Generally, indeterminate sentences include the a pronouncement by the judge as to the maximum and minimum terms of confinement. For example, the judge may sentence the defendant to serve a period of confinement for not less than two years nor more than ten. The minimum term establishes the earliest release date (after adjustments for credits such as good time or time previously confined awaiting trial). The maximum term is the maximum length of time that the prisoner will be required to serve. The indeterminate sentence is based on the concept of rehabilitation. The defendant is to be released when he or she is rehabilitated. The decision as to when the defendant is rehabilitated is taken from the judge and transferred to an administrative agency. Most juvenile courts operate on the concept of indeterminate sentencing.

As can be noted from above, there are two levels of security, secure and nonsecure. Secure facilities are characterized by their locks, bars, and fences. Movement is generally restricted in a secure facility. Nonsecure facilities are characterized by their lack of bars, locks, and fences. In addition, nonsecure places permit a greater freedom of movement for the youths.

Juvenile parole is the conditional release of a juvenile from a correctional institution to the community under supervision of a parole officer. In theory, the juvenile is released from the correction institution at a time when he or she can best benefit from the release and continued supervision after release.

Other methods used to gain freedom included petitions for pardons. Since some of the early laws mandated long sentences, the juries would frequently petition the governor to grant pardons. In some cases, pardons were used to make more room in the overcrowded prisons. It is noted that prison overcrowding is an old and continuing problem with our correctional systems.

Parole is a broadly used term that refers to the release of any youth from custody. It differs from probation in that probation usually requires little or no confinement and probation is administered by the juvenile courts on a county-wide basis. Parole is generally administered by a statewide agency on a statewide basis. Normally, parole is granted only after serving a significant portion of the sanctioned confinement. Probation is considered a pre-institutional procedure, while parole, on the other hand, is considered a continuation of the correctional process. Release on parole is conditional and may be revoked if the terms of parole are violated.

In many states, the term "aftercare" is used in lieu of parole for juvenile cases. To many social service providers, the term juvenile aftercare is more acceptable than the phrase juvenile parole. It appears that about half the states use "aftercare" and the remaining use "parole." In this text, the two terms are used interchangeably.

The word "parole" is taken from the French. Its literal translation is "a word of honor given or pledged." It was first used by the military to release prisoners of war who promised to refrain from taking up arms against their captors or attempting to escape. Presently, it generally means a conditional release on good behavior from a correctional institution.

The parolee usually requires more supervision than a youth on probation due to the fact that the parolee has been confined and must readjust to society. In addition, the parolee may be bitter toward society, remorseful, and resentful of his or her confinement to an institution.

HISTORY OF PAROLE

Juvenile parole in America can be traced back to the houses of refuge that were established here in the latter part of the nineteenth century. Parole is, however, more English and European than American. It was first used by the English to offer a conditional release from prison for those prisoners who agreed to work for a certain period of time in order to regain their freedom. Parole, unlike probation, was originally motivated by economic rather than humanitarian pressures. Parole provided employers with cheap labor and relieved the British government from having to pay the expense of imprisonment.

In Colonial America, criminals were sentenced to prison for stated periods of time and were not released until the term had expired. "Good time" credit was not in existence until 1817, when New York passed the first good time law. The good time law allowed for a reduction in the fixed term based on the prisoner's cooperative good conduct and behavior while in prison. Other states soon passed similar statutes that were firm and straightforward. Generally, the good time laws permitted the

Alexander Maconochie
and
Sir Walter Crofton

The concept of parole is often credited to England's Alexander Maconochie and Ireland's Sir Walter Crofton.

Alexander Maconochie was born in Edinburgh, Scotland. After a distinguished career in the British navy, he was appointed the first Professor of Geography at University College in London. Later, he became involved in studying prison conditions at the Tasmania Island penal colony. In 1838-39, he published *Thoughts on Convict Management* and *Supplement to Thoughts on Convict Management*. He wrote that the proper object of prison discipline is to prepare men for discharge; the first object of prison is to reform prisoners and prepare them to separate with advantage both to themselves and to society after their release. Maconochie devised five ideas to serve the rehabilitation purpose:

1. Sentences should not be imprisonment for a period of time, but for the performance of a determined and specified quantity of labor. Time sentences should be abolished and task sentences should be substituted.

2. The quantity of labor a prisoner must perform should be expressed in a number of marks which he must earn, by improvement in conduct, frugality of living, and habits of industry, before he can be released.

3. While in prison, a prisoner should earn everything he receives; all else should be added to his debt of marks.

4. When qualified by discipline to do so, he should work in association with a small number of other prisoners, forming groups of six or seven, and the whole group should be answerable for the conduct and labor of each member of the group.

> 5.   In the final stage of the prison term, the prisoner should be given a proprietary interest in his own labor and be subject to a less rigorous discipline.
>
> Sir Walter Crofton used Maconochie's ideas in the Irish Prison System. Idea 5 (above) developed into the concept of conditional release, i.e., parole. The gradual approximation to freedom—in every successive stage of discipline from maximum security, to trustee, to conditional release or parole.

prison term to be reduced by one-fourth for terms of five or less years. The prisoner would need to obtain a certificate of good behavior from the principal confinement keeper to obtain the credit. By 1916, all states had adopted some form of good time statutes.

Other methods used to gain freedom included petitions for pardons. Since some of the early laws mandated long sentences, the juries would frequently petition the governor to grant pardons. In some cases, pardons were used to make more room in the overcrowded prisons. It is noted that prison overcrowding is an old and continuing problem with our correctional systems.

PAROLE TODAY

After release from institutions, most juveniles are typically returned to their original communities. Generally, juveniles are released from confinement long before the expiration of their maximum period of commitment. In some states, the juvenile must serve a minimum time before being released. In nine states, the judge who committed the juvenile must agree to the release prior to the youth being released early. The problem with this latter practice or requirement is that often the committing judge is too busy with other cases and does not have sufficient time to review the case and make a viable recommendation as to the release decision. In addition, since no new presentencing reports are prepared, the judge may act on dated or incomplete information. For these reasons, judicial involvement in the early release decision has been eliminated in most states.

Homicide cases had the greatest likelihood of court-ordered residential placement in 1996, followed by robbery, rape, obstruction of justice, and motor vehicle theft cases

| | Percent of adjudicated delinquency cases | | | |
| | Residential placement | | Formal probation | |
Most serious offense	1987	1996	1987	1996
Total delinquency	**31%**	**28%**	**56%**	**54%**
Person offenses	**33**	**31**	**55**	**53**
Criminal homicide	60	59	33	30
Forcible rape	42	43	52	43
Robbery	46	46	48	41
Aggravated assault	32	31	58	53
Simple assault	27	26	57	57
Other violent sex offenses	31	32	61	55
Other person offenses	25	28	59	59
Property offenses	**28**	**26**	**58**	**56**
Burglary	33	33	58	55
Larceny-theft	24	23	59	58
Motor vehicle theft	37	41	53	48
Arson	29	27	59	59
Vandalism	18	17	62	60
Trespassing	22	21	52	54
Stolen property offenses	28	28	58	49
Other property offenses	28	17	55	60
Drug law violations	**32**	**24**	**59**	**54**
Public order offenses	**37**	**32**	**49**	**49**
Obstruction of justice	47	42	46	45
Disorderly conduct	18	16	56	57
Weapons offenses	27	28	60	56
Liquor law violations	16	14	52	64
Nonviolent sex offenses	38	39	54	53
Other public order offenses	21	15	49	44
Violent Crime Index *	**39**	**37**	**53**	**48**
Property Crime Index **	**29**	**29**	**58**	**56**

- Cases involving youth adjudicated for serious person offenses, such as homicide, rape, or robbery, were most likely to result in residential placement.

- Cases involving youth adjudicated for minor offenses, such as vandalism or disorderly conduct, were least likely to result in residential placement.

- The relatively high residential placement rate for public order offense cases stems from the inclusion of certain obstruction of justice offenses that have a high likelihood of placement (e.g., escapes from confinement and probation and parole violations).

* Includes criminal homicide, forcible rape, robbery, and aggravated assault.

**Includes burglary, larceny-theft, motor vehicle theft, and arson.

Source: Authors' analysis of NCJJ's *National Juvenile Court Data Archive: Juvenile court case records 1987–1996* [machine-readable data file].

Most experts assign two goals to parole: first, protection of society, and second, the proper adjustment of the youth. Presently, it appears that the most important goal is the protection of society. Many see the two goals as conflicting ones involving society versus the youth. A better approach appears to be the concept of protecting society by rehabilitating the youth.

Parole includes the objective of assisting the parolee with integration back into the community. The youth must be assisted in coping with problems faced upon release along with the adjustment to the status of being a parolee. To be a permanent benefit to society, parole agencies must assist in the development of the youth's ability to make good decisions that are behaviorally acceptable to the community.

The functions of the institution include classifying the youth's readiness for release along with the risk factors upon release. The duty of the parole officer is primarily, among other things, to assist in the rehabilitation and reintegration of the youth into the community and the reduction in the likelihood of the youth committing further criminal acts.

THE RELEASE DECISION

In most states, parole in the juvenile justice system is administrated by the state agency that is also responsible for juvenile institutions. There are, however, no clear-cut organizational patterns as to who makes the early release decision. In some states, the decision is made by the youth authority, in others by a child welfare agency, an adult correctional agency, a lay board, or the correctional institution staff. In addition, many states have delegated the decisional authority to local agencies.

Unlike the adult parole process, most juveniles' release times are not determined at the postsentencing hearing. Generally, a juvenile's length of commitment is determined by the youth's progress toward rehabilitation. In some jurisdictions, progress is measured by a token system that awards a specific number of points for various actions. This is very similar to the "task sentences" referred to by Maconochie.

While there is general agreement that youths should be released as soon as they are ready, there are no valid measures to determine if a juvenile has been successfully rehabilitated or has undergone a real change of attitude. The criterion used to determine if the juvenile has been successfully rehabilitated and thus should be released is generally whether the juvenile conforms to institution rules or rebels. Thus, by appearing to have been reformed, the youth receives the earliest release date. Accordingly, the youth's conduct and behavior in the institution may be based solely on the desire to please his supervisors to obtain release.

The question of when to release the youth depends on predictions of the youth's future behavior. The policy considerations that are required to be evaluated before the youth is released include:

➤ Has the youth been reformed?

➤ Is it likely that the youth will committed another serious offense?

➤ Was the youth's behavior acceptable during his confinement?

➤ Does the youth have a home or other place, such as a group home, to live?

➤ Will suitable employment, training, or treatment be available for the youth on release?

➤ What is the youth's own perception of his or her ability to handle reintegration into the community?

➤ Is the seriousness of the youth's past offenses and the circumstances in which they were committed sufficiently severe so as to preclude release?

PAROLE SERVICES

Parole services consist of the various programs and components of the juvenile justice system necessary to facilitate the goals and purposes of parole. Parole services include classification tasks performed at the institution, counseling sessions, and education classes provided by the institution. Generally, prior to release, pre-parole investigations are conducted to obtain the necessary background information to devise parole plans for the youths. Parole services continue until the youths are released from parole.

The length of time that a youth spends on parole varies from state to state. Most youths are on parole for a period of at least one year. Generally, girls are kept on parole for longer periods than boys. This fact is most likely attributed to society's attitude that young females need greater protection than young males.

Juvenile parole officers, also known as aftercare counselors, are actually social workers and typically have training in the social work field. Unfortunately, many of the officers have little or no training in juvenile corrections. As with other areas of the juvenile justice system, we assume that the parole officer can be all things to all youths.

The President's Commission on Corrections Report called for a maximum caseload of fifty juvenile probation cases per officer or counselor. While there is no empirical justification noted for that caseload, it does appear to be a workable number. Unfortunately, most juvenile parole officers have caseloads so large that routine contact with the parolee is conducted only via the telephone. Many persons have advocated that reducing the caseload sizes would result in a greater success in rehabilitating the youths. Research indicates that the problems of rehabilitation are more complex and that reducing the caseload size alone is not sufficient to make the system more successful. One of the mistakes we learned from the LEAA experience of the late 1960s and early 1970s was that merely spending more money on a problem will not automatically solve it.

Juvenile parole conditions are generally less stringent than those for adults. The general conditions of a juvenile parole agreement include the below listed promises:

- Not commit further crimes
- Not use drugs and alcohol
- Attend school or be regularly employed
- Report regularly to the parole officer

- Not hang around persons who are known offenders or who could have a potentially damaging effect on the youth,

- Not leave the geographic area without permission from the parole officer

Some states have standard contracts that juvenile parolees are required to read, understand, and sign prior to being released. Conditions of release may be changed and renegotiated after consultation with the juvenile parole officer. The ability to change the contract is an attempt to make juvenile parole as flexible as possible. While violations of the agreement or contract may be grounds for revocation of the parole, as a practical matter parole is usually only revoked when there is clear evidence that the youth has committed other serious offenses or that the youth cannot function properly in the community.

The major issues associated with juvenile parole that still remain unclear include:

➢ The conditions of parole may have on constitutional freedoms such as freedom of religion, privacy, and freedom of speech.

➢ Whether or not the conditions of release lack precision and create needless uncertainty for both the parolee and the community.

REVOCATION OF PAROLE

Generally, it is the function of the juvenile paroling agency to revoke a youth's parole. *Morrissey v. Brewer* (408 U.S. 471 1972) involved two parolees in Iowa who were originally sentenced for forgery. About six months after being released on parole, their parole was revoked for violation of parole conditions. The two parolees appealed the revocation decision on the grounds that their paroles were revoked without a hearing and that the lack of a hearing deprived them of their due process rights. The Supreme Court held:

The liberty of parole, although indeterminate, includes many of the core values of unqualified liberty and its termination inflicts a "grievous loss" on the parolee and often on others. It is hardly useful any longer to try to deal with this problem in terms of whether the parolee's liberty is a "right" or a "privilege." By whatever name, the liberty is valuable and must be seen as within the protection of the Fourteenth Amendment. Its termination calls for some orderly process, however informal.

The Court then stated that the *orderly process* included the below minimum standards of due process:

➤ Written notice of the claimed violations of parole

➤ Disclosure to the parolee of the evidence against him

➤ Opportunity to be heard in person and to present witnesses and documentary evidence

➤ A hearing before a neutral and detached hearing body

➤ A written statement by the fact finders as to the evidence relied on and the reasons for revoking parole

The Court also held that before requiring a parolee to face a revocation hearing, a preliminary hearing should be conducted to determine if there is probable cause or reasonable grounds to believe that the parolee has committed acts that would constitute a violation of parole conditions. Although *Morrissey v. Brewer* dealt with adult parolees, it appears that the requirements are also applicable to juveniles.

DISCHARGE FROM PAROLE

In many states, the juvenile may be released or discharged from parole at any time after the juvenile's release from the institution. In some cases, the release is automatic after a certain period of time. Most states require juveniles to be on parole for a minimum time before they may be discharged, usually one year. Release from parole may also be conditional. To be effective, however, enough time is needed to work on the youth's long range goals and needs and help achieve independence from the juvenile justice system.

After discharge, most juveniles are left to their own devices and are no longer supervised by the system. The decision to discharge the youth from parole may have many pitfalls. For many youths, survival in the community was mainly possible due to the assistance of their parole officer or counselor. Once this support mechanism is removed, the parolee may regress into the behaviors and attitudes that were the underlying causes of previous encounters with the law.

Many consider juvenile parole or aftercare as the poor stepchild of the juvenile justice system. Postparole follow-up seems to be an even poorer stepchild. In addition, there is a noticeable lack of research and analysis on postparole success.

DISCUSSION QUESTIONS

1. Describe the differences between probation and parole.

2. How does the historical development of parole differ from that of probation?

3. What are the major goals or objectives of parole?

4. What factors should be considered in releasing the youth on parole?

Chapter 13

Group
Home
Programs

As noted in Chapter 12, one type of institution used in juvenile corrections is group homes. A group home has been defined as a long-term juvenile facility in which residents are allowed extensive contact with the community, such as attending school or holding a job. The below report is reprinted from *Federal Probation*, September, 1993. It discusses the current environment in which group home treatment programs exist and provides a complete discussion, for purposes of this text, of this topic.

SUCCESS/FAILURE OF GROUP HOME TREATMENT PROGRAMS FOR JUVENILES

BAHRAM HAGHIGHI AND ALMA LOPEZ

Significant changes have occurred in the juvenile justice system in the last several decades. Due to recent emphasis on rehabilitation, reform, and, above all, concern for the welfare of young offenders, the juvenile justice system has employed a wide variety of options in treating young offenders. Optimism about rehabilitation and dissatisfaction with the traditional "lockup" in detention homes has caused many to consider residential treatment and the rehabilitation of juveniles in a family-type center rather than conventional incarceration. The popular trend, therefore, has been deinstitutionalization of young offenders. Due to this dominant philosophy, group home treatment programs, one of oldest options in treating young offenders, gained a special momentum during the 1960s and 1970s. The availability of federal dollars, the rising concern of numerous child-caring institutions, and, above all, the dissatisfaction with detaining juveniles have caused group homes to proliferate as a viable alternative and supplement to juvenile institutions.

Unlike many alternatives for juveniles, group homes have been recognized for providing a family-type atmosphere where the youth and house parents (counselors and case workers) often establish the same warm and intense ties that one would hope to find in healthy families. Stewart and associates, by tracing 906 juvenile offenders in a 3-year period, recorded that such family-type atmosphere has a significant impact on the recidivism rate of juvenile offenders. Group home treatment programs, as they found, are particularly effective when first-time offenders are referred to such programs. Similarly, Gaier and Sarnacki suggested that group home treatment is an effective approach in interrupting delinquent behavior, since it is designed to alter the delinquent's environment and provide a meaningful family-type setting. According to Murray and Dox, institutions have a greater "suppression" rate on subsequent arrests than do group home treatment programs.

Group home treatment programs are also recognized for their cost efficiency in providing a workable alternative for unruly and delinquent children. At the time that most local governments are pressed with budgetary concerns, group home treatment programs are viewed as a promising alternative. One recent investigation by the Department of Justice regarded group home treatment programs as a viable option in saving the juvenile justice system from budgetary problems. The investigation further revealed that group home treatment programs have been appealing to juvenile court judges due to both their effectiveness in treating young offenders and their cost efficiency.

Despite these developments, recently group home treatment programs have come under criticism. A steady increase in the rate of serious offenses committed by juveniles has encouraged many to conclude that the group home phenomenon has failed to live up to its intent. Some believe that group home treatment programs, the same as other alternatives in the juvenile justice system, have failed to produce a significant difference in overall rate of delinquency. As a result, the recent "get tough" approach has inspired many states to rethink their liberal stance, thus replacing the group home treatment approach with the traditional incarceration option. What appears to have emerged from the dissatisfaction with group home treatment programs is the combination of punishment with the dominated rehabilitation philosophy. Some states, such as Washington, Colorado, and Delaware, have already "adopted legislation that focuses more on punishing the juvenile delinquent."

In this article, therefore, the success/failure of group home programs in treating and reforming juvenile delinquents is reexamined. Special attention is given to identifying the underlying factors leading to the success/failure of such programs, By comparing the juveniles' backgrounds and their dispositions as to type of treatment, suggestions are made to maximize the success of such treatment facilities, consequently reducing the rate of recidivism by those treated in group home treatment settings.

The Treatment

The group home treatment program in this study was established in the mid-1970s by a local juvenile probation officer due to his dissatisfaction with the local juvenile court's referral of the majority of unruly and delinquent children to state facilities. The program began by housing a few unruly, disturbed, and runaway children in the 1970s, and later accepted juveniles with various problems and backgrounds in the 1980s. The program started with a few hundred dollars donated by local businesses and grew to have an operational budget of over $350,000 in the late 1980s. Despite the rapid growth in a short period, the program solely functions on donations and charitable contributions by citizens and local businesses without relying on local or state funds.

The treatment program rests on providing a therapeutic community, elevating children's self-esteem, reducing stress, and providing group orientation. The program offers community service projects (helping senior citizens, beautifying the community, etc.), assists in obtaining employment, organizes athletic activities, and helps residents with educational and vocational programs. Overall, the program centers on building a positive mind and respect for others. In particular, being in a position to provide service to others enables the juvenile to be a help rather than a hindrance.

Methodology

During a 2-year period (January 1988—December 1990), a total of 410 juveniles were referred to a group home treatment program in a Midwestern state. Juveniles were referred by the local juvenile court, juvenile probation department, or alternative schooling for juveniles, or they were directly placed in the group home program by parents or school officials. The intake reflected 304 referrals from the juvenile court, with the rest placed at the center by other sources. The average stay for residents was 5 weeks, ranging from a 1-week stay up to 12 months. The program is a 52-bed center which usually is fully used by the juvenile court due to recent overcrowding in the state detention facilities. Of the total 304 referrals by the juvenile court to the facility, 152 residents were randomly selected for this analysis.

While most group home treatment programs exercise some degree of discretion in selecting nonviolent and nonaggressive children, this particular program has accepted all types of referrals regardless of their delinquent activity, prior incarceration, or the type of offense they have committed (with the exception of murder). In fact, a majority of residents were referred to the group home treatment program subsequent to unsatisfactory results from probation, detention, and other alternatives in the juvenile justice system.

Despite disagreement among experts as to how a program should be evaluated and what factors should be included in assessing the success/failure of a program, a great majority of researchers believe that such spectrum must include the goals the program intends to accomplish. In that respect, the end result or the interruption in delinquent behavior has been recommended as a valid indicator in measuring the success/failure of a program. One group home director defined his success by "children being able to return to normal lives in the community... to adopt a normal life-style where they can be responsible, where they can have a family, where they can keep jobs, and act in their own best interest."

Since the goal is to reform delinquent juveniles and the purpose is to deter children's involvement in future delinquency, juvenile treatment programs are repeatedly examined based on their effectiveness in keeping young offenders from repetition of delinquent acts. In that sense, recidivism and reappearance in the juvenile justice system is commonly ranked as a "failure" of rehabilitative efforts, while the absence of such return is classified as "success" of the treatment program.

In this study two factors were chosen in determining the "success/failure" dichotomy. First, the residents were routinely evaluated by program staff (probation officers, counselors, or case workers), reflecting the youngsters' performance during the treatment program and predicting their performance in the future. The juveniles were categorized as either "improved," meaning gaining continuance in the treatment program or preparation to be referred to their families, or "failed/no change," reflecting the ineffectiveness of the treatment program in changing their delinquent personality. The latter category was commonly an indication that the child attempted to escape, engaged in fighting with other children, disobeyed the house rules, or engaged in a delinquent act. The "failed/no change" commonly resulted in referral of the child to a more appropriate agency. In our analysis, "improved" juveniles were defined as "success" while the latter categories were grouped as "failure." Secondly, reappearance of the individual in the juvenile justice system (after release from the group home treatment program) was an indicator in reassessing the prior evaluation.

Results

Of the 152 reviewed cases, 95(62.5 percent) successfully completed the group home treatment program. This group was evaluated as "improved" by program staff and did not reappear in the juvenile court system until the age of 18. The remaining 57 (37.5 percent) of the cases failed the program, reflecting that they were either referred to another agency or had committed a delinquency subsequent to release from the group home treatment program. The sample included 31 girls and 121 boys, reflecting 94 whites and 58 blacks.

The analysis of the data revealed that the success/failure of the group home program depends highly on when the juveniles were referred to such treatment program. As shown in table 1, prior treatment of the juveniles was a significant factor in successfully completing the group home program. The treatment was highly successful when delinquent children were referred to such program in the early stages of delin-

Table 1. Success/Failure of Group Home Treatment Program in Relation to the Number of Prior Referrals

Placement After	Total	%	Success	%	Failure	%
First Offense	35	100	27	77.1	8	22.9
Second Offense	40	100	32	80	8	20
Third Offense	30	100	22	73.3	8	26.7
Fourth Offense	25	100	9	36	16	64
Fifth Offense	9	100	3	33.3	6	66.7
Sixth or more	13	100	2	15.4	11	84.6
Total	152		95	62.5	57	37.5

quency (73 to 80 percent). More specifically, the group home was successful in interrupting delinquency behavior in four out of five cases when the child was placed in the group home treatment program following the first, second, or third offense. Conversely, the group home program was least effective when such option was considered after the commission of the fourth delinquent act. In fact, as the number of prior dispositions increased, so did the inefficiency of the group home treatment program in helping juvenile offenders.

The analysis of reviewed cases revealed that the group home treatment program was effective in helping juveniles, thus reducing the rate of offenses committed by youngsters. But, as presented in table 1, accomplishing such a goal was associated with when such an option was considered by the juvenile court in dispositioning the subjects to the group home program. This finding, however, is inconclusive without considering the type of prior dispositions. The analysis of the sample cases revealed such an option is not prioritized by the juvenile justice judges. In the sample study, only 23 percent of the children were placed in the group home following the first offense. In fact, group homes, despite their efficiency, were considered as a dispositional option when other alternatives, such as probation and detention, had failed to help the juveniles.

As shown in table 2, the success/failure of the group home program equally relied on the type of prior disposition. Of the juvenile cases, those placed on probation prior to referral to the group home program had a proportionately higher rate of success compared to those who experienced incarceration in detention facilities (64.6 percent as compared to 39.5 percent). This finding concurs with the previous investigations in which detention facilities have been found to be effective in shaping delinquent personality rather than in controlling such behavior.

Table 2. Success/Failure of Group Home Treatment Program in Relation to Prior Disposition of Juveniles

Disposition	*Total	%	Success	%	Failure	%
Probation	79	100	51	64.6	28	35.4
Detention	38	100	15	39.5	23	60.5
Total	117*		66		51	

X= 6.56 df=1 p<.01
* 35 juveniles were placed in group home treatment programs following their first delinquent act.

Further, due to the intent of the group home program to provide a family-type atmosphere, it was presumed that such setting would produce a higher rate of success among juveniles from single parent families. The analysis of the data, however, failed to support such expectation. As portrayed in table 3, both groups of juveniles (single parent and both parent family structures) equally gained from the group home treatment program. Similarly, race did not appear to be a *predicting* factor in assessing the success/failure of such program. Although whites were referred to the group home setting in a higher proportion than blacks, both groups produced comparable rates of success/failure from such setting.

While family structure and the race of the referred juveniles appeared to have no impact on the overall success/failure rate of the group home program, the sex of the juveniles tended to be a predicting factor. Overall, girls completed the group home

Table 3.
Success/Failure of Group Home Treatment
Program in Relation to Demographic Factors

Demographic	Total	%	Success	%	Failure	%
Living With						
Single Parent	45	100	27	60	18	40
Both parents	107	100	68	63.6	39	36.4
Total	152		95		57	
x = .17 df = 1 p > .05						
Race						
White	94	100	58	61.7	36	38.3
Black	58	100	37	63.8	21	36.2
Total	152		95			
x = .06 df = 1 p > .05						
Girls	31	100	22	71	9	29
Boys	121	100	73	60.3	48	39.7
x = 1.04 df = 1 p > .05						

Table 4. Referral of Delinquent Boy/Girl to Group Home Treatment Program Following a Delinquent Act						
Referral After	Total	%	Boys	%	Girls	%
First Offense	35	100	24	8.6	11	31.4
Second Offense	40	100	33	82.5	7	17.5
Third Offense	30	100	23	76.7	7	23.3
Fourth Offense	25	100	19	76	6	24
Fifth Offense	9	100	9	100	0	0
Sixth or more	13	100	13	100	0	0
Total	152		121	62.5	31	37.5

program with a higher rate of success than boys (71 percent to 60.3 percent). The fact that girls succeeded with a higher proportion than boys in such program was more a matter of their disposition rather than differential acceptance of the program. Analysis of the data showed that girls were frequently referred to the group home program in earlier stages than boys.

In fact, over 80 percent of the girls were referred to the group homes following the first, second, or third offense. Relating this finding to table 4, it appears that the disposition decision rather than the juvenile's sex was a predicting factor in the success/failure of such program.

Conclusion

Treatment of juveniles in the community and rehabilitation of young offenders in a group home setting has become a hotly debated subject. The recent get tough-on-crime policy, coupled with the national concern regarding the drug problem, has motivated many decision makers to reevaluate the juvenile justice process. During the last few years, a number of states have moved toward more stringent and punitive measures to deal with young offenders. Motivated by the increasing number of serious offenses committed by juveniles and the ineffectiveness of community treatment programs in reducing recidivism, proponents of stiffer sentencing have proposed departure from the rehabilitative efforts and reimplementation of punitive measure. In such debates, group home treatment programs have been attacked frequently for their leniency and their inability to punish and change young offenders.

Some believe that the entire juvenile justice system is becoming tougher. A few states have already revised their juvenile justice system, reflecting more concern for retribution and deterrence than for rehabilitation and reform. In Washington, for instance, the entire juvenile justice code has been revised to include detention and determinate sentencing. By dropping the family court's jurisdiction over status offenders, the Washington legislatures have explicitly noted that the aim of the new legislation is more the protection of citizens and community through tougher sentencing than the welfare of juvenile offenders. Other states have followed the same path. California, Colorado, Delaware, Florida, and New Mexico have adopted legislation which focuses more on retribution and deterrence than concern for juveniles. It is believed that the remaining states will adopt more punitive measures in dealing with young offenders before the turn of this decade.

Many believe that this recent development will undermine the entire rehabilitative effort. Recent concern for punishment will ultimately jeopardize the existence of community treatment programs and, in particular, group home program facilities. Proponents of stiffer punishment, however, believe that nothing will be lost. A high recidivism rate, in their view, is an indication that group home programs, the same as other alternatives, have failed to live up to their intent.

The present investigation, however, showed a different outlook. The analysis of sample cases revealed that the productivity or success of group homes could be maximized if certain factors are taken into consideration. First, it was found that group home programs would be highly effective in the rehabilitation and reform of young offenders if such an option is considered in the early stages of delinquent behavior. Precisely, group home programs are most effective (77 to 80 percent) if juveniles are dispositioned to such treatment programs immediately following the first or second delinquency act. Conversely, are least effective (33 to 15 percent) when group home facilities were considered after five or six delinquent acts.

Secondly, the get tough approach to young offenders may not reduce the number of repeated offenses committed by this group. The present investigation recorded that group home programs are the least effective when the child has served a period of time in state detention facilities prior to his/her referral to group home programs. In comparison, those previously placed on probation had a higher rate of success in group home programs. This finding leads one to believe that the reimplementation of determine sentencing and the application of punitive measures by confining juveniles to detention facilities may result in a higher rate of recidivism and ultimately the elevation of offenses committed by juveniles. While on face value, the get tough approach may appear promising, it may cause unexpected results. In the long run, such an approach will cause a dramatic increase in the population of adult felons, since the juvenile justice system will have failed to serve its clientele properly.

Finally, to depart from a productive alternative which has proven to be effective in reforming young offenders while reducing the cost of juvenile justice system is premature. Particularly, in light of the recent war on drugs and the substantial cuts in juvenile justice system budgets in favor of efforts to combat drug kingpins, it does not seem logical to revoke an alternative which has proven to be cost effective. Group home treatment programs could become productive if they are used accurately. To maximize their success and reduce the rate of repeated offenses by juveniles, this option must be made a priority rather than considered an option after dissatisfaction with other alternatives in the juvenile justice system.

DISCUSSION QUESTIONS

1. Do you agree with the authors opinions that group homes should be used earlier in the correctional process?

2. What problems do you foresee from a more extensive use of group homes?

3. Is the group home approach too soft for young criminals?

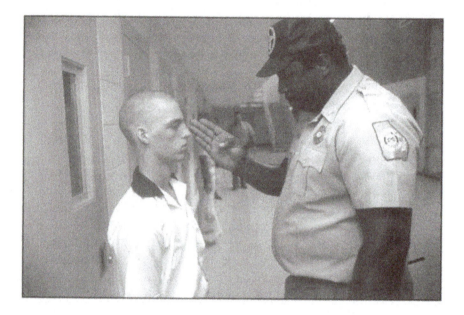

Chapter 14

Shock Incarceration

Since 1983, shock incarceration/probation programs, also known as boot camps, have enjoyed considerable popular support. Like other intermediate sanctions, these programs are intended to alleviate institution overcrowding and to reduce recidivism. In addition, because they are perceived as being "tough" on crime (in contrast to some other intermediate sentences like probation), they have been enthusiastically embraced as a viable correctional option for delinquent youths. The presumed combination of cost savings and punitiveness has proven irresistible to politicians as well as communities.

There has been a remarkable nationwide growth of boot camp prisons. In January 1984, only two states, Georgia and Oklahoma, had boot camp programs. By 1992, 25 states and the Federal Bureau of Prisons were operating a total of 41 programs. Two years later, in 1994, five more states had either opened boot camp programs or were planning openings. In 1984, Georgia's program capacity was 250 beds; by 1994, the capacity had expanded to over 3,000 beds. These figures pertain only to those programs developed statewide and do not include the programs developed at the county level.

CHARACTERISTICS OF SHOCK INCARCERATION

As the name suggests, boot camp programs are modeled after military boot camp training. Participation in military drill and ceremony, physical training, and hard labor are mandatory. Inmates begin their day before dawn and are involved in structured activities until "lights out," approximately 16 hours later.

This military-style training is generally supplemented with rehabilitative programming, such as drug treatment education and/or academic education. The emphasis placed on such programs varies. New York, for example, has structured the program as a therapeutic community. Rehabilitative programming, therefore, plays a central role in the program. In other states, rehabilitative programming is peripheral to the military boot camp experience.

As the boot camp programs have developed, rehabilitative programming has come to play a more prominent role in the day-to-day routine. The earliest boot camp models devoted little time to such programs. Most of those pioneering programs have since been enhanced with additional therapeutic services. Many programs developed in recent years seemed to place a primary emphasis on rehabilitative programing.

The boot camp programs are designed for, but not limited to, young male offenders convicted of nonviolent offenses. Eligibility and suitability criteria were developed to restrict participation to this type of offender. For example, a March 1992 survey of shock incarceration programs revealed that the majority of programs (61.5 percent) then in operation limited participation to individuals convicted of nonviolent offenses. Fifty percent of the programs further restricted participation to individuals serving their first felony sentence. Most programs have minimum and maximum age limits. The minimum age limit is generally 16 years of age and the maximum 23 years of age. Female offenders are permitted to participate in about 50 percent of the programs. The number of beds available to females, however, has been limited. Several state courts have ruled that failure to include female offenders in the programs is a gender discrimination violation.

EVALUATION OF BOOT CAMP PROGRAMS

As noted earlier, a major goal of the programs was to reduce recidivism by means of rehabilitation and deterrence. Specific rehabilitative strategies include teaching accountability or responsibility, developing self-worth or self-esteem, or providing education or substance abuse education or treatment. In addition, the shock incarceration programs are designed to serve as specific deterrents.

It is hoped that the difficult nature of the military-style training or the harsh reality of prison life would deter participants from future offending and, thus, reduce recidivism. An examination of a core element of military style training, which includes military drill and ceremony, physical training, strict discipline, and physical labor, is necessary to determine if there is any value to the regimented military routine.

Research on specific deterrence has not been promising. Researchers have previously reported limited or no deterrent effect as the result of incarceration in a training school. In addition, similar research on the Scared Straight program has failed to find evidence of a deterrent effect (E. Zamble and F. Porporino, "Coping, Imprisonment, and Rehabilitation: Evidence from the 1980s," *Criminal Justice Behavior*, Vol. 17, No. 1, 1990). Realistically, it is unlikely that the boot camp experience will lead to increased perceptions of either the certainty or severity of punishment. In terms of general deterrence, there is no reason to believe that individuals on the street will be deterred by the threat of serving time in a boot camp prison. In fact, camp participants interviewed revealed that prior to arriving at the boot camp, they did not believe that they would have trouble meeting program requirements.

Aside from deterrence, however, the experience of a day-to-day routine may have some beneficial by-products. Political support for these programs seems to be based, in part, on the idea that the regimented life-style and discipline of boot camp will be transferred to life on the outside. Completing the highly structured and demanding program is further expected to inspire a sense of accomplishment and higher self-esteem that may transfer to other activities. This sense of accomplishment is reinforced in many programs by graduation ceremonies that are attended by family and friends.

Former shock incarceration participants reported that the program helped them to "get free" of drugs and to become physically fit. Other advantages mentioned by offenders included learning to get up in the morning and being active all day. Thus, the military regimen appeared to promote both physical and mental health by ensuring a drug-free environment, balanced diet, sufficient exercise, and higher self-esteem.

Nearly 70% of public facility residents were held in facilities operating above their design capacity on February 15, 1995

Design capacity	All public facilities		Residents	
	Total	Percent operating above design capacity	Total	Percent held in facilities operating above design capacity
All public facilities	1,080	40%	69,929	69%
Fewer than 31 residents	595	21	8,543	29
31–110 residents	324	58	18,506	59
111–200 residents	90	63	13,141	66
201–350 residents	39	82	10,075	82
More than 350 residents	32	88	19,664	91

- In 1995, 40% of public facilities housed more residents than they were constructed to hold—a greater proportion than in 1991 (36%).
- The larger a facility's design capacity, the more likely it was to be operating overcapacity.
- Facilities designed for fewer than 110 residents accounted for nearly three-quarters of overcapacity facilities.

Compared with public facilities, a substantially smaller proportion of private facilities were crowded on February 15, 1995

Design capacity	All private facilities		Residents	
	Total	Percent operating above design capacity	Total	Percent held in facilities operating above design capacity
All private facilities	1,989	8%	39,706	15%
Fewer than 31 residents	1,694	7	17,377	10
31–110 residents	259	14	14,078	16
111–200 residents	25	20	3,672	17
201–350 residents	5	20	1,345	19
More than 350 residents	6	33	3,234	32

Note: Design capacity is the number of residents a facility is constructed to hold without double bunking in single rooms and without using areas not designed as sleeping quarters to house residents.

Source: Authors' analysis of OJJDP's *Children in Custody Census 1994/95* [machine-readable data files].

Contrary to popular opinion, however, it is unlikely that the long hours of hard labor characteristic of shock incarceration will improve work skills or habits. The labor that is often required of shock incarceration participants is largely menial, consisting of picking up trash along highways, cleaning the facility, or maintaining grounds. Researchers have noted that for work programs to be successful (i.e., promote rehabilitation) they must "enhance practical skills, develop interpersonal skills, minimize prisonization, and ensure that work is not punishment alone." Considering the type of labor generally required of inmates, it appears unlikely that it will be of much value in and of itself.

In short, the basic shock incarceration model may have some merit independent of rehabilitative programming. Positive by-products attributed to the core elements of shock incarceration alone may include physical fitness, drug-free existence, structured life-style, and a sense of accomplishment. It is the hope that these positive by-products will remain during parole and throughout life.

CATALYST FOR CHANGE

The basic shock incarceration experience is designed to induce stress. Incarceration, by its very nature, produces stress. Stress levels peak early during a period of incarceration and gradually taper off. Research has revealed that prison inmates were most receptive to personal changes (e.g., self-improvement classes, education, or training) during this period of high emotional stress. Within a period of several months, as stress levels tapered off, however, so did the desire to change. Inmates who, for example, had enrolled in self-improvement classes dropped out in favor of institutional jobs. In one study, researchers concluded that the desire for change was related to the emotional distress experienced at the onset of the prison term. They argued further that treatment programs should begin as early in the prison term as possible to take advantage of the motivation to change.

These research findings appear relevant to shock incarceration. Not only are inmates incarcerated, but they are forced to participate in a physically demanding and stressful program. At the same time, most programs require participation in rehabilitative programming ranging from academic education to drug treatment, and individual counseling. Generalizing from the findings then, the basic shock incarceration experience may make participants particularly receptive to early rehabilitative programming. Thus, the program experience may initiate a period of self-evaluation and change.

The implications of this approach are twofold. First, the basic program may function predominantly as a catalyst for change. Therefore, shock incarceration programs that do not also offer rehabilitative programming will have no effect other than those previously discussed. Secondly, if shock incarceration programs function primarily as catalysts due simply to the stress-inducing nature of the program, attention then must shift to the adequacy of rehabilitative programming.

REHABILITATIVE PROGRAMMING

Over 20 years have passed since a researcher, referring to correctional treatment, appeared to suggest that "nothing works." In response, prominent researchers in the field of corrections reviewed the extant literature on the effectiveness of treatment programs and concluded, on the contrary, that effective treatment existed and that on average appropriate treatment reduced recidivism by 50 percent. The key, of course, was the word "appropriate."

Appropriate treatment was defined as treatment guided by three psychological principles:

1. Intensive treatment should be matched with high-risk offenders.

2. Treatment should address "criminogenic needs."

3. Treatment should follow general strategies of effective treatment (e.g., anti-criminal modeling, warm and supportive interpersonal relations) and match type of treatment (e.g., cognitive or behavioral) to individual characteristics.

On the other hand, intervention strategies that have generally been found to be ineffective are those that are nondirective, use behavior modification techniques that focus on incorrect targets, and emphasize punishment.

The first principle suggests that more intensive treatment should be reserved for offenders who are considered higher risk. This is because high-risk offenders respond more positively to intensive treatment than do lower risk cases who perform just as well or better in less intensive treatment. Examination of the types of offenders targeted by this study's multi-site programs reveals that participants tended to be young, male, first-felony offenders. Many of these offenders were drug-involved as well.

The second principle requires that treatment programs target the criminogenic needs of offenders. Criminogenic needs are dynamic needs of offenders that, when addressed, reduce the likelihood of recidivism. Criminogenic needs may vary from individual to individual. Important criminogenic needs include substance abuse treatment, prosocial skill development, interpersonal problem-solving skills, and prosocial sentiment.

By and large, current shock incarceration programs attempt to address criminogenic needs. Seven states incorporated substance abuse education and treatment; six states provided job preparedness training; six states included academic education; and four states taught problem-solving or decision-making skills. Three states also provided intensive supervision upon release, which extended treatment and education to the community and sometimes also provided job training and opportunities.

There are, however, additional program characteristics that may influence the effectiveness of programming. The length of the program itself is one such example. Four of the programs in the multi-site study were 90 days long. Others ranged from 90 to 180 days. It would appear that six months of substance abuse treatment and/or education is more likely to have a positive outcome than three months. In fact, researchers have reported that length of drug treatment is related to successful outcome. This may be true of other program components as well. Programs that provide intensive supervision upon release tend to more effectively address criminogenic needs.

Another important component that may influence programming is the voluntary nature of the program. In some programs, participation was completely voluntary. Participants could drop out of the program at any time. In others, participation was mandatory. It has been hypothesized that offenders who volunteer to participate in shock incarceration possess a greater sense of control that those for whom participation is mandatory. Therefore, a sense of control may consequently lead to higher levels of commitment to the program.

The third principle, responsivity, outlines styles or modes of effective treatment programs. Effective styles of treatment use firm but fair approaches to discipline, anti-criminal modeling, and concrete problem solving. Workers in these programs relate to offenders in interpersonally warm, flexible, and enthusiastic ways while also being clearly supportive of anti-criminal attitudes and behaviors. Furthermore, effective programs must be cognizant of the fact that individual characteristics may interact with treatment style or mode of delivery. For example, highly anxious individuals are not as likely to benefit from stressful, interpersonal confrontation as are less anxious individuals.

What is most evident from the media reports and visits to boot camp prisons, though, is confrontation (e.g., drill sergeants screaming at inmates). Although staff and inmates directly involved in the program say discipline and staff authority is firm and relatively fair, outsiders who view the program and some program dropouts accuse the staff of domination and abusive behavior. Program staff generally attempt to act as anti-criminal models, reinforcing anti-criminal styles of thinking, feeling, and acting. However, few programs hire psychologists or others experienced in behavior modification techniques who work closely in the training of staff.

ATTITUDINAL CHANGE

A frequent assumption made regarding incarceration is that the pains of imprisonment will be accompanied by the harms of imprisonment. That is, it is assumed that the pains of imprisonment lead to negative attitudes toward prison, staff, and programs (i.e., prisonization) and, thus, prison will have a detrimental impact on offenders.

Inmates are thought to form a "society of captives" characterized by anti-staff attitudes. As a consequence, offenders just reject constructive aspects of the prison such as treatment or education programs that may give them the skills needed to succeed when they return to the community.

An equally destructive influence of incarceration may be the development (or exacerbation) of general antisocial attitudes. Reviews of the evaluation literature indicate a positive association between antisocial attitudes and criminal activities. Most theories of crime also recognize the significance of criminal cognitions or attitudes.

The impact of shock incarceration on inmate attitudes has not yet been fully understood. It has been hypothesized that the boot camp environment with its strict rules, discipline, and regimentation may increase the pains of imprisonment and as a result promote the development of increased anti-staff, anti-program, and antisocial attitudes. According to this view, the regimental routine may have a negative impact on participants. Offenders may leave the boot camp prison angry, disillusioned, and more negative than they would have been had they served time in a traditional prison.

On the other hand, the negative effect of the regimented routine may be offset or mediated by the rehabilitative programming required of inmates. As discussed earlier, though, the amount of daily routine varied among programs in this study. In New York, where program emphasis is on rehabilitation, inmates may have developed more antisocial or anti-program/staff attitudes. Changes in inmate attitudes, then, may vary as a function of the type of program. Offenders graduating from more treatment-oriented programs may not change at all or may change in a positive direction, while offenders graduating from programs that emphasize work and physical training may develop more negative attitudes over time.

The impact of boot camp prisons on inmate attitudes during incarceration (attitudes toward the program/staff and antisocial attitudes) was assessed in this phase of the evaluation. The attitudes of offenders serving time in shock incarceration programs were compared to the attitudes of demographically similar offenders serving time in traditional prisons. Attitudes toward the shock incarceration program (or prison) and antisocial attitudes were assessed once after the offenders arrived at the boot camp (or prison) and again three to six months later—depending upon the length of the shock incarceration program. Programs differed on critical dimensions such as the emphasis placed on rehabilitation, the voluntary nature of the program, and program difficulty—dimensions that might be expected to influence attitudinal change.

Changes in attitudes may also be related to the characteristics of the program, such as the amount of time devoted to rehabilitation versus work and physical training, the number of offenders dismissed from the program, and the voluntary nature of the program. Neither time devoted to rehabilitation nor voluntary exit was significantly related to program attitude. However, time devoted to rehabilitation, program rigor, and voluntariness appeared to lead to greater reductions in antisocial attitudes.

Despite differences among the programs in content and implementation, the results of this study were surprisingly consistent. Boot camp inmates became more positive about the program over time, while offenders serving prison time did not develop more positive attitudes. Both groups reflected less antisocial attitudes over time. This was true of enhanced boot camp programs that emphasized treatment as well as programs that emphasized military training, hard labor, and discipline.

The finding of the study, that boot camp inmates and prison inmates become less antisocial during incarceration, supports some current research indicating that prison may have some positive influence on some inmates. However, it is important to remember that these offenders were different from the general prison population. By and large, they were young and had been convicted of relatively minor offenses.

RECIDIVISM

One of the first questions asked about boot camp programs is "Are they successful?" By successful, many people mean, "Do they reduce the criminal activity of offenders subsequent to release?" The researchers concluded that the impact of boot camp programs on offender recidivism is at best negligible. The

While many States had increases from 1992 to 1996 in the number of under-18 youth newly admitted to State adult prison systems, some States with the most admissions in 1996 had decreases

State	Youth under age 18 admitted to State adult correctional systems		
	Number newly admitted in 1996	Proportion of 1996 admissions	Percent change 1992–1996
All reporting States*	5,599	2.3%	–6%
Upper age 15			
New York	624	3.5	–10
North Carolina	378	3.6	–51
Upper age 16			
Illinois*	460	2.7	29
South Carolina	353	5.3	56
Michigan	295	3.7	29
Georgia	219	2.3	99
Wisconsin†	196	4.1	165
Missouri	180	2.4	53
Louisiana	138	2.0	24
New Hampshire	6	1.1	–
Upper age 17			
Florida	773	4.1	–21
California	394	0.8	116
Youth Authority only	286	39.6	81
Mississippi*	217	4.4	117
Ohio	206	1.6	94
Alabama*	172	3.1	66
Oregon	141	5.7	–
Maryland	139	1.8	–5
Colorado	125	3.0	–
Washington	86	1.7	146
Pennsylvania	76	1.4	69
Virginia	71	0.9	18
Iowa	56	1.8	93
Nevada	54	1.9	–
Minnesota	52	2.1	–
Nebraska	50	3.6	67
New Jersey	49	0.5	32
Arkansas	27	3.6	–85
Utah	22	1.7	–
South Dakota	11	1.6	–
Tennessee	10	0.2	–
Kentucky	10	0.2	–
North Dakota	5	1.3	–
Oklahoma	5	1.0	–
Maine	1	0.2	–
Hawaii	0	0.0	–
West Virginia	0	0.0	–

*Count has been adjusted for admissions that were missing age data, based on admissions that had age data.

†In 1996, Wisconsin changed its upper age of juvenile jurisdiction from 17 to 16.

– Too few cases to calculate a reliable percent change.

Source: Authors' analysis of the Bureau of Justice Statistics' *National Corrections Reporting Program 1992–1996* [machine-readable data files].

results suggest that offenders who are released from shock incarceration programs appear to perform just as well as those who serve longer prison terms. Accordingly, the longer prison term does not serve as an additional deterrent.

Shock incarceration programs are still experimental. The researchers concluded that it would be irresponsible to continue placing offenders (particularly juveniles) in such programs without more carefully monitoring their effect at both the individual and system levels. If success is measured in terms of recidivism alone, there is little evidence that the in-prison phase of boot camp programs has been successful.

Are boot camp programs successful in achieving their objectives? To answer this question, objectives must be clearly defined. Programs that reported two major objectives—reducing prison overcrowding and changing offenders indicated that they were effective in reducing prison crowding. Results of program effectiveness in changing offenders is less positive. There is some evidence that some positive things happened during the in-prison phase of the programs. There is little evidence, however, that the programs have had the desired effect of reducing recidivism and improving the positive activities of offenders who successfully completed the program.

DISCUSSION

Shock incarceration programs provide a combination of punitive and rehabilitative program elements that are expected (in many programs) to both deter and to rehabilitate. The basic program model contains the more punitive elements including hard work, physical training, and military drill and ceremony. These elements may have some positive value. For example, they may promote physical health, a drug-free environment, and a sense of accomplishment. However, it is unlikely that any of the individual program components will lead to increased discipline, accountability, or improved work habits as frequently hypothesized. Based on previous research on deterrence, it is also unlikely that they will have a deterrent effect.

Rehabilitative programming in shock incarceration programs has received increased emphasis over the years. If the basic military model is viewed primarily as a catalyst for personal change, rehabilitative programming is of great importance because the other benefits of the program are minimal and, most importantly, are not related to recidivism.

Examination of the three guiding principles of effective treatment, however, reveals that shock incarceration programs probably do not maximize their treatment potential. Although rehabilitative programming attempts to target criminogenic needs, the effects of such programming are mediated by the responsivity principle, which stipulates that treatment is most effective when counselors relate to offenders in a warm and supportive manner and provide anti-criminal modeling and problem solving. Thus, although staff may try to provide anti-criminal modeling, the authoritarian atmosphere may not be conducive to effective treatment.

DISCUSSION QUESTIONS

1. Explain the advantages of boot camps over other dispositions that may be made by the court.

2. What are the disadvantages of using shock incarceration as a disposition?

3. Explain the community benefits of a boot camp program.

Chapter 15

The Future of Juvenile Courts

T he following article is reprinted with permission of Professor Robert Dawson and the *Journal of Criminal Law and Criminology*. In the article, Professor Dawson discusses the need and future of juvenile courts.

THE FUTURE OF JUVENILE JUSTICE: IS IT TIME TO ABOLISH THE SYSTEM?

Robert O. Dawson

I. Introduction

The juvenile justice system in the United States is approximately ninety years old. That age is old for a person and maybe also for a social-legal institution. There are signs it may be time to begin thinking about whether that system has served its purpose and should be abolished.

Initially, it is necessary to define what I mean by the juvenile justice system. I have in mind only that aspect of the jurisdiction of a juvenile court that includes criminal conduct and certain noncriminal conduct. Modern juvenile statutes normally label the former "delinquency" and the latter—often called status offenses—by various names, such as "Persons (or Children, or Juveniles, or Minors) in Need of Supervision." Usually included in the latter are running away from home, truancy, and (less often) incorrigibility or ungovernability. I exclude from consideration other elements of the possible jurisdiction of a juvenile court, such as adoption, termination of parental rights, child abuse and neglect, paternity, custody, and support.

I include within my definition of the juvenile justice system not only court proceedings but the entire legal process, beginning with law enforcement, through court intake and detention, informal and formal probation, and ending with the juvenile correctional process.

It is also necessary to state what I mean by abolition. I have in mind abolishing the juvenile justice system as a system separate from the criminal justice system. The result of abolition would be a merger of the two systems or, perhaps more accurately, an acquisition of the juvenile justice system by the larger criminal justice system. Abolition would not mean that all distinctions based on age would be obliterated; there would still be differences in how the criminal justice system treats defendants based on their ages. There would, for example, still be separation of youthful from older persons in pretrial and post-trial detention, treatment, and correctional institutions. The separations would not, however, be as rigid as they now are.

II. Why the Time May Be Right to Consider This Question

If one were to do an analysis over time of legal rights and legal structurez, comparing the juvenile justice to the criminal justice system, with a view to determining the legal differences between the two systems, the results would not be uniform. Were it possible to conduct such an analysis with some precision, one would probably find relatively little difference between the two systems initially, say in the beginning of this century. Legal structures establishing juvenile justice as a separate system were just being established, but resources were slower in coming. The system initially existed more in name than in reality. It was not until about 1925 that virtually every American state had enacted legislation establishing a juvenile justice system separate from the criminal system. There was initially more overlap in personnel operating the two systems. However, as the treatment philosophy underlying the juvenile justice system gained wider acceptance, the differences in legal rights and structure grew. Those differences were probably greatest in the late 1950s and early 1960s when the driving legal philosophy of the juvenile justice system was to entrust maximum discretion to the court and treatment staff with the absolute minimum of legal control.

But, beginning in the early 1960s, voices of dissent from the dominant legal philosophy grew. There was increasing skepticism about the ability of the system to perform on its promises and increasing concerns about whether the abuses of power that occurred were really aberrations or whether they were the norm.

This criticism of the system culminated in famous opinions of the United States Supreme Court in *Kent v. United States* in 1966 and *In re Gault* (387 U.S. I 1967) in 1967. The immediate reaction to these decisions was often to declare the juvenile system dead, but that pronouncement proved premature. The system survived that round of constitutional domestication, but did not remain unchanged. The major legacy of *Kent* and *Gault*—and, later, *In re Winship* (397 U.S. 358 1970) was the development and enactment of modern juvenile justice statutes.

That legislation reflected a different philosophy from the original statutes. The emphasis shifted from entrusting maximum power and discretion to system officials to limiting and controlling those powers. Room was made in the system for lawyers—as defenders. prosecutors, and judges. And, with the presence of lawyers, the system changed even more in the direction of a law-driven system and away from a treatment-driven system. To that extent, the juvenile system came increasingly to resemble the criminal system. The differences had narrowed as a consequence of those landmark Supreme Court decisions and the legislation they spawned.

Since the time of the "reform" legislation, there have been further developments that have narrowed the differences. We have lost even more of our faith in treatment and have replaced it with shadows of the criminal system philosophies of individual responsibility and punishment. We have increasingly embraced restitution, community service, and even fines in the juvenile system—concepts that would have been anathema only a few years earlier. We have become increasingly concerned with the violent juvenile offender and have responded to that person by adopting even more of the characteristics of the criminal system. In a few jurisdictions, we have even replaced the traditional, broad dispositional discretion of the juvenile court judge with a system of determinate sentences much like those now in vogue in the criminal system.

In summary, the *legal differences* between the juvenile and criminal systems are now narrower than they have been at any point in our history since the juvenile system was created. We have, in a sense, returned full cycle to the beginning. To be *sure,* both the criminal and juvenile systems have undergone many changes in the past ninety years; but looking only at the legal differences between the two systems, we do appear now to be very close to the beginning.

I have included an impressionistic chart of the differences in the extent of departure of the legal rights and structure of the juvenile system from the criminal over the past ninety years. Landmark events are noted on the chart. Of course, the chart lacks quantitative validity; it is instead intended merely to suggest visually the magnitude of differences I have observed.

One now encounters juvenile court judges who state (with disgust) when an appellate court requires adherence to a rule of procedure normally associated with the criminal system. "We might as well give up and abolish the juvenile system." One also encounters prosecutors and defense attorneys who articulate the same thought, some with disgust and some with relish. To the juvenile justice traditionalist, the system seems to have changed far beyond any recognition.

Taking a "legal snapshot" of the two systems at this time shows differences that are more nominal than substantial. We apply similar rules for both arrests of adults and for taking children into custody and for custodial interrogation. Identical rules for searches and pretrial identification apply. There is pervasive plea bargaining in both systems, only we are more likely to acknowledge it openly in the criminal system than the juvenile. The government is required to prove its case beyond a reasonable doubt in both systems and exclusionary rules apply with equal force. The guilt/innocence phase of court proceedings are separated from the sentencing phase in both systems, with the broad judicial discretion historically associated with the juvenile system now largely confined to the sentencing phase, as has long been true in the criminal system.

A cynic would examine the legal structure of the juvenile justice and criminal justice systems and conclude that one is an exact parallel of the other. The cynic might add that the only difference is in terminology and that such a difference exists only fraudulently to mask the underlying sameness. Thus, adults are "arrested" but juveniles are "taken into custody" even when the same law enforcement officer exercises the power and takes the person to the same police station. Adults are "hooked" into custody, while juveniles are "processed." Adults are "jailed" awaiting trial or release pending trial, while juveniles are "detained." Adults plead "guilty" or "not guilty" to the "charge" in the "indictment" or "information," while juveniles plead "true" or "not true" to the "allegation" in the "petition" or "complaint." Adults "plea bargain" most of their cases, while juveniles "stipulate" most of theirs. Adults have "trials" while juveniles have "adjudication hearings." Adults are found "guilty" or "not guilty" while juveniles are found to be "within the jurisdiction of the court" or "not within the jurisdiction of the court." An adult case proceeds to "sentencing" if the "defendant" is found guilty, while a juvenile case proceeds to "disposition" if the "respondent" is adjudicated. While both can be placed on probation, an adult who does not receive probation is likely "sentenced" to "prison" while a juvenile is "committed" to a "training school." An adult in prison is an "inmate" while a juvenile in a training school is a "resident" or a "student." An adult frequently is released from prison conditionally on "parole," while a juvenile often is released from training school conditionally on "aftercare."

An adult who is found guilty of having committed a crime is a "criminal"; a juvenile who is found to have committed the same crime is a "delinquent" or simply "within the jurisdiction of the court." The law specifically and in no uncertain terms declares that the juvenile adjudication is not a conviction of crime and carries none of the legal disabilities associated with such a conviction. In certain circumstances, we find even the term "delinquent" too harsh a judgment to place on the shoulders of a juvenile; instead, he or she is called a "Person in Need of Supervision" or some such similar euphemism. So ingrained is the difference in terminology, yet so self-consciously maintained, that when a judge or attorney is speaking about a juvenile case and accidentally says the child was "convicted," he or she is likely immediately to correct the error, with a slight smile, by saying, "I mean adjudicated, or whatever you want to call it."

If the only justification for maintaining a separate juvenile justice system were the advantages that accrue from a distinct legal structure, a compelling case for abolition might be made. And, as will be shown later, there are substantial advantages that could accrue from "folding" the juvenile system back into the criminal. But there are considerations, some of which have little to do with different legal structures, that might give us pause in such an undertaking. Here, we are going to look at the advantages and the disadvantages of abolition. As in most such matters, conclusions depend upon the balance that can be struck between the two.

III. The Case for Abolition

There are two major clusters of arguments for abolition, which will be discussed in order: resource savings and eliminating frictional costs.

A. Resource Savings

Initially, it is important to observe that the wall that separates the systems is more complete in some jurisdictions than others, and in some places in the same jurisdiction than in other places. This fact has an important bearing on the recourse savings that may be expected from the proposed merger. In some states, the same administrative structure, both line and staff, services both juvenile and criminal courts. In most, however, there is either a different structure from top to bottom or parallel divisions of the same state-wide department. In any event, in many jurisdictions there are adult probation officers and juvenile probation officers who are different people and work out of different offices with different support staff. In other jurisdictions, a probation officer's caseload may include some juveniles and some adults.

Similar distinctions may be found in the judiciary. In rural areas, the only judge available will be both the juvenile and the criminal court judge (and would also hear probate, divorce, general civil, and other types of cases). In urban areas, there are likely to be separate judges for the juvenile and criminal courts. In any event, the central point is that we already have in some parts of the country a substantial integration of resources between the systems. Abolition would not save resources in those places.

However, in jurisdictions without resource integration, the savings could be substantial. Duplication of many staff positions and functions could be eliminated—from computer systems to personnel officers to auditors to receptionists. Whether such duplication would be eliminated is, of course, another question. Merger would also permit more efficient use of courtroom space and personnel, such as bailiffs and court reporters. It should be observed, however, that in many localities such a savings would be difficult to achieve because the juvenile courtroom is located in a juvenile or family justice center several miles from the courthouse.

It would be possible, with relative ease, to combine juvenile and adult field probation officers and parole officers. Substantial savings might result from such a merger, especially in the elimination of duplicated staff positions and functions. However, juvenile probation officers perform many functions for which there are no counterparts in adult probation work. Juvenile officers frequently serve as intake and screening officers for the court system and also work directly with juveniles in pretrial detention facilities.

Merger might make some resource savings possible in detention and correctional facilities. It would at least create some opportunities for greater flexibility, both in assigning inmates (residents) to facilities and in transferring them from one facility to another. An old juvenile facility might be converted into a minimum security adult facility. One wing of an adult facility might be converted into a facility for youthful offenders. Of course, there would emerge a substantial turf battle between the county sheriff, who operates the local adult detention facilities, and the (former) juvenile probation department, which operates the local juvenile detention facility. Probably, the sheriff would win and would take over the juvenile detention facility.

In summary, the extent of resource savings resulting from merger would vary widely from place to place. It would depend upon the extent of pre-merger administrative integration, the configuration of physical facilities, and the extent to which officials wish to effect a resource savings or to maintain their own turfdoms after merger. The savings could range from great to almost none at all.

B. Frictional Costs

The juvenile justice and criminal justice systems are not totally separate from each other. There are bridges over which cases can and do pass from one system to the other. However, the fact that the systems are legally distinct makes those passages more difficult and more costly than if the systems were merged together.

1. Eliminating Transfer Costs. Almost all juvenile systems have some mechanism for dealing with the case or the respondent that is beyond the capability of the system. Typical is the *"Kent* style" transfer procedure. A case is filed in juvenile court against a respondent in the upper juvenile court age range. A prosecutor has discretion whether to handle that case as an ordinary delinquency case or to seek transfer of the case to criminal court for prosecution as an adult. Typically, a petition or motion for transfer must be filed, social and psychological studies conducted, and an extended, adversarial hearing held before the question of whether to retain the respondent in the juvenile system or to transfer him or her to the criminal system can be presented to a juvenile court judge.

Although transfer hearings undoubtedly occur in substantially fewer than one percent of the eligible cases that flow through the juvenile courts, they occupy a disproportionate amount of the time and energy of juvenile officials. Because transfer is extremely serious and the stakes are great for the respondent and society, the process is protracted and the hearing extremely adversarial. A transfer hearing is to the juvenile court what a capital murder case is to the criminal court.

The result of a transfer decision is merely to place the case in criminal court. It is not a trial. All of the trial and pretrial steps in the criminal court remain yet to be taken. A merger of the systems would totally eliminate the need for a transfer mechanism of any kind. The resource savings could be substantial.

2. Avoiding Frictional Miscarriages. The separation of the juvenile justice from the criminal justice system is ordinarily based on the age of the offender at the time the offense is believed to have been committed. Thus, in many jurisdictions, if the offense is committed a day before the actor's seventeenth (or eighteenth) birthday, he or she must be treated as a juvenile and can be treated as an adult only if a transfer mechanism is invoked successfully. However, if the offense is committed on or after the seventeenth (or eighteenth) birthday, the case is a criminal case from the very beginning and the juvenile *court* has no involvement.

The difficulty with the system is that it assumes the appropriate officials will know the actor's true age. It happens that sometimes the arrested person will misrepresent his or her age in order to be handled in one or the other of the systems. Also, it is not uncommon for there to be official uncertainty about the age of the person arrested because of the lack of reliable documentation. When this occurs, it can cause substantial problems. In some systems, if the ruse is carried out long enough, it can mean that the actor goes free.

Certainly, merger of the systems would eliminate any problems that occur because of the misrepresentation of the age of the accused or even official uncertainty as to age. While one cannot assert that such events occur often, they do occur, and when they do, the results are quite disruptive.

3. Providing for Continuity of Services. One of the abiding ironies of our handling of the chronic offender is that, although upon each pass through the juvenile system he or she is dealt with more harshly, upon becoming an adult, he or she is given a fresh start. A hardened juvenile offender a few days ago, he or she is now a first offender in adult court.

To some extent, this effect results from the confidentiality of records in the juvenile system that impedes the easy flow of information to criminal system officials. But, even when full information about juvenile involvement has been disclosed, there is an undeniable tendency on the part of criminal justice officials to discount that information substantially in making adult dispositional decisions. The person is treated as a first offender because he or she is a first offender in the system that is making the decision.

The "fresh start" phenomenon reflects more than anything else the attitudes of criminal justice officials toward the juvenile justice system. They view themselves as the real legal control system and the juvenile system as a "kiddie court" that only plays at legal control. This macho attitude ironically leads criminal justice officials to adopt a fresh start approach when a juvenile violator graduates to the criminal system.

That attitude is one reason why a surprising number of juveniles transferred to adult court for protection end up on adult probation supervision and why at least some persons of juvenile age and with prior juvenile system experiences who are arrested without identification misrepresent themselves as adults. A merger of the two systems would probably eliminate this totally inappropriate notion of a fresh start on crime when adult age is reached.

IV. The Case Against Abolition

The case against abolition is based on the same reasons the system was established in the first place. To a degree, then, it is an examination of the extent to which those initial reasons still have validity. The case against abolition is based on three clusters of arguments: (1) the notion that minors have less responsibility for their misconduct than do adults; (2) the greater rehabilitation potential of minors, justifying greater devotion of resources: and (3) the avoidance of inappropriate legal rules.

A. Lessened Responsibility

One reason for having a separate juvenile justice system is a belief that it is inappropriate to hold children to the same standards of responsibility as adults. Based on this same belief, the common law recognized a defense of infancy to a charge of crime. The matter of where to draw a line between childhood and adulthood is subject to different views and is ultimately arbitrary, but most people would agree that a line must be established and maintained. We simply react differently to misconduct by a twelve year old than to the same misconduct by a twenty year old.

We attach severe legal consequences to misconduct by the twenty year old. We label it a crime and the offender a criminal. We say that person has chosen to act badly. While we may recognize social and other restrictions on his or her freedom to choose, we believe that a choice was made and that one can be made by others in similar circumstances. We attach severe legal consequences in part to influence the choices others will make. We feel free to select the worst of adult malefactors for punishment, sometimes quite severe punishment. We save those we can and punish those we cannot.

With children, we are more likely to look outside the actor to understand the misbehavior. We are likely to look at parents, school, neighborhood, and companions. We view the education and development of the child as incomplete and, therefore, do not hold him or her to adult standards of conduct. We find it much easier to forgive the misconduct of a child than an adult. After all, the adult should know better.

So, for children we seek to avoid the imposition of the same severe sanctions that we affirmatively desire to impose on adults. We avoid the label "criminal" and its legal and social consequences. We solemnly declare that the juvenile justice system, which looks much like the criminal system, is civil in nature and that the child has engaged in delinquency, not criminality. We carefully provide for confidentiality of proceedings to protect the child. We protect court and other records from public inspection and, often, destroy or seal them once the process has expended itself and the child has been "rehabilitated."

For children, we believe they will behave as they are labeled by adults-that if we call the child bad, that is the way he or she will view himself or herself and, consequently, behave in the future. Therefore, we attempt to avoid labeling in the juvenile system because we fear that with impressionable children it will have the opposite effect we believe it to have with adults.

If the juvenile system were merged with the criminal, this philosophy of lessened responsibility would, to some extent, have to change. We would have to be willing to call the ten, eleven, and twelve year old who commits a crime a criminal, even though in the criminal system we might treat the child differently from the twenty year old who engages in the same conduct. One might question whether this is a step that we are prepared to take.

There is also the problem of status offenses, such as running away, truancy, and incorrigibility. If we merge the juvenile system into the criminal, we will lose this subsystem. That might be good or bad, depending upon whether one believes the juvenile system to have any business dealing with those problems-a matter of some current controversy. The loss would be almost certain, however, since it is doubtful that a state legislature would be willing to make it a criminal offense for a child to run away from home, or to be truant from school, or to disobey parents' orders. It is, of course, quite another matter to make such conduct a subject of juvenile court jurisdiction, especially when we label it something less serious than delinquency, such as "PINS" or "MINS." The fact that we engage in juvenile sublabeling is strong evidence that we would be unwilling to handle such problems in the criminal system. After all, if we are unwilling to call such conduct delinquent, would we be willing to call it criminal?

To merge the juvenile back into the criminal system is inevitable to abandon all or part of the notion of lessened responsibility of children for their conduct. Childhood would, to be sure, still be taken into account by prosecutors, judges, and juries in the criminal system and would undoubtedly be a major mitigating factor in individual cases. But the labeling would remain that of the adult and many of the legal disabilities of that label would apply to children in the criminal system.

How would the merged system work in those jurisdictions in which judicial sentencing discretion in the criminal system has been replaced by salient factor scores, offense severity scales, and matrices of the two? It might be necessary to reexamine the applicability of various determinate sentence schemes to youthful criminal offenders, since those schemes are premised in part on notions of adult responsibility. But that is a detail that could be worked out. Perhaps a new scale of mitigation could be added to take account of childhood.

B. Greater Rehabilitation Potential of Children

It is now fashionable to doubt the capability of the criminal system to rehabilitate offenders. Too many recidivism studies have been conducted with too many dismal results to permit many knowledgeable observers to maintain the faith. To a lesser extent this agnosticism has even crept into the juvenile system. We now think of "managing" juvenile offenders, rather than "rehabilitating" them. Those who still believe in the rehabilitation of children are likely now to place emphasis upon keeping the juvenile system from interfering with the natural process of maturation into adulthood rather than upon affirmative steps the system can take to rehabilitate an offender: first do no harm, then cure if you can.

It was, of course, one of the prime beliefs of the early juvenile system that children's behavior would respond to the intelligent application of public resources—that we could cure delinquency with the proper effort and with sufficient resources. To some extent, that belief even penetrated the criminal system and spurred the development of probation services, residential treatment facilities, and even treatment programs within the fences of prisons. There are people in both systems who still believe in rehabilitation, but there are proportionally more of them in the juvenile system than in the criminal.

Why is that? Some are merely traditionalists who still hold the beliefs of the pre-1960s. Others acknowledge the obstacles to rehabilitation, but believe that if the juvenile system can shelter a child from the destructive consequences (including legal ones) of his or her conduct until he or she has passed through the difficult years of adolescence, he or she may have a fighting chance of law-abiding adulthood. For them, there are sufficient success stories to cancel the depressing statistics. For them, the goal of the system is to keep the government off the children's backs until they can mature. In any event, many people believe that adolescence is a period of great life change during which anything is possible, and that if public and private resources are likely to be effective, it is during that period.

That belief likely accounts for the undeniable truth that children attract resources. It is easy to be sentimental about children, even those who misbehave in significant ways. They do, after all, have less responsibility for their conduct than do adults. There is always room for the belief that resources applied to children may actually make a difference in adulthood.

Children attract public resources. That is why juvenile probation officers almost always have lower caseloads than their adult counterparts. That is why juvenile institutions are smaller and comparatively better staffed than adult facilities. That is why there are comparatively more public facilities for children than for adults. We are simply willing to put our public monies on children more than on adults.

But the big difference is in private resources. An integral part of any juvenile justice system is a network of private, charitable, or religious institutions, facilities, and programs. These can be used by juvenile courts and their staff for placement or referral. These private "correctional" resources are used by the juvenile system thousands of time each year. There really is no adult counterpart to this private segment of the juvenile system, at least not in anything like comparable size.

What would happen to these public and private resources if the juvenile system were merged with the criminal? Would they continue at their current levels, or would they recede because there is no longer an easily identifiable beneficiary—the children of the city, county, state, or nation? Of course, no one really knows what would happen, but there is a risk that these public and, particularly, private resources would gradually recede. Juvenile and adult caseloads on probation, in institutions, and other facilities would gradually equalize at closer to the adult level than the juvenile.

This would likely occur because it would be difficult to maintain that part of the clientele of the criminal system is ripe for rehabilitation, while other parts are not. We would probably have more resources for younger criminals than for older, but the difference would not be as great as it now is. There would be a tendency to blur our devotion to rehabilitation as a consequence of merger, just as there would be a tendency to blur our concepts of responsibility as a consequence of the same merger.

Perhaps these public and private resources could be better spent elsewhere, perhaps not. In any event, one likely consequence of merger would be a net decrease in the resources now devoted to the two systems combined. But, new found efficiencies might cause a net increase in the effectiveness with which those diminished resources are used.

C. Avoiding Inappropriate Legal Rules

The legal rules of procedure that govern the criminal and juvenile systems are virtually the same as a consequence of the due process decisions by the United States Supreme Court and the round of reform legislation that followed. There is a right to counsel and to provision of counsel at public expense if the accused is unable to afford counsel. (*In re Gault* 387 U.S. 1 1967). There is a privilege against self-incrimination in each system, despite the juvenile system being nominally civil. There is a right to confrontation and cross-examination of witnesses. There is a right to notice of charges and to a requirement that the government prove its charges beyond a reasonable doubt. (*In re Winship* 397 U.S. 358). There is also protection against twice being placed in jeopardy for the same offense. (*Breed v. Jones* 421 U.S. 519 1975). The Fourth Amendment, with its exclusionary rule, applies in both systems, as do the requirements of *Miranda* (*Fare v.*

Michael C. 442 U.S. 707 1979). The only federal constitutional right adults charged with a criminal offense enjoy that a juvenile charged with the same conduct does not is the right to trial by jury. The Supreme Court halted the due process revolution in juvenile justice at that point. (*McKeiver v. Pennsylvania* 403 U.S. 528 1971). A handful of states provide for jury trials as a matter of state law, but most do not.

If the juvenile system were merged into the criminal, there would be no denying children charged with criminal offenses the right to trial by jury. That would be a healthy development in the law—one the Supreme Court should have taken years ago when it had the opportunity. In any event, it could potentially create a major change in the way we do business in the juvenile system—a change that many a juvenile justice traditionalist would contemplate with horror.

But there is another change that might occur that would be unqualifiedly catastrophic. Children in the criminal system would have the right to bail. Bail is a peculiar constitutional right. It is beneficial to the accused only if he has no other means of being released from pretrial confinement. Otherwise, it is a burdensome and corrupt system. In some communities, bailbondsmen control who is released and who is not before trial; in many, they exert great political influence over the local criminal justice system.

Increasingly, in the criminal system, bailbondsmen are being replaced by public bail systems. A quick investigation is conducted and if the accused shows ties to the community and, therefore, is likely to appear for trial, he or she is released on his or her own recognizance without the necessity of posting security or purchasing a bail bond. In a variation on that practice, he or she may be required to deposit a percentage of the bond amount with the court. Unlike a bail bond premium, however, this amount is returned to the person posting it if the accused makes all of his or her court appearances. Fortunately, in many communities, these public systems have totally displaced the traditional bailbondsman—but not in all.

Where bailbondsmen exist, they are extraordinarily powerful. They are likely to view adolescents as poor risks to appear for trial and are likely to be less willing to post bond for them than for an adult with a proven record of appearing for trial each time he or she is arrested. There could be no denying the applicability of the bail bond system that happens to exist in any community to juveniles now charged in criminal cases.

Bail has been handled in the juvenile system by pretending that it does not exist. The modern juvenile statute does not provide a right to bail and does not deny the right to bail. It simply ignores the subject entirely. Instead of providing by statute for a right to bond in juvenile proceedings, modern statutes typically provide for a prompt judicial detention hearing to be conducted under statutory release criteria. While there are a few appellate opinions holding that such a hearing is an adequate substitute for bail, the matter has not been fully tested, for no one has the heart to risk opening the doors of the juvenile justice center to the bailbondsman.

Yet, if the juvenile system were to be abolished, it would be difficult not to treat adolescents charged with criminal offenses like adults charged with the same offenses. Bail schedules would have to apply to all. Because of the volume of cases, bond would be set without much attention to the individual characteristics of the arrestee. In some communities fortunate enough to have release on recognizance programs, many adolescent offenders would be released. However, in those communities without such programs, release would depend upon the willingness and financial ability of the adolescent's family to post bond and upon the willingness of a bailbondsman to write a bond.

Since most adolescents involved in the juvenile process are totally dependent upon their families for money, whether they would be released on bond would depend not upon their resources, but upon those of parents and other relatives. Usually, that money could be better spent elsewhere, and the parents appreciate that fact. Further, they are very likely feeling quite hostile to their arrested child at that moment and, even if resources are available, may be unwilling to pan with them for bail.

In summary, the bail bond system is a major problem in the criminal justice system. It is a problem that has, by common consent, been avoided in the juvenile justice system. Merging the two systems would likely make bail bonds a problem in the juvenile system for the first time. Bail bonds are, further, even less appropriate in the juvenile system than in the criminal because children lack resources of their own.

V. How Would Life Be Different Under the Merged System?

The answer to that question depends in part on how different it is under the separate systems. The practical consequences of a merger would be great or small depending upon the legal structures and allocation of resources to the juvenile and criminal systems prior to merger. Here, we shall take a case through the merged system in an effort to detect differences. We shall assume that the now abolished juvenile system was fully implemented both legally and in terms of resources. That will suggest a maximum model of difference as a consequence of merger.

Bill Bob, fifteen years of age, is taken into custody for a felony offense-burglary.

Before merger, he would have been taken from the streets to a special division of the police department, called the Youth Services Division. He would have been processed, but probably not photographed or fingerprinted. His parents would have been contacted by a Youth Services officer. That officer would have screened the paperwork submitted by the arresting officer for factual and legal sufficiency. It is possible that the officer might have questioned Bill Bob in an attempt to clean up several recent unsolved burglaries. In any event, if this were Bill Bob's first felony offense, and if his parents were moderately concerned and stable, chances are that Bill Bob would have been released by Youth Services from its custody to that of the parents on the promise of the parents to bring him to juvenile court when required. The paperwork generated by the taking of Bill Bob into custody would probably have remained at a local law enforcement level, not sent to a central state or federal depository of criminal records.

If Bill Bob had not been released to his parents, he would have been transported by a Youth Services officer to the intake office of the juvenile court, located at the juvenile detention facility. If the arrest had been newsworthy, the local papers would merely report that a juvenile had been taken into custody for burglary, without identifying Bill Bob.

Under the merged system, Bill Bob would be taken from the streets to Central Booking. There he would be photographed and fingerprinted. He might immediately be placed in a cell, probably in a cellblock reserved for youthful criminal offenders, or might be taken to the Burglary Division for questioning, where an effort might be made to clean up recent unsolved burglaries. Someone in the police department might or might not attempt to contact Bill Bob's parents: that would be a matter of local law enforcement policy, since the state law would no longer require it. Once Burglary is through with him, Bill Bob would be returned to his cell to await his first appearance in court. The next morning, his fingerprints and a record of his arrest would be mailed to the central state depository for criminal records and to the F.B.I.

If newsworthy, the local paper would fully report the arrest, including Bill Bob's name.

Before merger, Bill Bob, if not released to his parents by police, would have been interviewed by a juvenile court intake worker, who would have attempted to determine how serious the matter was. The worker would have examined, by computer or manually, the available records to determine whether Bill Bob was already on juvenile probation and whether he had any prior referrals to the juvenile court. The worker would have attempted to contact Bill Bob's parents. If they showed an interest in Bill Bob's release, chances are he would be released to them, pending further court processing. If Bill Bob had not been released by intake, he would have been processed into the juvenile detention facility, where he would have been enrolled in academic classes in an effort to prevent a major interruption of his schooling. A detention hearing might shortly have been held, at which Bill Bob would probably have been released if his parents were sufficiently interested in him to show up at the hearing.

After merger, in some communities, Bill Bob would be called from his cell to be to interviewed by a personal recognizance program worker in order to determine whether he would be a suitable candidate for release without security. In other communities, bail would be set from an offense schedule and Bill Bob would remain in jail until a bail bond could be purchased by his family or until a lawyer was appointed (or was hired by the family) who could persuade a judge to reduce bond to an amount the family could raise. Bill Bob would be brought before a judge, probably the morning after his arrest. There, he would be warned of his legal rights, informed of the bond amount, and, perhaps, given the opportunity to apply for the appointment of counsel if indigent. If unable to make bond, Bill Bob would remain in the county jail, where he would watch television.

Before merger, Bill Bob's case would have been evaluated by an intake officer and, perhaps, by a prosecuting attorney. A decision would have been made whether to handle the case informally or to file a petition in juvenile court alleging the offense of burglary. The case would likely have been handled informally unless Bill Bob had an extensive record of prior referrals to the court. If a petition had been filed, a date for an adjudication hearing would have been set and Bill Bob, his lawyer, and his parents would be expected to be in court for that hearing. If the evidence against Bill Bob was strong, it would be expected that his attorney would have advised Bill Bob to stipulate to the evidence in the expectation that such a step would guarantee that the judge would give probation in the case.

In the merged system, the complaint filed by the police would be forwarded to the prosecutor's office for review of legal sufficiency. In some jurisdictions, the case would in due course be presented to a grand jury for an almost-certain indictment. In other jurisdictions, Bill Bob might receive a short probable cause hearing in front of a magistrate before the prosecutor filed an information.

Before merger, all of the court proceedings in Bill Bob's case would have been non-public, as would have been all of the court and other legal papers filed in the ease. After merger, all of the court proceedings would be open to the public, although, unless the case is extremely newsworthy, at most only a few courthouse regulars might be expected to be present (unless Bill Bob is unfortunate enough to be in court the day Miss Jones brings her eighth grade civics class to observe justice in action). All of the papers in the case that were filed with the clerk of court would also be open to public inspection, although that is not much of a problem because finding the file (even for a court proceeding) often presents some difficulty.

After merger, Bill Bob's lawyer would plea bargain with the prosecutor, seeking a disposition that would permit his or her client to remain on the streets. Whether this materialized would depend mainly upon his prior record, all of which is open and available to the prosecutor and the court. If the record is extensive, Bill Bob, despite his youth, might receive a short prison sentence or perhaps a form of "shock probation," which might even include elements of the boot camp experience for youthful, male offenders.

Before merger, if Bill Bob had been committed to the state training school system, he would have been evaluated and probably assigned to a cottage or dormitory style living arrangement with children approximately his own age and under the supervision of house-parent types. He would have gone to school and perhaps received some vocational training and maybe even some counseling.

After merger, if Bill Bob was sentenced to prison, he would be transported to a large institution for youthful criminal offenders. There he would work and might also receive some vocational training or academic schooling. Forget about counseling. He would live with one or two other inmates approximately his age in a cell in a cellblock under the control of a correctional officer who most definitely is not a house-parent type. If he became a chronic disciplinary problem in the youthful offender institution, he could be transferred administratively to a less desirable facility.

Bill Bob would eventually be released on parole. Before merger, the time as a "resident" would probably be one-third to one-half the time after merger spent as an "inmate." Upon release, before merger, Bill Bob would have a record as a delinquent, although that record would not be public and would be relatively inaccessible from computer terminals. After merger, Bill Bob would have a record as a criminal, and that record would be universally available to any law enforcement officer in the nation with access to a computer terminal and with Bill Bob's full name and date of birth.

Before merger, Bill Bob might be eligible to return to juvenile court, after a respectable time following release from "aftercare," to petition the juvenile court for a sealing or expunction of his juvenile records. After merger, Bill Bob can forget about expunction. He had best spend his time memorizing an explanation for the arrest and subsequent events that he will be required to give for the rest of his life no matter how straight he goes.

VI. On Balance, Don't Abolish It

There are some very good arguments in favor of abolishing the juvenile system by merging it into the criminal. There might be some resource savings through efficiencies and some troublesome frictional costs would be eliminated. The criminal system's inappropriate concept of a fresh start on crime would likely be eliminated or greatly modified by merger.

These are all substantial gains. The losses would, however, be even more substantial. We would lose control over status offenses. While that is controversial, I wonder what a patrol officer is supposed to do when he or she observes a fourteen year old walking the streets at 3:00 if there is no justice system jurisdiction over running away from home. There are a number of communities that have invested considerable thought and resources into dealing with these status offenders. It is unlikely the legislatures would be willing to make such conduct criminal, and it would be inappropriate to do so. We would simply be withdrawing official authority over such conduct. Of course, status offenses could be made a type of parental neglect and some of the slack taken up in that fashion.

Do we really want to deal with bailbondsmen in our juvenile system? That would be a retrogressive step of giant proportions.

Finally, the undeniable fact is that children attract resources, both public and private, That is why the juvenile system is comparatively better funded and staffed than the criminal system. The juvenile system has a level of resources that officials in the criminal system can envy but not attain. Merger would have a leveling effect. Unfortunately, it would likely be a downward leveling effect. Public and private resources would flee from service to children in trouble with the law because the legislature abandoned all pretense of helping them by abolishing the legal system designed to deal only with them.

DISCUSSION QUESTIONS

1. Do you agree with Professor Dawson that we should retain our present juvenile justice system?

2. What changes should we make to the system to make it more effectively?

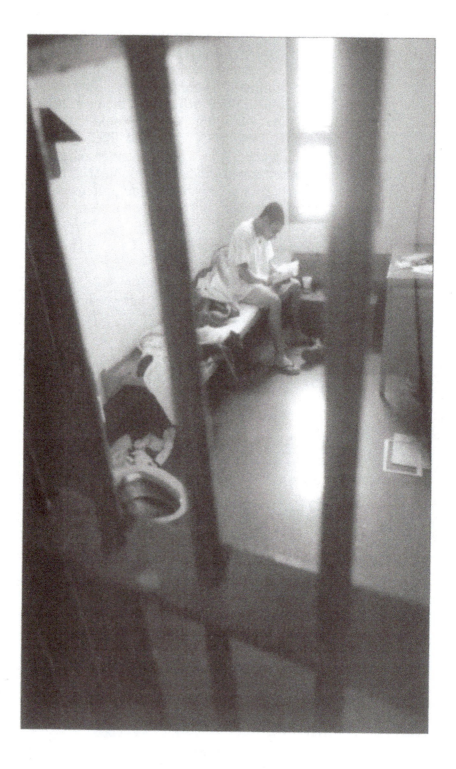

Chapter 16

Directions
for
Change

To bring this text to a close, excerpts from research reports and programs are included that may provide either a direction for change or points to consider in evaluating any proposed changes in juvenile justice for the future. As noted earlier, many researchers, including the author, believe that education is the key to reform and improvement.

As we start the new century, many media reports have highlighted the problems with violence in our schools and school shootings. Accordingly, the first section of this chapter is an extract from a *Juvenile Justice Bulletin* by OJJDP regarding this problem. The next article is regarding educating juveniles in corrections. The following article by Judge Lederman provides a brief review of the history of juvenile court and gives guidelines for the future.

It appears that youth gangs will continue to be a problem in the new century. A look at the last youth gang survey published prior to the year 2000 is also included in this chapter. Making juvenile justice work will go a long way toward solving the adult crime problem.

VIOLENCE AFTER SCHOOL

(U.S. Dept. of Justice, Office of Juvenile Justice and Delinquency Prevention, *Juvenile Justice Bulletin*, November 1999.)

Shay Bilchik, Administrator OJJDP

In the midst of our national anxiety about recent violent tragedies in and around our schools and our search for solutions, we must be careful to act on the basis of fact, not fear, and to solve real problems, not imagined ones. Reliable data indicate that students are safer at school than away from school and commit fewer crimes during school hours than after school ends.

The real problem area is not the school itself but the world our children return to after the dismissal bell rings. In today's society, fewer and fewer children have a parent waiting for them at home when school lets out. As a result, youth often supervise themselves and younger siblings after school with varying degrees of oversight by parents and guardians. Most juveniles are responsibly engaged in an array of positive activities, such as sports, clubs, or homework, or they "hang out" harmlessly with friends. However, for youth who have few activities available, whose friends are prone to negative behavior; or who experience other risk factors, the unsupervised hours between school and dinnertime offer ample opportunity to go astray. Statistics show that serious violent crime committed by juveniles peaks in the hours immediately after the close of school.

At the same time, we should not fail to recognize that during these afterschool hours, juveniles are most likely to become victims of crime, including violent crimes such as robberies and aggravated assaults. In this unsupervised time, youth are more vulnerable and more likely to be exploited, injured, and even killed.

The data reported in this bulletin document the need for schools and communities to develop strategies for youth during afterschool hours. The information provided here demonstrates the desirability of exploring policy changes, such as flexible work schedules so parents can provide more direct supervision during these crucial hours. Local school districts and communities need to consider initiating or expanding recreational, sports, employment, mentoring, tutoring, arts, and homework programs as positive alternatives to unsupervised time in a child's day.

Knowledge is indeed power. Although we may not always be able to prevent isolated incidents of extraordinary violence, we can work together to develop programs and strategies that prevent juvenile crime and violence where and when they occur, most predictably—away from school during afterschool hours.

There are many youth-focused programs with afterschool initiatives and activities for children and youth. For comprehensive information on resources that support children and youth during out-of-school hours, visit www.afterschool.gov. This website, which is sponsored by the Interagency Federal Support to Communities Initiative, provides a data base of more than 100 Federal grant and loan programs; information on community success stories and networking opportunities for afterschool programs, federal publications and clearinghouses, and websites designed for children and teenagers; and access to information on food and nutrition, health and safety, learning, recreation, technology, transportation, and volunteers.

Answers to frequently asked questions about juvenile justice statistics, as well as periodic updates of data presented in *Juvenile Offenders and Victims, 1999 National Report,* are available on the Internet in the OJJDP Statistical Briefing Book, which can be accessed through the OJJDP home page at www.ojjdp.ncjrs.org through the JJ Facts & Figures prompt. For information on OJJDP initiatives related to the reduction of juvenile crime, violence, and victimization, contact the Juvenile Justice Clearinghouse (JJC) at www.ojjdp.ncjrs.org.

JUVENILE CORRECTIONAL EDUCATION: A TIME FOR CHANGE

Robert J. Gemignani

For too long, education has been regarded as just another service for incarcerated youth. For too long, yesterday's pedagogy has failed to educate delinquent youth for today's world. It is time for change. This need for change is reflected in an 18-month study conducted by the National Office for Social Responsibility (NOSR). Dr. Osa Coffey and colleagues looked beyond traditional correctional education literature and research to include lessons learned from Job Corps and Job Training Partnership Act educational programs. The researchers analyzed the findings from Effective Schools research and from the U.S. Secretary of Labor's Commission for Achieving Necessary Skills.

Today's labor market demands a more comprehensive and advanced academic vocational training curriculum. Incarcerated youth should be afforded the opportunity to develop their competitive skills and move beyond drill to tackle increasingly complicated tasks.

Addressing juvenile offenders' academic skills without paying equal attention to their social and moral reasoning is futile. Teachers in correctional institutions should incorporate innovative teaching methods to stimulate incarcerated youth to learn. Examples of effective educational practices follow.

Effective Schools

➢ A school's learning and working environment determines its effectiveness.

➢ Education is regarded by facility administrators as the most important component of the rehabilitation process.

> ➤ Education and training are priorities, not competitors with other programs.

> ➤ The comprehensive education program includes basic academic skills, high school completion, general equivalency diploma (GED) preparation, special education, preemployment training, and other programs aimed at enhancing students' social, cognitive, and life skills.

> ➤ Student/teacher ratios reflect needs of the students, demands of the subject area, availability of equipment and resources, and legal mandates.

> ➤ Academic achievement is reinforced through incentives, including diplomas and certificates.

> ➤ Academic programs ensure educational equity for all.

> ➤ Teachers are competent, committed, and active.

> ➤ Parents and community volunteers are involved in the academic program.

Administration

Effective administrators stress the need for education to be regarded as the centerpiece of the rehabilitation process by educational and correctional staff. They recruit high-quality teachers and provide them with equitable remuneration and adequate training opportunities.

> ➤ Education is regarded by correctional facility staff as the key component of each youth program.

> ➤ Appropriate correctional school accreditation is maintained.

> ➤ Periodic assessments are made of student and staff needs.

➤ Staff are trained in the procedures and principles of providing educational services in a correctional school setting.

➤ Staff are kept informed of current research on effective instructional strategies.

➤ Site-based management affords administrators and teachers the authority to change structures and practices while accepting responsibility for outcomes.

Academic Programs

A fundamental assumption underlying academic curriculum in the past is that basic skills have to be mastered before students are given more advanced tasks, such as problem solving and cognitive reasoning, reading comprehension, and written communication. Current thinking challenges this concept. The new paradigm is based on the assumption that all students can succeed and that educationally disadvantaged students can profit from more challenging tasks.

Classrooms in correctional settings often reflect the old model, which emphasizes workbook exercises, remediation, drill, and practice in the basics. Under this model, educational assessments have focused on what students cannot do in order to provide remedial instruction. Classroom management has centered on discipline and control, with time-out periods in which unruly offenders are separated from other students. A more effective model involves changes in educational philosophy, curriculum, and instructional techniques.

➤ The academic curriculum features comprehension and complex problem-solving tasks, allowing students to develop their cognitive skills.

➤ The curriculum integrates basic skills into more challenging tasks that allow students to apply these skills to real-life situations.

➤ The curriculum allows for a number of discrete skills to be combined and applied to more complex tasks.

➤ Knowledge sharing is emphasized through cooperative learning, peer tutoring, and team problem solving.

➤ Teachers model cognitive process through a variety of instructional strategies, including externalizing thought processes, encouraging multiple approaches to problem solving, and focusing on dialog and reciprocal learning.

➤ A variety of assessment and evaluation measures are used. Progress is based on mutually defined student goals emphasizing competence.

➤ Instruction involves multiple strategies appropriate to each learner's interests and needs.

➤ Reading, writing, and oral expression are interrelated.

Special Education

As many as 40 percent of youth in correctional facilities may have some form of learning disability. It is essential that correctional education employ trained and certified staff with the capacity and resources to provide a full spectrum of special education programs and services.

➤ Incarcerated youth with learning disabilities must be provided special education in full compliance with Federal and State law.

➤ Correctional staff should be trained to meet the mandates of the Americans With Disabilities Act.

➤ Essential components of an effective special education program include: (1) assessment of deficits and learning needs, (2) a curriculum that meets each student's needs, (3) vocational training opportunities, (4) transitional services that link correctional special education services to prior educational experiences and to educational and human services needed after release, (5) a comprehensive range of education and related services, and (6) effective staff training.

> Youth with learning disabilities should be included, to the greatest extent possible, in regular academic programs, classrooms, and educational activities.

> Independent living, social, and vocational skills that prepare students for adult living supplement the regular academic program.

> The special education program should help youth in their transition between public schools and corrections or between corrections and independent living and work.

Psycho-Educational Programming

Delinquents are often deficient in the cognitive problem-solving skills, moral reasoning, and communication and social skills essential for successful functioning in daily life. Sound juvenile correctional education programs enhance offenders' thinking and social skills while ameliorating their academic and vocational deficiencies.

> Such programs include a social meta-cognitive skills curriculum focusing on such areas as social interactions and communications, moral and spiritual values, problem solving, and conflict resolution.

> Students are assessed in social skills and cognitive reasoning.

> Social skills education is integrated into life at the facility.

> Opportunities are created for practicing and applying social skills in the community.

> Students are afforded opportunities to participate in school and facility governance.

➢ Academic and vocational instructors are trained in such instructional techniques as modeling, small-group discussions, and cooperative learning.

Employment Training

The majority of delinquents age 16 and older do not return to school after release from a correctional setting or do not graduate from high school. While correctional educators must find better ways of motivating students to return to school, they must also provide students with the knowledge, skills, and attitudes needed in entry-level jobs.

➢ Education programs should afford students the opportunity to develop competencies in: (1) basic skills such as reading, writing, and mathematics, (2) thinking skills such as creative thinking, decision making, and problem solving, and (3) personal qualities such as responsibility, sociability, and honesty.

➢ Students should develop workplace competencies: (1) using resources and staff, (2) working productively with others on teams, (3) acquiring and using information, (4) understanding and utilizing systems, and (5) using technology.

➢ Students should be provided with opportunities to apply knowledge through on-the-job training, work experience, internships, apprenticeships, mentorships, or observing workers on the job.

➢ Students should develop a portfolio that includes credentials, work samples, work history, resume, letters of recommendation, relevant community service, and extracurricular experiences.

➢ Partnerships with employers should be developed to enhance current programs and provide post release support for students.

Transitional Services

Expanded and improved transitional services are needed to bridge the gap from community schools to correctional facilities, and from correctional facilities to home or independent living. Lack of services may undo many of the benefits students have received through their educational programs while incarcerated. Effective transitional programs will increase the students' rate of reenrollment in school, their high school graduation rate, and their success in independent living and employment.

➤ Incarcerated youth are provided opportunities to acquire social skills, survival skills, independent living skills, preemployment training, and law-related education.

➤ Incarcerated youth have access to a comprehensive library that contains a variety of materials related to transitional services.

➤ Student records are transferred in a timely fashion between the releasing and the receiving institutions.

➤ Educational information is used to make prompt and appropriate placements.

➤ Students are scheduled and preregistered prior to their reentry into community schools.

Program Evaluation and Research

Progress in correctional education requires an increased level of research. Process as well as outcome research—especially scientifically designed, rigorous evaluation studies of effective educational programs and practices—is needed to assist practitioners. Legislators and funding agencies demand proof of effectiveness in determining policies and allocating resources.

➤ Student intake data are collected and maintained in a systematic manner to provide a baseline for student achievement. Performance data are linked to specific skill areas and competencies.

➢ Each student's progress is evaluated regularly, and cumulative data are maintained for evaluating programs and staff. Evaluations are curriculum-based and assess mastery of specific competencies by students individually and in the aggregate.

➢ Juvenile correctional administrators encourage and provide time and resources for correctional education staff to participate in and conduct correctional education evaluation and research.

➢ Corrections education research should be conducted in accordance with conventional standards of social science research.

➢ Research findings are published and disseminated to other practitioners, researchers, policy makers, and legislators and disseminated via existing information systems and clearinghouses.

THE JUVENILE COURT: PUTTING RESEARCH TO WORK FOR PREVENTION

(U.S. Dept. of Justice, Office of Juvenile Justice and Delinquency Prevention, "Juvenile Justice: 100th Anniversary of the Juvenile Court, 1899-1999". The Honorable Cindy S. Lederman is the presiding judge of the Miami-Dade Juvenile Court. Citations have been omitted, and the article has been condensed.)

Cindy S. Lederman

The juvenile court is a noble institution—a noble, underfunded, often unappreciated institution charged with the most important duty imaginable, protecting and reforming our children when all else has failed.

The scrutiny the 100th anniversary of the juvenile court has brought to bear on the institution is welcome. It provides an opportunity to examine the court's record in attempting to achieve its virtually impossible charge. More important, it provides a forum to discuss the modifications that need to be made to design a juvenile court that can meet the challenges of the next century. This discussion, involving legal scholars, researchers, judges, lawyers, historians, social scientists, and others, is taking place at a time in history when society is scared of its own children.

Society is permeated with rhetoric about how children are its most precious resource, but too often those words ring hollow. In reality, the needs of children are not a national priority. One in five children lives in poverty, more than 11 million (1 in 7) have no health insurance, and among industrialized countries, the United States ranks 18th in infant mortality. Some children who have recently immigrated to the United States appear to be protected from these and other risk factors (e.g., those involving physical and mental health), but this advantage wanes with length of residence and from one generation to the next.

The juvenile court is one of the few places in society where the needs of children are paramount and where a passion for helping children defines its work. In the juvenile court, children are the absolute priority. The juvenile court is doing a creditable job under adverse circumstances toward achieving these goals; however, a better job is needed and, fortunately, it can be achieved.

Most citizens see the juvenile court as an institution designed to deal with young offenders who commit crimes. Although this may be its most public function, the juvenile court is much more. The dispositions of child abuse and neglect cases and cases involving the termination of parental rights are equally and increasingly important functions that are essential to understanding the relationship between dependency and delinquency. There are more than 3 million reports of child abuse and neglect each year, almost half of which are substantiated. These children, who have been beaten, raped, starved, burned, maimed, neglected, and abandoned, are at increased risk for delinquent behavior. Many of the children who are arrested for committing offenses are already familiar with the juvenile court as dependent children. Data indicate that 75 percent of violent juvenile offenders suffered serious abuse by a family member, 80 percent witnessed physical violence, and more than 25 percent had a parent who abused drugs or alcohol.

From Rehabilitation to Punishment

In the past decade, the juvenile court has undergone a major shift toward a more punitive and less therapeutic institution. There have been significant changes in state juvenile codes based not on data or research, but on the misconception that America is in the midst of a violent juvenile crime epidemic. Contrary to such perceptions, the record shows:

> The juvenile crime rate, while cyclical in nature, is declining.

> Adults—not youth—are responsible for most violent crime. Seven out of eight violent crimes are committed by adults.

> Although juvenile violence remains at a higher level than a decade ago, it is declining.

> Today's youth do not commit more acts of violence with greater regularity than their predecessors, but more juveniles are being arrested for violent acts. This means that the "superpredator epidemic" does not exist.

Despite these facts, virtually every state has enacted legislation during this decade to significantly alter the philosophy of juvenile justice and promote the view that the juvenile justice system should mirror the criminal justice system. Increasingly, judicial authority and discretion have been taken away despite the belief that properly constrained judicial discretion in charging and sentencing is more effective than prosecutorial or legislative control. Limitations on juvenile jurisdiction, mandatory sentencing, and the creation of more punitive programming have seriously affected the ability of the juvenile judge to dispense justice in a therapeutic environment. The juvenile court has undergone a major shift toward a more punitive and less therapeutic institution.

The social reformers who created the juvenile court 100 years ago believed that children's culpability for their actions was limited and that delinquency was closely related to poor parenting, neglect, poverty, and lack of moral values. They believed that children were malleable and that rehabilitation could occur under the jurisdiction of a benevolent juvenile court through which the state adopted the philosophy of *parens patriae*.

Since that time, the juvenile court has undergone significant change, from being an institution focused on social welfare and acting in a child's best interest to one. . . focused on accountability and punishment. None of these, alone, is enough. Today, the court must somehow simultaneously afford children due process, deliver swift and appropriate punishment, and endeavor to rehabilitate and meet the therapeutic needs of juvenile offenders and their families.

Juvenile or Criminal Justice?

The "adultification" of the juvenile justice system continues to this day. Increasing numbers of youth—some 17,000 per year—are transferred to the criminal justice system, often without benefit of judicial intervention in the decision making process. Florida researchers, led by Donna Bishop, compared 3,000 transferred Florida youth with 3,000 non-transferred Florida youth and found that the former group was more likely to be incarcerated and for longer periods of time. When released, transferred youth were more likely to reoffend and reoffend earlier than those who were not transferred.

There is no question that some juveniles merit transfer. Serious, violent, and chronic juvenile offenders may demonstrate by the nature of their offenses or offense history, their failure to benefit from treatment programs in a manner indicating a lack of amenability to treatment, and in other ways that transfer to the criminal justice system is appropriate. However, the wholesale transfer of juveniles on the basis of factors other than individual characteristics and without judicial intervention is imprudent. It is crucial that juvenile courts be allowed to make carefully defined, individual determinations regarding transfer.

Accountability is a crucial goal of the juvenile justice system. When necessary, punishment should be swift, measured, and well reasoned. In some cases, secure confinement is appropriate. Juveniles must learn that delinquent behavior is intolerable and that they will be held accountable for their actions. Tough sentencing laws for crimes involving firearms, often involving mandatory confinement, have proven effective. While there are children in the juvenile justice system who can be classified as serious, violent, and chronic offenders, they constitute a small minority of the juvenile offender population. These offenders may need to be confined to receive long-term treatment and to ensure the safety of the community.

At the same time, the juvenile justice system should not be redesigned to respond disproportionately to the behavior of a small number of offenders who are uncharacteristic of the population as a whole. Juveniles often stop committing crimes as they mature and become employed . Increasingly punitive in nature, juvenile justice legislation must not abandon the critical goal of rehabilitation. The juvenile court needs to adopt a rational, measured, and scientific approach to the continuing problem of violent juvenile crime. Such an approach should include balancing accountability and rehabilitation. Education, counseling, and training of youth increase the chances that those adjudicated for delinquent acts, whether confined or not, will be helped to avoid lives of crime. It is essential to avoid creating a one-dimensional juvenile justice system with rules, laws, practices, and goals designed to adjudicate Billy the Kid when most of the juveniles in the system more closely resemble Dennis the Menace.

Intervention

Reliance on scientific research is key to realizing the promise of the juvenile court. Decades of research in juvenile and criminal justice, developmental psychology, epidemiology, and other disciplines, including evaluations of promising program interventions, should inform policymaking, decision making, and the development of programs and treatments. Working as a multi-disciplinary team, juvenile justice and child welfare system practitioners, researchers, and experts in the community should combine their clinical experience with this growing body of knowledge.

Some argue that the juvenile justice and child welfare systems have been one huge experiment. Children are assigned to a variety of treatments or programs, and child welfare and juvenile justice practitioners have little to say about the comparative benefits of these interventions or the quality of decision making by those who operate the system.

Most practitioners believe—as does the public—that a well-meaning intervention designed by competent people will have a positive effect. Whether a program could have unintended negative effects or no effect at all is seldom considered. Initial progress may be short lived. These factors underscore the need for rigorous program evaluations across the entire spectrum of child welfare and juvenile justice services to ensure that interventions benefit children and society and do not produce unintended effects that may even increase the risks of delinquent behavior. The juvenile justice system must be vigilant about the quality of its programs, services, and service providers and must work with researchers to design an agenda that will make a positive contribution to the body of evaluation research.

Working collaboratively, juvenile justice officials and researchers can develop study designs and outcome measures that more accurately assess the effectiveness of treatment programs. Measures of success should embrace more than the customary outcome measures of efficient case management and reduced recidivism. Intermediate outcomes also should be measured, and evaluators should determine whether participating children received other benefits from the program, such as academic success, conflict resolution skills, and reduced use of alcohol and drugs.

Risk and Protective Factors

For decades, juvenile justice researchers and social scientists have been studying the causes and correlates of delinquent behavior and identifying a variety of risk factors for delinquent behavior that could assist the court in designing and adopting earlier and more effective interventions. A major risk factor for delinquent behavior is family dysfunction; other risk factors include negative peer influences, parental neglect, low academic achievement, early onset of antisocial behavior, substance abuse, and exposure to violence. The risk factors for maladaptive behavior are all too prevalent in dependent children and are often seen well before they begin to engage in acts of delinquency. Early childhood victimization has demonstrable long-term consequences for delinquency, adult criminality, and violent criminal behavior, providing strong support for the "cycle of violence" hypothesis. Research enables us to identify those juveniles most in need of intervention.

From a developmental perspective, it is now possible to identify risk factors facing children before birth. The potential for offending is higher among individuals with multiple perinatal complications, particularly when coupled with other risk factors. Examination of risk factors for delinquency leads to the conclusion that if delinquent behavior is to be prevented, the juvenile justice system must work at the earliest possible opportunity not only with the child but with the child's family, peers, school, and neighborhood.

Developmental experts have identified a variety of protective factors that counter risk factors and thus reduce the likelihood of delinquency. Protective factors range from a strong and involved grandmother to parental involvement, a commitment to school, and personal self-esteem. The research on risk and protective factors can be used by practitioners to develop risk assessment instruments that measure exposure to risks and to design interventions that reduce the impact of risk factors and strengthen protective factors. It is important to note that protective factors can change over time. Being a female was once considered a significant protective factor against delinquency, but today girls make up 26 percent of all juvenile arrests. Learning more about the needs of these girls should be a priority of the juvenile justice research agenda. With knowledge delivered from research, courts can expand their influence over children and their environment and not be limited to merely adjudicating cases and making educated guesses about their appropriate disposition.

There are several clearly defined developmental pathways to delinquent behavior, and every child responds differently to risk and protective factors. Sound intervention by the juvenile court requires specific inquiry into a particular child's family, school performance, social activities, and other circumstances to identify risk and protective factors present in the child's life. The factors that cause youth to commit delinquent offenses do not disappear when they return home from the juvenile system, and rehabilitation will fail if a youth returns to the same environment without the support and services needed to succeed (effective aftercare services involve the family, school, and community and take into account the child's therapeutic and academic needs).

Early Intervention and the Dependency Court

In addressing delinquent behavior, it is important to consider its developmental origins and intervene at the earliest opportunity to prevent it. Prevention efforts should include intensive, individualized intervention in the lives of dependent children so that the dichotomy between interventions with delinquent and dependent youth, and between the way their cases are handled, can be dissolved. Such efforts would ensure that the juvenile court may act to prevent delinquency before it takes root rather than simply prevent recidivism, a traditional outcome measure of the juvenile and criminal justice systems. Simply preventing another offense is inadequate.

Unless society devotes significant attention and resources to abused and neglected children, the juvenile court will not realize its potential. More than half the children who enter the child welfare system as a result of child maltreatment are under 7 years old. For these young victims, the juvenile court needs to consider their developmental and mental health needs. With a comprehensive picture of the child in mind, the juvenile court has its best opportunity to provide needed services.

Comprehensive and Interdisciplinary Interventions

The response of the juvenile system must be collaborative and interdisciplinary because children at risk are often the victims of cumulative disadvantage. Juvenile justice system professionals, in particular service providers, need to take into account the relationships between child maltreatment and other problems, including violence, substance abuse, and other high-risk behaviors. More research on how these factors combine to place dependent and delinquent youth at risk is essential, and the knowledge gained from this research should be used to reform practice, guide policy, and influence the design of interventions.

The Dependency Court Intervention Program for Family Violence, a national demonstration project in Miami, FL, provides an example of interdisciplinary work in jurisprudence. Funded by the Violence Against Women Office, Office of Justice Programs, U.S. Department of Justice, this demonstration project seeks to address the co-occurrence of child maltreatment and family violence in a juvenile court setting. Advocates are provided to battered mothers of dependent children, assessment instruments have been designed to measure the extent and impact of violence on children, and collaboration between the child welfare and domestic violence community has been fostered as the foundation of a communitywide approach to handling child abuse cases in which other forms of family violence are also present.

Because infants and toddlers can tell the court about their development through their actions, an assessment for use with children from 1 to 5 years old has been developed through this program, with assistance from Joy Osofsky, Ph.D., Professor of Pediatrics and Psychiatry at Louisiana State University Medical Center. Parents and dependent children are videotaped in a number of structured and unstructured interactions. The developmental and cognitive functioning of the young child and his or her bonding and attachment with a caregiver are assessed. Preliminary data indicate that, while many of these dependent children are developmentally delayed, the developmental delays often go undetected. The Miami court is now able to reach these children earlier, enhancing their ability to develop in a healthy, age-appropriate manner.

The program is undergoing a rigorous process and outcome evaluation. A quasi-experimental research design is being used to develop data on the needs of children and their families when multiple forms of family violence are present. The demonstration project already has resulted in institutional reform intended to enhance child safety.

Other innovative interventions have been developed to address the comorbidity of substance abuse and child maltreatment. By 1995, dependency and delinquency courts, building on the success of adult drug courts, had begun to experiment with similar collaborative processes that focus on a juvenile's recovery from drug dependency rather than on punishment. In addition to drug treatment, a variety of psychosocial interventions were marshaled to encourage recovery. The juvenile drug court team could look beyond the individual to the family and seek to change behavior by attacking problems that permeate the juvenile's environment: drug use, mental health needs, poverty, and poor parenting skills. There is hope that a youth's behavior can be modified by relying on some of the same processes used in adult drug courts, such as interdisciplinary teamwork, intensive judicial supervision, close monitoring of drug use, rewards, and sanctions. Long-term evaluations of juvenile drug court programs are under way.

Every person or institution that touches a child's life and interacts with his or her family can contribute positively to that child's development. The juvenile judge's role should be expanded to include leading the community in responding to the needs of its children. The California Rules of Court, for example, encourage juvenile judges to provide community leadership in determining the needs of at-risk children and families and obtaining and developing resources and services to address them. The larger society that contributed to the problem should also be part of the solution. It is essential to learn more about collective efficacy and how neighborhoods can organize to protect and supervise their children. The heart of any institutional reform must begin with a community partnership for child protection and a collective realization that every citizen is responsible for the well-being of all children, a responsibility that cannot be delegated to the juvenile justice and child welfare systems.

School and community interventions are key to serving children's needs. The following types of interventions have demonstrated positive effects on reducing risk factors and enhancing protective factors:

➤ School organization interventions

➤ Comprehensive community interventions incorporating community mobilization

➤ Parental involvement and parental education

➤ Classroom-based social and behavioral skills curriculum

➤ Intensive police patrolling, targeting hotspots in particular

➤ Media campaigns to influence public attitudes

Aftercare programs, specific to each child and each treatment program, are also important. The progress made by program participants will be limited unless it is followed up, reinforced, and monitored in the community.

Tomorrow's Juvenile Court

Modernizing and professionalizing the juvenile court requires that interdisciplinary training be provided to court staff—judges in particular. Knowing the law is not enough. Judges should be aware of available diagnostic tools, sensitive to the developmental needs of children and possible risks that they face, and proactive in efforts to prevent youth crime and violence.

There should be no need to wonder whether the juvenile court's work makes a difference. Juvenile court judges need to take the lead in promoting program evaluation as an integral part of each new intervention by demanding that services have been proven effective or are based on sound principles of proven effectiveness before more children and families are sent to participate in them. With the resources to conduct evaluations of promising and innovative programs, dedication, and a willingness to collaborate across disciplines, juvenile court and juvenile justice practitioners can answer the question of what works empirically.

The juvenile court should also stress its nonadversarial nature, keeping the child's best interest in mind by promoting a more sophisticated, less confrontational manner of adjudication. The juvenile justice system should avoid duplicating the criminal court model, while protecting the fundamental rights of juveniles. A one-dimensional system dealing exclusively with adjudication would limit the juvenile court's potential to promote rehabilitation and the well-being of youth while protecting the community and serving victims. Adjudication culminating in individualized dispositions and based on the need for accountability and the best interest of youth and society should be the cornerstone of the juvenile court's work.

Despite the lack of resources and respect accorded juvenile courts, their overwhelming caseloads, and the many other challenges that confront them, they are staffed with professionals who reflect talent, dedication, and commitment. A fully functioning professional juvenile court has the potential to be the most effective prevention tool in the juvenile justice system. However, this cannot occur unless judges take the lead in revitalizing and professionalizing America's juvenile courts, using the results of scientific research, the promise of creative innovation, and the resources of the community. The nation's societal pledge that "children come first" must not be allowed to ring hollow in, of all places, the halls of justice.

YOUTH GANG SURVEYS

(The material in this section was taken from a recent OJJDP Youth Gang Survey. For a copy of the most recent survey, visit the website of OJJDP.)

The proliferation of youth gangs throughout the United States and the growth of youth gang violence have heightened the awareness of the youth gang problem among public policymakers, law enforcement agencies, and social scientists. To measure the extent of this problem, the U.S. Department of Justice, Office of Justice Programs, Office of Juvenile Justice and Delinquency Prevention, conducts an annual survey of law enforcement agencies. Nearly 5,000 law enforcement agencies were surveyed.

A youth gang was defined as "a group of youths or young adults in (the respondent's) jurisdiction that (the respondent) or other responsible persons in (the respondent's) agency or community are willing to identify or classify as a 'gang." The National Youth Gang Survey was sent to two groups: a statistically representative sample of 3,018 law enforcement agencies and a comparative sample of 1,951 law enforcement agencies that were surveyed in a previous National Youth Gang Survey but not selected for the representative sample. The response rate was 92 percent for the representative sample and 81 percent for the comparative sample. Information and analyses included in this summary are limited to the survey responses for the statistically representative sample, because the data are more comprehensive and allow for a more complete nationwide perspective.

The statistically representative sample was composed of jurisdictions in four area types: all large cities with populations greater than 25,000; a random sample of small cities with populations between 2,500 and 25,000; all suburban counties; and a random sample of rural counties. Surveys were sent to the appropriate local law enforcement agency within each jurisdiction in the representative sample.

Based on the results of the survey, the percentage of jurisdictions with active youth gangs has decreased slightly from 53 percent in 1996 to 51 percent in the present survey. The greatest decrease appeared in large cities, especially those with populations ranging from 25,000 to 49,999. Despite these decreases, the nation's largest cities continued to experience gang activity.

In the surveys conducted to date, 100 percent of respondents in cities with populations of 250,000 or more reported active youth gangs in their jurisdictions. The estimated number of jurisdictions with active youth gangs was 4,712, down slightly from 4,824 in 1996. The number of youth gangs and gang members also decreased. An estimated 30,500 youth gangs and 816,000 gang members were active compared with 31,000 youth gangs and 846,000 gang members in 1996. Although the prevalence of youth gangs and gang members declined overall, the number of gang members rose in small cities and rural counties.

Despite the decreases in the number of gangs and gang members, 45 percent of respondents indicated that the gang problem in their jurisdictions was staying about the same, while 35 percent indicated it was getting worse and 20 percent said that it was getting better. In contrast, 49 percent of respondents to the 1995 National Youth Gang Survey believed that their problem was getting worse, 41 percent that it was staying about the same, and 10 percent that it was getting better.

Youth gang members were estimated to be involved in 3,340 homicides, almost two-thirds of which took place in large cities. Youth gang involvement in other types of criminal activity remained high. Respondents reported a high degree of gang member involvement, most often for aggravated assault and larceny/theft (28 percent), followed by motor vehicle theft (27 percent), burglary (26 percent), and robbery (13 percent). However, for all of the above crimes, the estimated degree of involvement in criminal activity by youth gang members was less than in 1996. These apparent decreases are consistent with the national downturn in both adult and juvenile violent crime arrests, as reported by the U.S. Department of Justice.

Youth gang involvement in drug sales and distribution has become a growing public concern in recent years. Results of the survey indicated that youth gangs played a key role in the sale and distribution of drugs. Respondents estimated that 42 percent of the youth gangs in the country were involved in the street sale of drugs and 33 percent were involved in drug distribution for the purpose of generating profits for the gang. The street sale of drugs by youth gangs was especially high in large cities and suburban counties. Nationwide, youth gangs were involved in an estimated 33 percent of crack cocaine sales, 32 percent of marijuana sales, 16 percent of powder cocaine sales, 12 percent of methamphetamine sales, and 9 percent of heroin sales. These data may indicate increased youth gang involvement in drug activities since the 1996 survey.

In contrast to the slight decrease in gang activity, reported gang migration increased from 1996. Eighty-nine percent of respondents indicated that they experienced some gang migration into their jurisdictions, up from 84 percent in 1996. In addition, an estimated 23 percent of youth gang members in the United States were migrants compared with 21 percent in 1996. The vast majority (70 percent) of respondents who experienced some gang migration cited social factors (e.g., to move with families, to find legitimate job opportunities, to join relatives, or to join friends) as reasons why youth gang members migrated to their jurisdictions.

In response to the proliferation of gangs throughout the country, most law enforcement agencies (66 percent) have established specialized response units. More specifically, 35 percent reported having a youth/street gang unit or officer(s), 18 percent reported having a gang prevention unit or officer(s), and 29 percent reported having a unit that combined both types of units.

Index